Suzanne,
   It's all about —
world we all love so much

for T. L
Aug 26, 1998

COLD OCEANS

COLD OCEANS

ADVENTURES IN KAYAK, ROWBOAT, AND DOGSLED

JON TURK

HarperCollins*Publishers*

To Chris Seashore, my ski buddy

HarperCollins books may be purchased for educational, business, or sales promotional use. For information please write: Special Markets Department, HarperCollins Publishers, Inc., 10 East 53rd Street, New York, NY 10022.

FIRST EDITION

Designed by Joy O'Meara
Maps by Nathan Young

Library of Congress Cataloging-in-Publication Data

Turk, Jonathan.
    Cold oceans : adventures in kayak, rowboat, and dogsled / Jon Turk.—1st ed.
        p.   cm.
    ISBN 0-06-019147-3
        1. Turk, Jonathan—Journeys—Arctic regions.   2. Arctic regions—Description and travel.
    3. Ocean travel.   4. Explorers—United States—Biography.   5. Adventure and adventurers—
    United States—Biography.   I. Title.
    G635.T83A3   1998
    910.4'5—dc21   98-7175

98 99 00 01 02 ❖/RRD 10 9 8 7 6 5 4 3 2 1

CONTENTS

ACKNOWLEDGMENTS

I would like to thank

    All the people who offered me tea and cookies along the way,

    And my expedition partners:

    Chris Seashore,

    Dave Adams,

    Mike Latendresse.

    My father, Amos Turk, has patiently edited my manuscripts for forty years, starting with book reports in Miss Maroney's fourth-grade class.

    Finally, thanks to my agent, Richard Parks, and my editor, Megan Newman, who believed in me.

PROLOGUE

1

In the high Arctic, the cold can be so intense that the moisture in your eyes freezes to form tiny icicles between your upper and lower lashes. On a bright day in February the sunlight refracts through the crystals and spreads dancing rainbows across your retina. You live deep inside the tunnel formed by the hood of your anorak. Only your breath ventures into the polar landscape, and as it escapes the moisture freezes on the fur ruff of your hood, forming icicles that tinkle softly when you walk, like crystalline wind chimes. Part of you wants to push the curtain aside and step into the outer world, but your body selfishly contracts within itself and draws its warmth toward the center. Eventually the body wins, and your mind withdraws to the deepest, most protected places. The hostility of the environment becomes abstract. Even the cold lives in a different time and place, and all that remains is a peaceful eternity of ice.

In the Arctic summer, when the sun circles lazily around the sky and compensates in persistence for what it lacks in intensity, the ice breaks apart and floats away. Life returns to the land, and the polar oceans lose their white veneer to become gray and nasty. People have argued this point with me. They claim that on a warm day, high-latitude oceans don't look or feel ominous. I disagree. Even on the most perfect, glorious day, when the seas are flat, a double rainbow dances on the horizon, icebergs bob gently in the foreground, and a pod of white whales chase each other across your port bow—even on these days, if you block out the incredible panorama and look into the ocean itself, it is gray and nasty.

2

I can trace the events that led me to Cape Horn, the Northwest Passage, the east coast of Baffin Island, and northwest Greenland. But I can't tell you why an offhand joke told in a bar over a third pitcher of beer propelled me toward some of the coldest, wettest, most remote regions on the earth. Of course the drunken chatter that afternoon didn't light the fuse; it had been smoldering from my earliest childhood.

When I decided to kayak around Cape Horn nearly twenty years ago, my friends thought that my dreams were suicidal. Tired of ridicule, I set off alone, guided by the adventures of Elizabethan explorers. However, after paddling through the rain and mist of southern Chile, I miscalculated and shipwrecked.

I also failed on the second expedition, an attempt to row the Northwest Passage. At the end of the summer, while waiting for the once-a-week flight south, I shared tea and bannock with an old woman named Nora. We were camped on the tundra, and she squatted by her fire with the grace of a person who was born in an igloo and hadn't seen a chair until she was a teenager. She asked me whether I had stopped at Letty Harbor, an abandoned trading post along my way. I said I had.

Then she asked, "Were you visited by the spirits while you were there?"

I pictured the place in my mind: the abandoned Hudson's Bay store, the tundra with its summer flowers spreading pinks and purples in a world otherwise ruled by browns and yellows, and the gray limestone cliffs. "No, I wasn't. . . . Why?"

She looked across the land and said, "That's where we threw the babies off the cliffs during the hungry times."

Children were playing on the hillside below us. Men and women were loading nets into a small speedboat. My girlfriend, Chris Seashore, was airing our sleeping bags in the afternoon sun.

Nora removed a burning stick from the fire and used it to light the tundra mosses around her. As I watched silently, she beat out the flames, leaving a thin line of smoke rising from the ground.

"Keeps out the mosquitoes. Terrible, those mosquitoes!" and she grinned.

The wrinkled grin pushed away the spirits, and we were back to the present on a warm day in a peaceful landscape.

During the Northwest Passage attempt, Chris and I shared the same hunger, fatigue, and danger. But Chris always saw our destination as secondary while I often focused beyond the horizon at an arbitrary dot on the map, which I called the goal. Frustrated by our differences, I half blamed Chris for our failure and planned a third expedition without her.

Two years later, I traveled to the eastern Arctic and attempted to run a dog team up the east coast of Baffin Island. Again, I failed. My partner and I had made our final camp beneath an iceberg locked into a frozen sea. As I prepared to turn the team around and admit defeat, the morning sun colored the tip of the berg orange, while the windblown snow at my feet remained in shadows. It would have been easy to blame my failure on the sixty-below temperatures, the winter blizzards, or my own inexperience, but that would have been a lie. I failed because I lacked Nora's sense of humor and her acceptance of the land. I hadn't learned that adversity isn't the enemy.

In 1988 Chris joined me to paddle sea kayaks along an ancient migration route from Ellesmere Island to Greenland. The journey had been done in the mid-1800s, led by a man who was a shaman, a murderer, and perhaps a madman. Following in the footsteps of the old ways and finally listening to the land, its people, and its ghosts, we crossed into Greenland, finding the goal within the journey.

3

I worked on this manuscript for a decade, writing about adventures as I completed them, uncertain how the tale would unfold. Then, on January 26, 1997, an avalanche swept me off a mountainside in British Columbia. The next day, after the surgeons had bolted my pelvis back together, I lay on my hospital bed, dazed on morphine, staring at all those tubes transporting fluids into and out of my body. My roommate was watching television. I pushed the call button and asked the nurse to close the curtains; I knew that Oprah wasn't my salvation. When I returned home, Chris rented a small hydraulic crane from a hospital supply company. Every morning for the following six weeks, Chris jacked me out of bed, lowered me into a recliner, and spread all the necessities around my chair: lunch, a few cookies, a water bottle, a telephone, a book, and a laptop computer. Then she put on her parka and left to ski powder. I always ate my cookies as soon as the door closed. Munching slowly, I traveled back across the remote landscapes, trying to understand where my journeys had led me and where they would take me as soon as I could walk again.

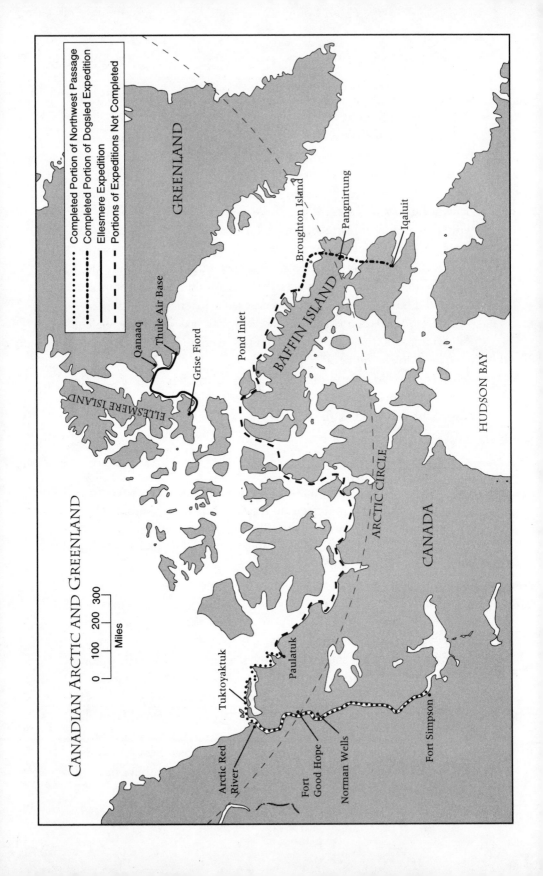

CANADIAN ARCTIC AND GREENLAND

Completed Portion of Northwest Passage
Completed Portion of Dogsled Expedition
Ellesmere Expedition
Portions of Expeditions Not Completed

GREENLAND

ELLESMERE ISLAND

Qanaaq
Thule Air Base
Grise Fiord

Pond Inlet

BAFFIN ISLAND

Broughton Island
Pangnirtung
Iqaluit

HUDSON BAY

ARCTIC CIRCLE

CANADA

Paulatuk

Tuktoyaktuk

Arctic Red
River

Fort
Good Hope
Norman Wells

Fort Simpson

Miles
0   100   200   300

Part 1

CAPE HORN

No, it is impossible; it is impossible to convey the life-sensation of any given epoch of one's existence—that which makes its truth, its meaning—its subtle and penetrating essence. It is impossible. We live, as we dream—alone.

Joseph Conrad,
Heart of Darkness

1

The back porch of the 1890s bar is perched over a narrow slough that washes kelp, cannery wastes, and sea life back and forth with the tides. One Saturday afternoon in 1975 I was drinking beer with a group of Pacific Northwest fishermen and boatbuilders. As the empty pitchers accumulated, the talk veered to sailing, and my friend Craig announced that only people who had sailed around Cape Horn could toast the queen with their feet on the table. Craig wiped the foam off his beard and grinned. Another friend thought that you were allowed only one foot on the table, but no one was sure.

A second tide change reminded me that I had been drinking for over six hours and it was time to go home. I walked toward my apartment, which was one unit of four clustered duplexes that were slowly sinking into a common swamp. A week before, a public health official had flushed purple dye down our toilets to test the septic system, and no one was surprised when the swamp behind our buildings turned purple. Craig went on a midnight foray, stole a plastic pink flamingo from someone's lawn in suburbia, and set it among the cattails in the purple muck. Then he spray-painted THE GETTO on the west wall of the duplex.

I looked at the wall, turned back to town, staggered into the hardware store, and bought a can of fluorescent pink spray paint. Then I returned home and added a capital H between the G and the E.

I had chosen my lifestyle. As I told the counselor during the breakup of my second marriage, I didn't want a good job, respectable career, house, new car, mortgage, and membership in the country club. I was on a different journey, and I didn't mind living in a few ghettos along the way. But at least I would spell the word right.

As I walked unsteadily toward my sagging front porch, I reflected that my grand journey had taken me only as far as La Conner, Washington, the ghetto, and the 1890s bar. An early evening breeze blew in from the slough, and small purple waves circled around the flamingo's skinny legs. I tried to imagine the huge rollers of the southern ocean.

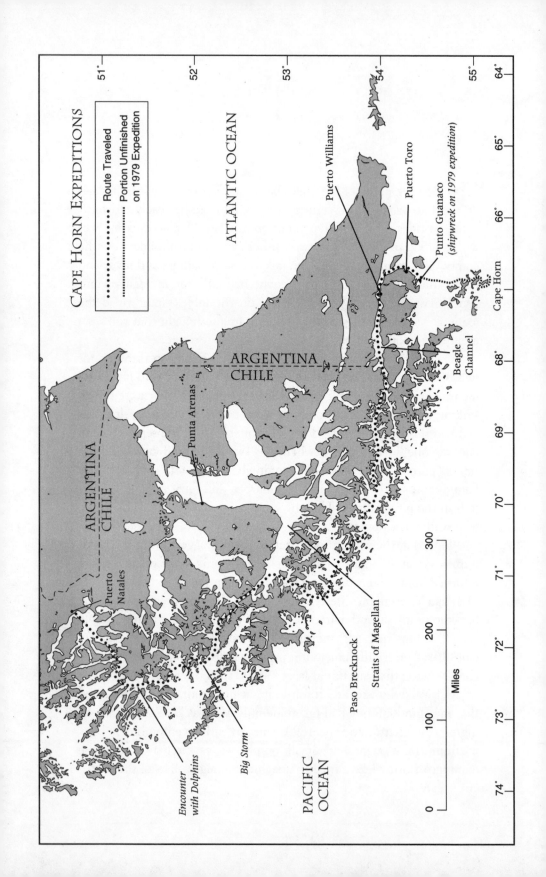

CAPE HORN EXPEDITIONS

•••• Route Traveled
•••• Portion Unfinished
      on 1979 Expedition

ATLANTIC OCEAN

PACIFIC OCEAN

ARGENTINA
CHILE

ARGENTINA
CHILE

Puerto Natales

Punta Arenas

Puerto Williams

Puerto Toro

Punto Guanaco
(shipwreck on 1979 expedition)

Cape Horn

Beagle
Channel

Paso Brecknock

Straits of Magellan

Big Storm

Encounter
with Dolphins

Miles

0   100   200   300

51°
52°
53°
54°
55°

64°
65°
66°
67°
68°
69°
70°
71°
72°
73°
74°

A few days later I told my friends at the bar that I was thinking about sailing around the Horn.

No one said anything for a few moments, then one man shook his head. "It was just a joke, Man. That's serious shit. I mean, you're not a sailor. Buy a small sloop, sail around the San Juan Islands for a few years, take a test passage to Hawaii, learn about boats, buy a better yacht, then think about Cape Horn."

He was right and I knew it, but I didn't care. I had earned my Ph.D. in chemistry four years earlier. Then I had run away—from my career; from my first wife, Elizabeth, and our daughter, Reeva; and from my second wife, Debby, and our two children, Nathan and Noey. I had intentionally created a huge void to be filled by something else. But what? I had been earning a living writing science textbooks, but the job didn't fill the emotional vacuum. What about a sloping deck, wind in the rigging, spray in the air? I was too excited to plan this expedition over several years, so I drove to Seattle and bought *Hussy*, a forty-six-foot wooden sloop. On the way home I stopped to visit Debby, Nathan, and Noey. Despite our differences and divorce, Debby and I remained good friends, and she asked me to stay for dinner. We chatted about trivia and I played with the kids, but I didn't mention the yacht.

After dessert, Debby asked, "Did you just fall in love?"

"No, why?"

"Well, you're acting different; something happened in your life."

She knew me so well.

I told her about *Hussy* and my dream. Debby agreed with me that the mechanical details would fall in place if the journey was important enough.

I wanted to hug her and be close again, but her frightened eyes warned me away.

"It's late. I'd better go."

She walked me to the door, but I couldn't find my shoes. We searched the house—no shoes. Finally, Noey, who was three years old, approached. "Well, Daddy, if you can't find your shoes, maybe you'll have to stay. You could sleep with me but my bed is too small. Maybe you'll have to sleep with Mommy."

I knelt down and sat Noey on my knee. She smiled and snuggled. I asked, "Where are my shoes?"

She lifted her tiny hands. "I don't know."

I laughed and asked again, then spoke sternly. Finally she led me to her room and pulled back the bedcovers to reveal the hidden shoes.

2

Throughout that fall and winter I scraped, painted, polished, overhauled engines and winches. In the early spring three friends and I sailed out of Seattle harbor for "around the Horn and around the world." We beat our way westward into a building storm and then swung south. A sixty-knot gale and rising seas arrested our progress and drove us back northward. Then the storm veered to the west and increased to ninety knots, generating new waves that collided with the old ones at right angles. Water flew straight upward, as if it had been sucked into the air. By midnight of our third day we were surfing down giant combers under bare poles. Each time we fell into a trough, the boat slammed into the cross sea, shuddered, and stalled beneath a waist-deep wall of green water that washed across the deck. One of my shipmates, who was a cabinetmaker, proclaimed that nothing made of wood could withstand such punishment. We worked together to tie everything down, then he went below. I remained alone in the night, listening to every creak and trying to feel the flex of the hull. Our navigation system had broken down so I was unsure of our location. As we rode the waves eastward toward land, I hoped that the rocks were still far away.

When the wind subsided the next morning, we were afloat, land was fifteen miles away, and no one had washed overboard. The mast stood, and we hadn't lost any sails. There was ample reason to celebrate, except that lines were frayed, hardware bent, varnish chipped, and the engine had been washed thoroughly with saltwater, inside and out. We limped back to our home port, and for the next few weeks I scraped, painted, polished, overhauled engines and winches, and dug deeply into my savings to pay for parts. By the time I finished the repairs and was ready for sea again, my friends had drifted off to other ventures.

I motored out of the marina by myself to test the new engine. Bobbing in the protected bay, I went below, set the timing, adjusted the ignition points, and tightened the belts. I was sick of engines and paint and the mounting bills at the marina chandlery. I turned up the tape player and raised sail. The hull heeled and stabilized; I ran forward on the sloping deck and raised the jib. But the excitement wasn't there.

That afternoon I returned to port and hung a For Sale sign on the mast.

3

Driving southward along the interstate, I couldn't tell whether I was heading toward a new adventure or running from a failure. I reminded myself of the conversation with Debby: If a journey was important enough, the details would fall in place. Obviously Cape Horn hadn't been important enough. But for a time I had thought it was. I turned her words in a different direction. If our marriage had been important enough, would the details have fallen in place? Had she seen that twist of logic when she encouraged me to set sail? Or had she seen it earlier, when our marriage began to dissolve?

I used the money from the boat sale to buy a house in Telluride, a ski town in western Colorado. I met Marion, we fell in love, and she and her son, Adam, moved in with me. Nathan and Noey lived with us for a school year. Once again I was immersed in a happy family, and I spent five winters in that curious Colorado mixture of near desert sun and copious snow.

During the summers I learned to rock climb in the rugged San Juan Mountains. Eventually I became a competent climber and felt ready to face bigger mountains. When I invited Marion to join me on an expedition to the Himalayas, she said that she had a son to raise. We struggled and argued; I packed my climbing gear, and she moved back to her old home in Boulder.

My climbing party failed to summit in India and I returned to my empty house, feeling the weight of repeated failures. I climbed in Yosemite, hiked through remote canyons in northern Mexico, then, for lack of a better plan, drove home.

Even though I had left the sea, my interest in Cape Horn lingered. One afternoon I relaxed with Joshua Slocum's classic *Sailing Alone Around the World*. Slocum had spent his life as a trader and a captain of square-rigged sailing ships, but he lost his job after steamships became competitive. He found life on land unbearable and the prospect of working on a steamship even worse, so he bought himself a half-rotten thirty-foot sloop, renovated it, and set off to sail around the world, alone. He left Boston in 1895, headed south and then west through the Straits of Magellan. During this passage, local Indians attacked him from primitive canoes. Joshua, being alone, couldn't stand guard day and night, so he spread tacks on his deck. When the barefoot interlopers tried to sneak on board, they stepped on the tacks, screamed, woke him, and gave him time to charge out with a loaded shotgun.

I read the chapter, put the book down, and thought, "There's a message here that I'm not seeing." I fixed a cup of tea, walked out to the porch, and watched the sun set behind the tall peaks.

Right, I thought, the story isn't about Slocum, it's about the indigenous Fuegians, who lived on the land long before the arrival of Europeans. If they could paddle the Straits of Magellan in bark canoes, I could navigate the region in a kayak! Kayaks are cheap and low maintenance. A kayak can't weather a big storm, but when the winds howl and the waves roar, I could carry the boat up the beach and relax in my tent.

Although I had never paddled a sea kayak before, I had canoed down Arctic rivers and along the coast of British Columbia. Now I wanted to paddle around Cape Horn, and my self-confidence—or hubris—told me that I could do it.

I asked my climbing partners to join me, but they weren't interested. The journey was too dangerous, we had no experience in kayaks, no training, and no reason to succeed or even to survive. I felt foolish, but the idea wouldn't go away.

My life was full with skiing, climbing, and writing. I had friends, free time, money, a house at a major ski resort. There was no need to follow dreams into the dark rain forest and angry waves of Tierra del Fuego, Land of Fire.

I climbed with a retired ballerina who had learned to love the mountains rather than the dance floor. One evening I was fixing dinner while she was relaxing in the bathtub. She hollered through the door, asking if I would bring her a glass of wine, and when I did, she asked me to sit. I closed the cover on the toilet seat and sat down.

"You know, Jon, I've been thinking about this Cape Horn thing. You're a survivor; you'll come back. Don't worry about that. But remember, if you listen to your own quiet whisper that speaks of feeling and not reason, you won't be the same person after it's over. You better be sure you're going to like the new *you* before you set off."

This was a different kind of warning. I looked into her face, rising out of the soapy water.

"Maybe I already like him. Maybe I want to paddle to the Horn with him just to get better acquainted."

She shrugged and smiled. "You'd better go, Jon."

4

On a snowy day in December 1979, a friend drove me over the pass to the bus stop in Ridgeway, wished me luck, and returned home. Four years had passed since I had resolved to round the Horn. Now I stood by the side of the road in the middle of my pile of gear: two large duffels that held the collapsible kayak, another for the sail and accessories, one duffel of clothes, one filled with general camping gear, a camera bag, and two long paddles. The high peaks of the San Juan mountains appeared occasionally through a storm. I wondered, "Which way to Cape Horn?" Buttoning up my parka, I then asked myself, "Which way to Mars?" Both destinations seemed about the same at that point.

The bus was due at two in the afternoon. Two o'clock came and went, and no bus. I wandered into the gas station with the Trailways sign to warm up. A young man was tuning the four-barreled carburetor of his metal-flaked baby-blue Mustang. "The bus will be here any minute," he assured me. Afternoon turned into evening, and then the phone rang and we learned that an avalanche had closed the pass; there would be no bus that day. The mechanic bolted down the air cleaner, adjusted the idle to a moderate roar, and told me he was going to close up shop, grab a couple of six-packs, and party. I could join him if I chose. I started to explain that I was headed to Cape Horn, but it all seemed too ridiculous, so I hauled my seven parcels back out to the roadside to start a long night of hitchhiking.

I arrived in Boulder at dawn on December 24, spent Christmas in town, and then flew to Chile. Expeditions start where civilization leaves off. If there are wolves and bandits outside the castle walls, the expedition starts as soon as you cross the moat and the gate bangs shut. Puerto Natales was my starting place because it lies at the end of the road in southwest Chile. My plan was to paddle southward along the coast using a string of islands to protect me from the legendary waves of the southern ocean. Then I would continue eastward through the Straits of Magellan and south through the Tierra del Fuego Archipelago. Cape Horn forms the southernmost tip of the southernmost island, the last land before Antarctica. The total journey from Puerto Natales to Cape Horn is about five hundred miles.

I stepped off the bus in this strange town almost ten thousand miles from home and unloaded my gear in a steady rain. It was January 9, the height of South American summer. I would have to get used to the rain. The bus pulled away. Taxi drivers proclaimed the virtues of various hotels, each trying to shout louder than the others to attract my attention. I ignored the commotion.

A fresh wind blew. Peering down the street through the houses, I saw whitecaps in the strait and snowy peaks in the distance. I was alone, about to venture onto an uninhabited coast along one of the most tempestuous oceans in the world. Rescue could not be expected.

I bought food and organized my gear. The wind slackened by midafternoon of the following day, and even though a cold rain continued, I hauled my gear to the beach. A small crowd gathered as I assembled and loaded the collapsible boat. Travelers bring a spark of variety into people's lives. Bards and jugglers were people of the road.

The kayak was seventeen feet long, with one large cockpit in the center. I mounted a short mast forward, fitted with a homemade square sail. Finally, I strapped a harness around my chest. In this miniature sailing vessel, I was part of the rigging; the sheets would be tied to the harness with slip knots so I could spill the wind quickly should the need arise. I could not afford to capsize.

The whitecaps flattened to gentle ripples, and the afternoon sun dried the surface of my vinyl raincoat, even if it was too weak to attack the dampness beneath. I picked up my paddle and felt its balance and weight. The fiord curved to the west, appearing to pinch off between green hills. But I knew that when I rounded the first corner I would see a continuation of the channel, and after that another curve, and after another few hours the channel would open again, and again, and again, for the next few months.

I tied the last of my food bags securely. Then I looked out at the ocean. It had been easy to be brave when I was in a steamy room, drinking wine and talking philosophy with a naked woman bobbing in the bathtub. But now all the sober warnings from my climbing friends seemed more poignant. I had never been in a sea kayak before.

People looked at me expectantly. They had patiently watched me pack, and now they waited for me to paddle off across the fiord. I nodded, and half a dozen people helped me lift the boat and set it in the water. My share of the load was light, but I knew that from now on I would have to drag the boat up and down the beach alone. I slipped into the cockpit and waved jauntily. Eager hands pushed me into the channel. The load shifted and the boat listed until I found the center of gravity.

The storm had subsided; the water was calm. I searched for danger on the horizon, found none, and felt afraid anyway. I paddled slowly, thinking, "I'm not physically prepared for this; my arms are tired already; this is really stupid."

The sun shone weakly in and out of the clouds. The temperature hung in the midforties, and the ninety percent humidity chilled me despite my warm clothing. I reached the curve in the channel after two hours and looked back on the town for the last time. It was six-thirty, and although the high-latitude summer sun promised many more hours of daylight, I set up camp. I built a smoky reluctant fire from damp wood and boiled a stew with meat, potatoes, and vegetables—a luxury for my first meal.

Mist fingered its way down the mountain canyons and spread into the fiords. I stood on the balls of my feet and bounced gently, like a tennis player about to receive a serve. I was camped north of the Straits of Magellan, Tierra del Fuego, Cape Horn. I wasn't going to turn back. Self-doubt wasn't a useful emotion. Alertness and balance were the only important virtues right now.

5

The earth comes alive when the forces of nature collide. Hurricanes and tornadoes arise when hot and cold air masses smash into one another. The steepest, most dangerous waves develop along the boundaries between opposing currents. When two tectonic plates grind into one another, the earth buckles to form lofty mountain ranges. There are a few places, called triple junctions, where three opposing influences, such as three different currents, wind systems, or tectonic plates, collide. There is only one place on earth—Cape Horn—where three triple junctions meet at the same point.

Three oceans, the Pacific, the Atlantic, and the Antarctic, converge at Cape Horn; each one is ruled by a different current. The South Pacific Gyre approaches from the west, strikes the west coast of Chile, and deflects to the north. The South Atlantic Gyre moves down the east coast of Argentina and then veers sharply west. Finally, the Antarctic Circumpolar Current girdles the globe. There is no land to impede the wind south of Cape Horn, so, in the Antarctic Ocean, waves build from the west, circling the globe forever.

Each current is driven by its own prevailing winds. Thus it's not only the water that collides, but also the air above it. I could expect, as the norm, erratic seas, high and often unpredictable winds and almost constant rain.

Two of the most violent geological environments are rift zones, where tectonic plates pull away from one another, and subduction zones, where plates converge and one sinks into the mantle. Both of these environments are characterized by rising magma, mountain building, and frequent earthquakes and volcanoes. At the Chilean triple junction, an active rift zone is colliding with a subduction zone. Thus two plates are pulling apart and simultaneously colliding with and diving under a third. For the past three hundred thousand years, the rift has been falling into the trench formed by the subduction and is slowly oozing its way into the hot plastic asthenosphere one hundred kilometers beneath the surface. The descending plate churns the subterranean rock, forming magma, which rises and creates mountain ranges on the surface. The mountains along this triple junction are less than half as high as the Andes farther north, but they climb directly out of the sea and present steep rock faces to the storms arising from the vortex of the colliding oceans.

Tectonic plates move a few centimeters a year. Uplifted granite, twisted and contorted rock, and sinewy lava flows tell the story of collisions, but the motion itself is invisible. From the vantage point of a kayak, with your butt below the water and your eyes barely above the surface, you see only one ocean at a time, not three. Therefore, the triple junctions aren't visible marks on the land. But power expresses itself in different ways. Beyond the high tide line, a dense wall of tight interlocking trees grows in the abundant rain, but the barrier is stunted and bent almost horizontally by the wind. Thus the vegetation spoke of violent motion, so that the feeling of the wind was always present, even on calm days. Occasionally, granite spires rose through the clouds, and the fact that they were hidden most of the time made them feel more powerful.

6

ithin a few days, I learned to balance the kayak with subtle
movements of my hips, rather than by wild gyrations with
my paddle. My arms strengthened. I developed an efficient stroke that
reduced strain on my wrist tendons. Progress was steady, but my emotions collided in the vortex of triple junctions. I had chosen to paddle
in a harsh land, but I cursed the harshness because it impeded my
progress toward Cape Horn. I had pushed my life toward a romantic
notion of solitude, but during long afternoons in the boat, I frequently
became despondent over broken marriages and failed relationships. I
told myself that I welcomed the cleansing effect of imminent danger,
yet I couldn't dispel the weight of continuous fear.

When I stepped out of the tent in the morning, I tried to start the
day with a memorable and uplifting image: a tree so gnarled by the
wind that it stood out against a forest of gnarled trees, a sun ray highlighting a misty peak. But often I just felt the rain, pulled my hood
over my head, and allowed the vinyl to close me in, obliterating
three-quarters of the horizon and trapping that part of my soul that
otherwise would soar.

After breakfast, I carried my loads from the rain forest through the
intertidal zone to the kayak—three worlds ruled by wetness. Then I
set my course on the next point and started to paddle. A kayak moves
so slowly that you seem motionless. Initially, the trees at the far end
of a fiord blur together into a green wash, but gradually they resolve
into individuals, and then each tree becomes a unique entity composed of branches and leaves or needles. I told myself that every
minute was filled with changing beauty, but I felt empty and alone,
and I filled the emptiness with internal chatter, the mental equivalent of a roadside strip filled with gaudy signs and fast-food restau-
rants. The inner peace wasn't there. I wanted to get to the next
point, so I could get to the next one, and the next, so I could go
home and arrogantly toast the queen with my feet on the table.

I paddled about eight hours a day, and when I came to shore, I
worked for another hour or two setting camp before I could relax

with a cup of hot milk and sugar. First, I unloaded my boat and dragged it and all my gear above the high tide zone. As I had food for two months, that task, in itself, was arduous and time consuming. Then I set up the tent, spread out my sleeping gear, and built a fire if it wasn't raining too hard. Usually the shoreline was rocky and slippery, tent sites were hard to find in the wind-hammered brush, and I was already tired from the long day of paddling. I fantasized that I had a companion who was starting the fire as I set up the tent or someone to help me carry the heavy boat over the slippery kelp-covered rocks. I wished for someone to talk to so I wouldn't have to listen to myself.

Depression has a way of spiraling out of control. I had imagined that the wilderness would miraculously wash away the hassles that my civilized life had brought to me. However, when I realized that I was depressed, I became even more depressed.

A few days after leaving Puerto Natales, I had to paddle the length of a channel called Paso Kirke. When the tide rises and falls along a coastal archipelago, the islands funnel the moving water into currents. These currents increase in intensity, then decrease and eventually reverse themselves with the changing tide. If the channels are narrow, tidal currents are compressed to form rapids. When I reached Paso Kirke, the current was flowing full force against me. By all standards of seamanship and good sense, I should have waited three hours for slack tide, or better yet I should have waited longer until the tide turned and the current reversed and flowed in my favor. Certainly, any competent partner would have insisted on such a reasonable and conservative approach. But I didn't feel like huddling under a damp bush, in the cold rain, alone, for three hours waiting for the tide to change, and I had no wise or logical counsel to contend with. Even though the tidal current in the center of the channel was against me, it created a large eddy that flowed along the shore opposite to the main current. If I hugged the rocks, I could paddle with a current at my back. I was so close to shore that occasionally I had to duck my head beneath the overhanging bushes. Their thick, oily odor mingled with the salt smell of life, death, and decay along the intertidal zone. Unfortunately, the eddy ended at the neck of a constriction that created a tidal rapid. I stayed in the eddy until it reversed itself, and as I pulled out into the choppy current of the main stream, I hoisted sail and paddled upstream through the rapid into another eddy on the other side. The current pushed me backward; the wind pulled forward. I paddled hard. A whirlpool spun me halfway around, spilling the wind and tangling the sheets. The boat stalled and wouldn't respond to the rudder; then a gust of wind caught the corner of the sail and I rotated the boat with my paddle to catch more wind. The kayak made headway against the current and finally dropped into the eddy on the opposite shore. Yahoo, technical sea kayaking! I knew that it was a mistake to treat the expedition as a sporting event; I didn't need to court danger. But I was happy for the first time in the journey. My goal wasn't just to stay alive and to reach Cape Horn; with a positive outlook and a little ingenuity, this trip could be fun.

We don't live in a world where a single "aha" can change our lives, and I battled with my emotions throughout that first week. It was hard to reach any equilibrium at all. The next day a storm kept me on shore. As I sat in my tent, I wrote in my journal:

> *The wind howls and shrieks. How else can I say it; this is a land of cliches and here the wind howls and shrieks. It doesn't look like I'll go for The Horn. It is strictly a matter of facts and probability. Fact: I can't make headway against a strong wind. Fact: The winds are unpredictable. Fact: If an unpredictable strong wind comes up I'll get blown out to sea or dashed against the rocks. What are the chances? They don't feel good enough.*
>
> *And sitting here alone in my tent I cried today over what? Over loss of Earth, you know, moist growing Earth, not this impenetrable windswept land, half rain forest, half marsh that all of humanity has shunned—this coast and sea that I call home right now.*

The depression reverberated against the inside walls of the tent, so I donned my rain gear and sat outside in the storm. In the mountains wind chases animals into their burrows, and the blowing snow erases their tracks, leaving a lifeless landscape. But here in Patagonia, the storm that sent me scurrying for shelter was ignored by my fellow creatures. A flock of petrels skimmed over the surface, and a sandpiper scurried along the beach pecking at food uncovered by the falling tide. An albatross banked into view from around the corner of the canal and landed, delicately folding its wings like an exercise in origami. It was the first albatross I had seen. I thought of Coleridge, *The Rime of the Ancient Mariner*, and the albatross as a symbol of a caring and benign nature. But Coleridge dreamed romantic images from a comfortable desk in England and never traveled to the southern oceans.

I once read a story about a sailor who was washed overboard while rounding the Horn on a clipper ship. His shipmates immediately lowered a boat, and a few of them rowed to the rescue while the remainder of the crew dropped sail and brought the ship into the wind. The boat crew plucked the hapless sailor out of the sea, but the small boat broached on a steep breaking wave and capsized. As the men clung to the upturned keel, a flock of albatrosses circled overhead. The lookout on the main ship watched with horror as one of the birds dove, landed on a man's head, and plucked out his eyes. Then a second bird dove, and a third. Another rescue boat was dispatched, but the lines became tangled in the davits as the mother ship drifted downwind. The lost time was fatal. Blinded and bloody, the men in the water untied their life vests and one by one dove to their deaths rather than face the continued assaults.

I turned into the storm to let the rain beat against my face. So far, the land had been friendly to me. The albatross bobbed gently in the waves and didn't fly over to peck out my eyes. The storm raged, but I was camped safely on shore. The twisted trees that spoke of so many storms provided a tight shelter for my camp. I reminded myself that I wanted to be here. I spoke aloud, but softly, into the wind: "This is okay." Then I went for a walk along the beach. When the storm cleared the next day I was in my boat headed toward the Horn, not back to Puerto Natales.

7

The following day, a long, narrow peninsula of land blocked my passage to the southeast, and I had to paddle directly into the prevailing winds to round the headland. I focused on a rock in front of me, bent my head into the wind, and concentrated on a steady, powerful stroke, simultaneously pushing against the paddle shaft with one hand and pulling with the other. I continued in this manner for two days until I gained the headland and turned southeast. White-caps that yesterday had been nasty barriers pushing me away from my goal became friendly hands that lifted the tail of my boat and pro-pelled me onward. Although the wind freshened and the waves developed an ugly curl, I greedily stayed out in the channel for the free ride.

On the Chilean coast, you can see a gale before you can feel it or hear it. The wind drops invisibly down the mountainsides, but when it hits the water it tears at the surface. A sharp line forms across the sea; on one side of the line, friendly wavelets play on a green sea, while the other side is covered by angry foam. The waves generated by the first onslaught of a fast-moving gale have no majesty like the waves that have developed over thousands of miles of ocean. Instead, they are bunched up and agitated and jump chaotically like a rioting crowd.

The channel was bounded by cliffs, so I had to continue down-wind until I could find a harbor. I lowered sail, tightened the draw-strings of my hood, and felt the first onslaught of noise, wetness, and wind. Within fifteen minutes, the juvenile waves matured. A steep wave lifted the stern of my kayak; I drifted sideways and cranked hard on the rudder to avoid broaching and capsizing. Then I surfed the wave until it broke across my back and the white foam rolled over the deck.

I looked behind me to watch the next wave, but my body rotation disrupted my balance, so I faced forward and responded to the sound and feel of the water.

As another line of white approached unseen, I heard a loud *whoosh* that was a new sound, like rushing air, not water. I grasped the paddle tighter but didn't know what was behind me or how I should react. The sound grew louder, and I turned my head to stare into the eyeball of a dolphin, tail in the water and face in the air. A *whoosh* on the other side of my kayak announced that a second dolphin was surf-ing the wave with me, riding high on the crest, at shoulder level. Then the wave subsided and both dolphins disappeared. When the next breaker rose, four dolphins surfed along with me, smiling. I took a paddle stroke to stabilize myself. As one side of the double-bladed paddle dipped into the water and the other side rose, the closest dolphin darted under the uplifted paddle and dove beneath my boat. When I took the next stroke and lifted the opposite side of my blade, a second dolphin accelerated on the other side of my boat and dove. I was sure that the two creatures would collide underwater, but the second swam beneath the first, its dorsal fin crossing beneath the other's tail. The next wave came, and six or eight dolphins were diving under my boat in rhythm with my paddling, crossing beneath like a zipper closing in front of me. It was a magical zipper, because as it closed, it opened the way and carried me safely along. The game enforced my paddling rhythm; if I missed a stroke or took one too late, I would hit a dolphin on the back and that would be a rude thing to do to one's playmates. I also realized that if the dolphins lost their rhythm, one might sever my flimsy kayak with its sharp fin. But they were born in the water, had evolved aquatic precision for millions of years, and understood the rules of the game.

After about fifteen minutes, the wind died and the dolphins disappeared. It was a strange calm, both welcome and disappointing. A few miles beyond, I paddled into a small bay in the lee of an island. The sea was absolutely flat, and raindrops left circular patterns in the otherwise motionless water. Someone had been here before me and had cleared a tent site with a chain saw. In another place and another time I would have been upset to find such an ugly slash in the wilderness, but on that day I was thankful for the intrusion and the mess, for it meant that I would spend a comfortable night on level, dry soil.

I made camp and climbed to the top of a nearby hill. The rusted hulk of a freighter lay half sunk on a shoal to the southeast. Salvagers had removed anything of value, and loneliness and death hung over the ship's carcass. Ghosts are unwelcome companions after a close call. But the afternoon had been more than just an encounter with a storm; the dolphins had brought a playful affirmation of life. The desolation of this land that had been such a burden was now turning into a friend. It had entered me and run around inside scraping out the cobwebs. The dolphins had played with me only because I had become a creature of the sea with its lonely mists. They had not been there to help the folks on the steel freighter with its electric lights and throbbing engine. I sat there looking at death and feeling alive and then walked down to cook dinner.

8

The next day I paddled southward out of the narrow, protected channels into the Straits of Magellan. On its western edge, the straits fan out, and in the northern portion of this fan there is a collection of thousands of small islands, some a few acres in size, others as large as a house, and still others nothing more than a point of rock sticking out of the sea at low tide. A map is useless in this region because you can't match the islands with all the tiny dots on the map, so I took a compass heading, and paddled as if there were no land in sight. It was foggy, still, and pouring rain. My universe was reduced to a circle one hundred yards in diameter with me at the center. Islands entered from beyond and settled into nowhere behind me. A great, low-frequency Pacific Ocean swell gently lifted and dropped my boat and slurped against the rocks.

It was eerie and spiritual, but at the same time I was soggy, hungry, and lonely. In our normal lives we are constantly bombarded by noise and color. Although most of these stimuli are so meaningless that we forget them almost immediately, we seek new ones to maintain the habit. Living on the land, without any Pepsi ads to show how lively things really were, the monotony of paddling often dragged into boredom. Against the pale greens of the forest, the gray-green sea, and the white mists, one new image might appear in a day, or one new one every two or three days.

Some images were obviously powerful, like the storm and the dolphins, but others were strong only because of the setting. For example, Magellanic penguins would approach my kayak underwater without either of us being aware of the other. If they surfaced near the boat, they stared at me for an instant, took a gulp of air, emitted a strange cry, and quickly dove, leaving behind only a ripple on the sea and a phosphorescent image on my retina. After seeing the first one, I asked myself, "Did I really see a black and white bird with a smile-shaped line beneath its bill and another around its eye?" I searched the water for hours, waiting for the second one, and when I saw it I grasped at its rapidly disappearing image to confirm my earlier impression. These flashes of black and white became important to me; I tried to predict when they would arrive and spent long hours waiting for them. The penguin's cry sounded like a cross between a duck's quack and a cow's moo, so I called them Surprise Moo Ducks and was amused for weeks at my own humor.

9

A few days later, I took a shortcut through a narrow kayak-sized passage only twenty feet wide at low tide. A stiff breeze drove clouds across the hilltops, but only gentle gusts wafted through the corkscrew channel. However, when I turned into a wider passageway, the wind met me head-on. I wanted to pull to shore, but the channel was lined with cliffs. According to my map, a safe harbor lay a quarter of a mile ahead, so I raced against the storm. The wind intensified until it held me at a standstill and then it pushed me slowly backward. Shelter was so close, if the wind would only slacken for fifteen minutes I'd be safe. But it didn't, so I turned around and ran before the freshening gale.

A large, protected fiord lay a few miles downwind, but I didn't want to lose that much distance so I gambled that I could ride out the squall in my kayak by hiding behind a rocky point. I paddled into the small sheltered cove behind the rock and turned to face the channel. The wind howled a few feet to my right, hit the shore behind me, reflected off the bank, and eddied back. Thus, the wind eddy pushed gently at my back, coaxing me out of my shelter. For an hour I paddled backward to keep my position behind the rock. Gradually, the storm shifted toward the west and the wall of wind edged closer. First, it caught the tip of my paddle as I backstroked, then a gust hit me in the face forcing me to paddle forward, then backward again as the back eddy took over. The waves rose and I bounced against the rocks.

I gripped my paddle tightly, took a deep breath, paddled out into the storm, and turned toward the shelter of the fiord. The wind grabbed the tops of the waves and hurled foam horizontally across the water, blurring the distinction between sea and air. Riding in the kayak, I wasn't floating on the water as much as I was floating within a world where fresh water and saltwater met. I'd feel and hear a wave rising behind me, then the wind and howl would diminish as the wave curled, cradling me, protecting me from the storm, and embracing me in the calm air of the tube. At the bottom of the wave, there was no horizon, no universe, no future, just water poised in an improbably graceful arc over my head. Within moments the wet greenness descended, burying my boat and leaving me alone with only my head and shoulders protruding above the white foam. My spray skirt kept the water out of the cockpit so the boat shed its weight and bobbed to the surface. I was afraid that the wind would pull my paddle out of my grip; worse yet, if I exposed the paddle, a gust could catch the blade with enough force to flip me over. So I tucked the paddle flat against the deck, grabbed my tiller lines and hunkered low in the boat.

When a wave broke over me, I thought about nothing but the wave itself, but when I rose high on a crest and viewed the larger landscape, a new danger loomed. The wind was driving me directly toward the shore, where waves would quickly beat me to death against the cliffs. When a rising wave sheltered me from the wind, I paddled furiously beam to the storm, toward the fiord. Then, before the wave broke, I quickly turned downwind so I wouldn't broach and capsize. This zigzag motion led me toward shelter, but not rapidly enough. My course still pointed toward fatality on the rocks.

I rose to the next crest, took quick mental bearings, recalculated, and came up with the same answer. I paddled harder, started my beam run earlier, before the rising wave cast much shelter, and then held the course longer until I careened sideways on the steepening wave. I thought, "I might make it, but it will be close." My mind stepped outside the situation and told me, "Look around, Jon, remember this. You will never be here again." It was an odd voice: quiet, unhurried.

My inner voice was comforting, but it wasn't much help in my dash for the fiord. Then luck intervened. You can't stay alive if you depend on luck too often, but every once in a while, that's all there is left. The wind slackened for about ten minutes, I paddled hard, and when the storm intensified again I was in the fiord and headed for shelter. After a wild ride downwind, I found a small bay, pulled in, dragged my kayak up the beach, and crawled into the bushes.

A few yards up the hill, I found a protected platform beneath a thick barrier of trees. The forest canopy deflected the wind, filtered the sunlight, and dispersed the rain into a fine mist. The green mosses and yellow-green lichens on the forest floor were spongy and comfortable. A roar in the canopy overhead reminded me that the storm still raged, but that was another world, far removed from my burrow within the rain forest. I sat in the mist with my back against a rock, watched the water drip off my parka, and relaxed. Then I pitched my tent and crawled inside to brew a hot cup of tea.

The following morning I walked to a rocky point overlooking the fiord. The storm still raced across the water, throwing the tops of the waves against the falling rain. I tried to imagine a kayak in the middle of the mayhem, then returned to my den, read, brewed another hot drink, and took a long nap.

I awoke and lay in my bag, watching the trees through the pale yellow nylon and listening to the wind howling through the foliage. My mind drifted to another time: It was past midnight in the instrument room of the chemistry laboratory, and I was firing molecules toward fatal collisions with speeding electrons, giving the resulting ions one wild ride through a magnetic field before they would land, splat, against my detectors. Each molecule traveled alone, through a high vacuum, and my job was to figure out how the molecules vibrated and what held them together.

My results had been controversial, and I spoke at an international conference in Brussels. After my talk, several scientists invited me to lunch. I looked around the table at professors from renowned universities in several countries. Lunch droned on into our third cup of coffee. The men's faces were yellow and saggy, tanned by fluorescent lights and softened by the controlled temperature and humidity of the chemistry laboratory. We talked about designing a new experiment to confirm or contradict my conclusions.

I lazily wandered deeper into time, toward my life's earliest images: a dog that frightened me, a broken tricycle, a friend crying after I had pushed him and he had cut his head against an iron fence. My parents told me that before I could walk, I crawled into the bathroom, climbed onto the toilet seat, reached across for the sink, made a bold move, and pulled myself into the basin. They found me sitting there, apparently contented. Later, when I learned how to walk, I routinely explored—or was lost—among sand dunes near our summer bungalow at Rockaway Beach.

Christmas 1974, four years earlier, Debby and I drove to her parents' ranch near Santa Barbara. We took Nathan and Noey to Disneyland, ate too much Danish pastry, traded gifts, and headed back north. We spent a night at a friend's carpeted ranch-style house at the end of a cul-de-sac in suburban Portland. The following morning, as we continued north along the interstate, Debby told me that some day she hoped we would be successful enough to have a house like that: dishwasher, washer-dryer, guest room for visitors, and all the other amenities of a comfortable life. I told her not to plan on it, that it wasn't where I was headed. The following morning she told me that maybe it would be better if we separated so we could each follow our own dreams.

I pushed the thoughts aside. I was short on fuel but started the stove for a diversion, not because I needed another hot drink.

Damp unwashed underwear hung to dry on lines strung above my head. "Hung to dry!" Nothing would dry in this land of dripping mosses and perpetual rain. Maybe "hung to get less damp" or "hung so as not to get wetter on the tent floor." When the storm ended I planned to crawl into that clammy, smelly material, cover it with my heavy vinyl rain gear, and let my body shiver until I warmed up.

My thoughts drifted again. I remembered Noey, raising her hands in mock resignation, telling me that I would have to sleep with Mama if I couldn't find my shoes. Nathan stood behind her, watching silently. Nathan was always the quiet one, watching, listening, absorbing it all. And where was my daughter Reeva, whom I hardly knew? Reeva was growing up with Elizabeth somewhere, separated from me by a court order written by a hostile judge who had reacted to my long hair and defiant attitude.

All that was far away. I was camped on an uninhabited, windswept island, and to survive I had to wait out the storm and paddle toward civilization with a quick detour to Cape Horn.

10

The wind subsided after four days. On a calm, gray, glorious southern-latitude day I ventured out of my fiord, retraced my steps, and paddled back into the Straits of Magellan. Although the straits are narrow compared with the open ocean, they are considerably wider than the canals I had been paddling through. The open water was more dangerous, but I was less isolated because I had reached a shipping lane. If I needed help, a vessel would certainly pass within a few days. Although I saw no houses, ships, or people, I was temporarily close to civilization.

In 1520 Ferdinand Magellan sailed down the east coast of South America, exploring every major bay and river mouth until he found a path to the Pacific. Later, Spanish and Portuguese adventurers sailed through the narrow, dangerous Straits of Magellan in their clumsy vessels and then turned northward to colonize the west coast of North and South America and to steal gold from the Native Americans. In 1577 Francis Drake left England with five ships to steal gold from the Spanish and Portuguese. When Drake set sail, no one knew about Cape Horn and the ocean passage between South America and Antarctica. Explorers assumed that the Straits of Magellan formed the only passage through an otherwise continuous land barrier to the South Pole. Drake abandoned two of his ships after crossing the Atlantic and cleared the straits with the three that remained. Almost immediately he encountered a horrible storm, "the like whereof no traveller hath felt, neither hath there been such a tempest, so violent and of such continuance since Noah's flood; for it lasted full 52 days." * One ship was destroyed and a second fled back through the Straits and returned to England.

Aboard the only remaining vessel, the *Golden Hind,* Drake took advantage of a brief lull in the tempest, anchored near an island, and

---

*Nuó de Silva (Drake's pilot), quoted in Eric Shipton, *Tierra del Fuego: The Fatal Lodestone* (London: Charles Knight & Co., Ltd., 1973), p. 43.

sent eight crew members ashore to fill the water casks. He must have been in the eye of a hurricane, because the storm struck once again with sudden fury. Fearing for his ship, Drake ordered the anchor line cut, abandoning the water crew. The ship sailed south-west, running before the wind, which was the only thing that Drake could do. Owing to his limited knowledge of geography, he was sure that at any moment he would smash into a long peninsula that he thought extended all the way to Antarctica. But instead he sailed into the previously unknown passage to the south. According to some historians, Drake actually landed on Cape Horn Island and realized that he was standing on the southernmost bit of land in the Western Hemisphere. He climbed to the top of the bluff and ordered a sailor to hold onto his ankles so he could "cast himself down on the uttermost point, grovelling, and so reached out his body over the sea."*

In the meantime, the water crew had been abandoned on an uncharted island, thousands of miles from civilization, with a sixteen-foot open boat. They had knives and cotton clothes—no guns, no sleeping bags, no tents. They ate shellfish, crabs, and roots and rowed north. After reaching the Straits of Magellan, they caught fish and birds and occasionally killed a baby seal basking on the shore. A few thousand miles later, along the coast of southern Brazil, a Native American war party captured four of the sailors and killed two. The four captured men were never heard from again. The other two escaped; injured, they rowed to a small island. Their boat was smashed in the surf as they came to shore and they found no running water on the island. After two months of terrible thirst and hardship, they built a raft and sailed back to the mainland, but on finding water, one of the two drank himself to death. The last survivor continued on land, alone. He was befriended by a tribe of cannibals and taught them how to make shields for warfare. These were such a great success that his new friends achieved a momentous victory against their rivals and even went on to kill (and eat?) "certain Portugals and Negroes" that they came across. The tide turned when the sailor was captured by the Portuguese and sentenced to be a galley slave for the

*Richard Hough, *The Blind Horn's Hate* (New York: Norton, 1971), p. 214.

rest of his life. But he escaped and eventually made his way back to England.

Although I recalled this story to assure myself that, by comparison, I was fortunate and well equipped, I still felt overwhelmed by all that gray-green water, and I hugged the north shore tentatively. The following day was relatively calm so I crossed the strait and continued eastward toward Paso Tortuoso, named for its sinuous, twisting contours. The narrow passage afforded protection from storms and waves, providing the intimacy of the sea-land junction that I cherished and that captains of larger craft fear.

The sea was calm, and for a change the sun was shining. I stripped off my vinyl rain parka and let the gentle breeze blow through my shirt and across my body. My chest and armpits tingled as my pores greeted the wind, and my capillaries dilated and constricted until they reached equilibrium. As I rounded a bend, the massive hull of a supertanker appeared incongruously out of the wilderness. I hadn't seen anyone for a few weeks, and even though I knew that the ship would never stop, the proximity to people was exciting. I thought the crew would come out on deck and wave, I'd tip my paddle jauntily, and the captain would blow the big whistle. The tanker kept appearing for a long time. My kayak was a fraction the size of its lifeboats. I could paddle around inside the pipes used for loading and unloading oil. I probably registered as a floating log on its radar; I was too small to exist. These thoughts were interrupted by the realization that I was in the only channel, and if I didn't do something fast the tanker would run me over and grind me up with its massive propellers. I turned and paddled for the beach, and as I was making my escape, I looked up again for signs of humanity. Miles above me, halfway to the sun, I saw the bridge that housed sailors: sons of Drake, blood brothers of Slocum. The windows were copper-tinted one-way mirrored glass, so I couldn't look beyond the reflective metallic eyeballs of the monster that was bearing down on me. Behind the eyes, beneath the liver, within the fire-breathing bowels, men were drinking coffee and watching a video. We weren't destined to meet. It was an encounter with a ship, not with people. The ship wasn't being malicious, but it certainly had no intention of altering its course to avoid me.

11

There is limited storage capacity in a kayak, so I brought short rations and planned to supplement my diet with fish. I had assumed that fish would be plentiful because southwest Chile is geographically similar to southeast Alaska, where fish are abundant. I brought a hand reel with a jig for catching bottom fish and a stout eighty-pound line for yanking in the big ones. In the early days of the journey I religiously fished at likely points, but I always came up empty-handed. As miles went by, my attempts were more sporadic; the day after my encounter with the tanker, I tossed the line and all the lures overboard. If I wasn't going to catch any fish, I didn't want to be troubled with trying.

Later, when the trip was over, I asked a fisherman why I hadn't caught anything. He assured me that there was nothing to catch. "But there are seals," I protested, "and seals eat fish, so there must be fish." I had to repeat myself several times in my broken Spanish to be understood, but I persisted. Finally, my friend answered that the fish are very deep, three hundred feet or more.

The evening after my tantrum with the fishing line, I decided to concentrate on shellfish. Mussels had been abundant, but I couldn't find any that night. Instead, I walked the beach at low tide and collected limpets, which are small mollusks, like dime-sized abalone. Limpet eaters are on the bottom of the affluence scale as far as hunter-gatherers go. Sitting on the beach in a light drizzle, munching my bowl of rice and limpets, I thought about twenty-pound cod and became angry that evolution hadn't produced something good to eat to fill such an obvious ecological niche.

I usually ate only three-quarters of my dinner, saving the rest for lunch, because I didn't have room in the kayak for a two-month supply of bread or crackers. That evening I ate the whole ration, then broke into my special stash of treats and cooked a packaged tapioca pudding for the following day. But during the night, the smell of fresh pudding interrupted my dreams, and I awoke and gobbled it all. Chagrined at stealing from myself, I set off the next morning with just a few hard candies to chew on until dinner.

12

By the start of the third week, I was still in the Straits of Magellan, paddling eastward. I hadn't spoken with anyone, taken a shower, changed my underwear, put on dry socks, relaxed in a chair, or eaten a good meal for fourteen days. My clothes and sleeping bag had settled into steady-state dampness.

On the fifteenth day, while paddling along the rocky coast through a dense fog, I drifted over a whale skeleton. Its massive head was anchored on the rocks a foot underwater, and its torso and tail dropped off into the darker depths. Ligaments still held the bones together, and bits of flesh and skin drifted with the current. Small waves refracted the light so that the submerged tail appeared to undulate as if to coax the giant back into the sea. Death seemed natural, a simple embrace by the sea that had become my companion. With a simple mistake—or an intentional flick of my hips—I could capsize the kayak and join the whale where the frigid water would gradually begin to feel warm.

"Whoa! Wake up! Bad idea!"

The fleeting image of my own death scared me, and I pulled to shore for a midday break. I climbed a rocky prominence far enough inland to rise above the ubiquitous smell of decay along the intertidal zone. I wasn't despondent, but something had guided my morbid fantasy. Maybe I had left my normal world so far behind that all the barriers had disappeared.

I didn't talk aloud to myself often, but I needed a human sound to break the spell, so I talked into the wind,

"Don't worry, Jon, you haven't lost your senses. You had a momentary understanding of the way things are. Animals are born, they live, they die, they rot—you will too. You saw it all in one emotional instant. No big deal. You still know where the limits are."

My words drifted through the rocks like morning mist that lingers and then evaporates into still air. Time to change moods. I tried shouting, "Whooo! whooo! yeah! yeah!" That didn't work. No, my mood rested on a loneliness that I couldn't shatter.

I returned to the boat and carried my lunch back to the rock outcrop. Today's midday meal was the usual cold damp leftover rice from dinner. I had cooked this particular concoction with a package of dried asparagus soup and a few mussels. I ate a spoonful and looked into the tasteless mush; I unwrapped a hard candy from my pocket, carefully crushed it between two rocks, dusted the orange sugary splinters into the rice, mixed it up, and munched the mixture slowly. Much better.

I could contemplate loneliness and mortality some other time, as an alternative to reading or studying Spanish. Right now, clear thinking was my salvation and joy.

To dispel the mood, I reminded myself, "Watch the sky, watch the sea. Watch your steps, literally. Don't slip on the wet kelp-covered rocks, because even a small injury like a sprained ankle would be serious out here. Make a mental picture of where your foot will land, place it carefully, and then move on to the next step."

If I could live with such precision, not only would I increase my chances of survival and success, but also I would drive away all the sniveling mental distractions: "Oh, I am cold. Oh, I am wet. Death is okay. I am so sorry for myself because I am hungry, bored, and lonely."

Words were great, but paddling was going to get me to Cape Horn. I picked up my lunch pail and spoon, and walked back down to the boat.

13

That afternoon the wind was blowing strongly, but I raised the sail nevertheless. The kayak whistled through the water, its internal skeleton flexing with the waves, like the vertebrae of a whale driving its huge fluke. I tightened the shrouds and backstay to stiffen the mast and loosened the slipknots on the sheets so that I could spill the wind when gusts were too strong. Hanging onto the edge of danger, I whisked along at three times paddling speed. A tugboat appeared around a curve, heading north and pulling a gleaming, white passenger ship. The ship was far away, but I guessed, correctly, that she was the *Lindblad Explorer*, an elegant cruise ship for expensive Antarctic tours. I thought of dances on the afterdeck, the sudden screech as she struck a reef or an iceberg, the dull silence as her engines went dead. I felt proud to be afloat and sailing aggressively in waters that could disable such a large ship.

A few hours later, I turned south, out of the Straits of Magellan, down Canal Barbara, and toward the Horn. The mountains on my right provided shelter from the west wind, and I dropped sail and paddled through the calm water. Several tidewater glaciers groaned and spit icebergs into the sea. A gray flightless steamer duck squawked and raced away. These ducks have stopped midway in an evolutionary transition between graceful fliers and graceful swimmers. When frightened, steamer ducks quack vigorously and beat the water furiously with wings and feet, trying to gain enough speed to fly; instead they half-run, half-swim across the surface of the water. The splash and commotion continued until the duck was a small dot like a cartoon roadrunner disappearing on the desert horizon.

I took off my raincoat, and even though water dropped off my paddle and soaked my jacket to the elbow, my body welcomed the escape from its plastic covering. Two whales were making love in the bay, grasping each other with their fins, breathing hard, blowing, and rolling over and over. I stopped to watch, feeling a strange mixture of arousal and embarrassment. A male sea lion barked along the shore. Perhaps he had also been watching and was bellowing to reaffirm his transitory supremacy over his harem. Rain fell and the dots grew to form intersecting rings on the calm sea. Reluctantly I put my raincoat back on. A breeze spilled down off the glacier and ruffled the sea, the whales sounded and disappeared, and the sea lion slipped off the rocks.

Contentment washed through me. Few people had played with dolphins and glided unobtrusively through a whale's bridal chamber. I would remember these images long after I had forgotten the hardship and loneliness. I paddled toward shore to look for camp, but steep, timbered hillsides rose abruptly from the water. An hour later my back muscles ached and a cold chop splashed against me, but still there was no comfortable camp. I thought about the whales, about making love, and then I remembered skiing with Marion, followed by evenings drinking champagne by the wood-burning stove.

I wasn't going to think about Marion, the good times. Now she was gone and I was alone in this place, a creature of the sea. No! I

wasn't thinking clearly. I reminded myself that I had replaced one rich-
ness with another. But my mind couldn't win over my feelings, and I
couldn't hold onto the joy I had felt only an hour before. As I wearily
paddled the last half mile toward shore, I promised myself a positive
journal entry after dinner. I made camp, crawled into the tent to escape
the rain, shucked a few mussels into a pot of white rice, added a package of cream of tomato soup that tasted mainly of salt and flour, and
rummaged in my food bag for a few raisins to give the meal some flavor.
When I picked up my journal, I wrote about an uncomfortable morning
and barely mentioned the sights, sounds, and feelings of the afternoon:

> *Last night was the wettest and most miserable I've spent on this trip. It*
> *poured and the entire muskeg became an interminable bog, so camp in*
> *the bog or camp in the ocean; I chose the bog and it was wet and soggy.*
> *I think that the only thing that got me out of bed this morning was the*
> *knowledge that it was more miserable in bed than in the boat.*

The rain cleared by midmorning of the following day, and the sun
came out a few hours later. It was the first warm, dry afternoon since
the start of the journey, eighteen days before. I paddled to shore early,
took a bath in a cold stream, and broke out my only clean pair of
underwear. Then I built a fire to dry my clothes.

I turned my back to the fire and let the heat roast my hamstrings. Clearly
I needed more control over my wild mood swings. I was tired and the fire
felt good. It was too much work, just then, to sort through the emotions.

14

One day, out of the mist, one of my good friends came by to
pay me a visit. The visit was more intense than any normal
daydream. In a daydream, one thinks about things that would be fun
to experience. In this encounter I seemed to be experiencing the

event itself. I was carrying too much sail in a choppy sea, when one of my climbing partners appeared, perched on the deck just in front of the mast. In the past, in real life, I had used bad judgment in making a decision that led us both into a dangerous situation. He had never forgiven me, and on this visit he hadn't been with me long before he reminded me of past miscalculations and argued that we should drop sail and find shelter. I could hear the timbre of his voice, see the lines on his face, feel his presence. However, I found the conversation annoying, so I asked him to leave, which he did. Soon another friend came to visit. The previous fall he and I had planned a difficult climb, but friends warned that it was too hard for us and we would fail. We set out anyway and succeeded. He was excited by my reckless sailing and stood on the bow waving his fists in the air and yelling into the wind. He came to visit frequently, and I really enjoyed those times.

In many societies, people induce visions by practicing self-denial: Don't eat enough to feel full, shield yourself only incompletely from the elements, remain silent and alone. Self-denial wasn't my goal; it was only a necessary step toward my goal. Yet the hunger, cold, and solitude were taking me on their own journey, a curious subtheme to the slow progress plotted out on my map.

During my good moods I accepted the asceticism and embraced its rewards. I practiced my paddling mantra patiently, waiting for a rare but special image, and I had no problem accepting the obvious: You can go only so far every day, and if the tide or the wind turns against you, you have to stop. But during my bad days, I chafed at the agonizing progress of one person in a small boat in a hostile landscape. I just wanted to reach the Horn and go home.

15

At the southern edge of Canal Barbara, my route led outside the shelter of the islands and across an exposed portion of the

Pacific Ocean. The danger presented by an ocean wave is more closely related to its shape than to its size. A boat can fall off the face of a steep six-foot wave and be pounded by the breaking top. In contrast, a thirty-foot wave poses no threat to a small boat if the leeward face is soft and bosomy. As I swung into the large swells in Paso Brecknock, the waves broke against the rocks, sending foamy towers into the air. But there was no violence in deep water. At the bottom of a trough I was surrounded by three-story-high walls of water that blocked out the wind and left me within a protected calm. It seemed that a thirty-foot mountain of liquid should spill onto my head like water pouring out of a glass, but a wave obediently follows the laws of physics and slides under a boat. When I rose to the crest, the wind blew at my back and a two-foot chop danced across the surface. Then the wave slid out from under me, and I dropped gently back into the trough.

A fishing boat churned out of the canal into Paso Brecknock, heading northward. It towered on a crest, then disappeared. The craft looked so vulnerable every time it was swallowed that I watched anxiously for the radio antenna to reappear. Three men ran out on deck and shouted. Their voices were distorted by the wind and the sound of the diesel, so communication was impossible. Nevertheless, when I reached the next crest, I yelled back to ask for a cup of hot coffee and a dozen oatmeal cookies. It was an abstract request to the cosmos, and the men on the deck grinned and waved their hats, although I'm sure they couldn't hear my words. They puttered off to the north, while I made my slower way southeast. It was a small human contact but my first in nineteen days, and it felt warm and comforting.

The day after rounding Paso Brecknock, I was battling a nasty concoction of intermittent head winds, cross winds, adverse currents, and kelp, when I heard another motor sound around the corner. This was not the measured putt-putt of a small diesel but a high-pitched whine, almost like an airplane skimming along the surface. I didn't have to wait long to discover the source, for within a few minutes three sleek military patrol boats roared up the strait. I was tangled in the kelp and floundering against the rocks, so I set my paddle on my lap and watched them zoom up the channel. They almost passed me, but before disappearing alarms sounded, the boats veered abruptly in my direction, and men scrambled on deck, ripping covers off machine gun mounts and unclasping safety latches on torpedoes. It all seemed rather abstract; my boat was smaller than the torpedoes aimed at me. I tried to smile at these three heavily armed naval vessels, although I wasn't sure that friendly thoughts could penetrate the armor. The helmsmen drove those gray, camouflaged speedsters toward me quickly, but gently and elegantly. When the motors decelerated, the hulls stopped planing and the boats settled, blub, blub, blub, in a tight circle around me. I stared upward at fifty-caliber machine guns, an array of small arms, and those ridiculous torpedoes. A man with a megaphone called down in Spanish, "What language do you choose to speak in?"

It was the first voice I had heard in twenty-one days and it seemed friendly enough, so I yelled back that I spoke some Spanish but was best at English. He called back in polished English, asking me to come aboard. A sailor threw me a two-inch line that was fatter than my mast. When it landed on one side of my deck, the whole boat listed. The line wouldn't fit through any of my tie-off loops, so I hitched it around a duffel that was lashed securely, looked upward into the barrels of half a dozen M-16s, and tried to figure out exactly how I was supposed to climb aboard. I crawled out onto the edges of my cockpit on all fours and delicately stood up on the thin wooden edges of the cowling. It occurred to me that it would not be good style to lose my balance and fly off with a splash into the water. By standing almost on my toes, I reached up along the smooth overhanging hull and managed to grasp a bow stanchion with my fingertips. Letting my feet swing free, I pulled myself up by my arms. Halfway up, with my feet dangling in the air and my kayak now swinging out of reach in the current, I remembered that for the past few weeks I hadn't bothered to fasten my suspenders on my rain pants so that I could urinate easily when the need arose. Looking down, I saw that my drawers were sliding off and about to fall into the sea. By kicking my feet and holding my legs far apart, I squirmed aboard on my stomach with my rain gear at my ankles and my fly unzipped. The antics seemed to reassure my captors, because when I looked around the sailors were suppressing their laughter and no one seemed as alert and trigger happy as they had been a few moments earlier. I smiled and a sailor escorted me to the bridge.

The officer was cordial. I showed him my papers, we had a cup of coffee, and he asked with interest about my journey to the Horn. He assured me that the navy would keep an eye on my safety and requested that I stop in at the base in Puerto Williams to report to the *comandante*. I explained that Puerto Williams was several days out of my way and that I would have to regain my route by paddling against the wind. He responded: "Four or five days is so little, the Horn is so dangerous, we're concerned for your safety. We have had coffee together, we are both friends and gentlemen, we request it of you." He gave me a broad smile. "You will agree, won't you?"

Of course I had no choice.

"Do you need anything, anything at all? Food, clothing, are you all right?"

I was short on food but wouldn't admit it. We shook hands and I left. That night I wrote in my journal:

> *Negotiated the reverse overhang into my boat. Vroom! Vroom! Then silence; a few gulls, a seal in the kelp. And I'm glad and sad. It's much safer now; if I get stranded at the Horn, I can wait for rescue, which is sure to come. But it is sad in a way, for the exploring nature of the journey has changed; some exposure is lost. Well, I am living in the age I am living in and it's just as well because I could be dead otherwise. I still have quite a bit of serious ocean ahead of me.*

I later learned that I had been stopped because there were high tensions between Chile and Argentina. Apparently, the Chileans had feared that the Argentines might spearhead a surprise attack by sending commandos in by kayak.

Later that afternoon, I rounded a point and saw a crab-fishing boat at anchor in the bay. I felt that I had seen enough people for the day and almost didn't want to meet them. For a moment I started paddling away, but that seemed foolish so I turned in. They were friendly and talkative and deep-fat fried a batch of sugary pastries called *sopaipillas*. I ate heartily enough to get sick and throw up after they left. As I lay in my tent, nursing my angry stomach, I wrote:

After three weeks alone, people were people and I was just me. I didn't forget to talk or stand awkwardly alone. The solo concept is no big deal; outside of the work and danger, it doesn't feel that I am more alone than if I were doing the same trip with a friend. I'm glad to have learned that; it makes me feel strong.

I brewed a cup of hot sugary milk, but it made me sick again. I had sunk so far into dampness, limpets, and boiled rice that my body rejected normal food. I crawled into my bag but couldn't sleep until I admitted that I had lied to myself. I picked up my journal again and wrote:

Next kayaking trip will be to the fiords of Norway with reindeer milk, beer, and women between the cold, spray-filled days at sea.

16

Even though I was headed for the wilderness of Cape Horn, I was spiraling back toward towns and villages in the Beagle Channel ahead of me; there were people—there was war.

This pile of things and ideas that we call Western Civilization used to have better manners. Long ago it resided in a few isolated cities and only occasionally ventured into the countryside. But lately it has trespassed in places where perhaps it doesn't belong. It's not just that when you go out on an adventure and want to be alone, some PT boat bristling with torpedoes comes zooming up to you and harshens your meditative buzz. This encroachment doesn't only affect a few eccentric kayakers and climbers; it affects all of us, whole civilizations, to say nothing about all the plants and animals that don't write books about themselves. Where were the Yamana Indians who once paddled around these waters in their sewn bark canoes?* Why didn't I bump into one of them instead of the computerized, steel, turbine-powered jetmobiles? Well, with a few exceptions, the Yamana are all dead.

In the 1880s there were about twenty-five hundred to three thousand Yamana in western Tierra del Fuego. In the mid-1970s there were nine. In explaining what happened, encyclopedias use syntax like "disintegrative factors" were the effect of "white man's diseases and miscegenation." That doesn't sound too bad. The language is too flat to evoke terrible images like smallpox epidemics and genocide. You don't look into the page and see a people torn apart by invaders, ravaged by sickness and starvation, shot by bounty hunters, and then eliminated as the few survivors retreat from the canals and straggle into the cities to be absorbed. But I wasn't living in the library. I was living on the land.

I hadn't thought about the Yamana during the first portion of my trip. The land was so harsh and uncompromising that it seemed natural that it should be uninhabited. I had empathized with Drake's water crew. This wasn't an island paradise where one would dream of finding a wife and eating breadfruit until death followed a peaceful old age. This was a place to escape from, even if it meant rowing to England. But as I sat in my kayak, surrounded by kelp that subdued the tops of the waves, I finally began to feel comfortable here. The lingering diesel fumes contrasted sharply with the soft smells of the sea. The Yamana had a verb, *iya*, which means "to moor your canoe to a streamer of kelp." Another verb, *okon*, means "to sleep in a floating canoe," which is very different from sleeping in a bark hut or sleeping with your wife.

The Yamana traveled in small bands, built temporary stick dwellings, and moved constantly to avoid depleting the mussel beds that were their primary source of food. Charles Darwin, who visited the region aboard the *Beagle* in 1832, considered them among the poorest people on the earth. He wrote:

*The indigenous tribe that lived in the Beagle Channel and Cape Horn area is generally called Yaghan in English texts and Yamana in Spanish sources. Museum curators in Punta Arenas and Puerto Williams also prefer Yamana, so I defer to local usage.

While going one day ashore near Wollaston Island, we pulled alongside a canoe with six Fuegians. These were the most abject and miserable creatures I anywhere beheld. . . . These Fuegians in the canoe were quite naked, and even one full-grown woman was absolutely so. It was raining heavily, and the fresh water, together with the spray, trickled down her body. In another harbor, not far distant, a woman, who was suckling a recently-born child, came one day alongside the vessel, and remained there out of mere curiosity, whilst the sleet fell and thawed on her naked bosom and on the skin of her naked baby! These poor wretches were stunted in their growth, their hideous faces bedaubed with white paint, their skins filthy and greasy, their hair entangled, their voices discordant, and their gestures violent and without dignity. Viewing such men, one can hardly make oneself believe that they are fellow creatures placed in the same world. . . .

At night, five or six human beings, naked and scarcely protected from the wind and rain of this tempestuous climate, sleep on the wet ground coiled up like animals. Whenever it is low water, winter or summer, night or day, they must rise to pick shellfish from the rocks; and the women either dive to collect sea eggs, or sit patiently in their canoes, and with a baited hair-line without any hook, jerk out tiny fish. If a seal is killed, or the floating carcass of a putrid whale discovered, it is a feast; and such miserable food is assisted by a few tasteless berries and fungi.*

Darwin, one of the world's great scientists, who was such a careful and unbiased observer of the natural world, lost his objectivity when he contemplated the lives of his fellow humans. The Yamana didn't view themselves as "abject and miserable." The word *Yamana* means "to live, breathe, be happy, recover from sickness, and be sane," and to them their territory was a paradise compared with the outside world, which was hell.

The Yamana left no permanent physical mark on the land, no bent grasses where they slept, no stick-and-leaf shelters, no paintings of naked bodies snuggling warmly together against the icy rain. They

*Charles Darwin, The Voyage of the Beagle: Charles Darwin's Journal of Researches, ed. Janet Browne and Michael Neve (New York: Penguin, 1989), pp. 177–78.

didn't write books or establish nations. They lived on the land and now they are gone. The only remnant is a void. Voids are hard to see at first. We are not trained to look for them, but once they appear, they glare like neon.

17

The northwest arm of the Beagle Channel is lined with tidewater glaciers that tumble over the cliffs and cascade into the ocean. Yet the fatigue, the wetness, and the hunger overpowered any peaceful equanimity I could find in the soft mists. My journal entries concentrated mainly on winds, squalls, deteriorating equipment, and bad camps:

> *Sailed and paddled simultaneously through a cold, rainy morning and a warm afternoon for thirty miles through glacierville. Camped where the ice meets the sea. Tomorrow with a good run I should make it to Puerto Navarino. Houses, Food??!!*

The next day the wind was calm, and I felt the eternity of the paddling and the infinity of the journey. Rounding a point I came across a house, a snug white house like you might see on a flowered lane, inhabited by blond-haired children. There was no dock, so I pulled my boat up on the rocks. There was a lighthouse beacon on the roof, but the house was really a concrete bunker with recoilless cannons hidden in the bushes to either side. No one had seen me yet, and I mused that commandos in kayaks could easily sneak up on this isolated military outpost. I climbed the hill to knock on the door and meet the guardians of the light and the keepers of the guns, folks whose multiple job was to provide for the safety of passing boats and to protect the area against potential attacks from the Argentines. And what would the enemy attack? The penguins? The canals? The glaciers? The few poor fishermen with their diesel putt-putts and their leaky launches?

A man in a T-shirt answered the door, and after his initial surprise, he invited me in for coffee, cheese, and crackers. Four people lived at the base: an officer with his wife and baby, and a young soldier. When we finished our snack, the officer went out to butcher a sheep for dinner, and the younger man suggested that the two of us go out to hunt guanacos. He explained that my arrival was a rare opportunity because the guanacos live in a valley across the bay, which could be reached easily by kayak and only with great difficulty on foot. I said I'd be happy to oblige and then, out of curiosity, asked him what a guanaco looks like. He rattled on in Spanish, and somehow I translated his explanation to mean that a guanaco is a slightly stunted version of an Australian ostrich. (I later learned that a guanaco is a close relative of a llama.) My new friend, Phillip, retired to his room and returned wearing rubber galoshes, a camouflage marine fatigue suit, and a black beret with an insignia of a regiment *especial*. He carried a pair of binoculars, a sheathed knife slightly smaller than a machete, and an automatic assault rifle.

As we paddled across the bay, Phillip explained that guanacos are very intelligent so we must be quiet and sneaky. I was the bearer of the binoculars and was to follow Phillip and his submachine gun and hand him the glasses when he needed them. Then he presented me the knife. It was also my task to slit the creature's throat after it had been shot.

We landed, secured the boat, and started for the high country. Here, near the southern tip of Tierra del Fuego, Land of Fire, one hundred fifty miles from Cape Horn, where the last glaciated fragments of the continent fade into the ocean that surrounds Antarctica, I was following a man who was intent on tommy-gunning a guanaco or two.

My feet hurt. For the past twenty-six days my feet had been immersed almost constantly in cold saltwater. I wore a pair of loose-fitting tennis shoes over wet-suit booties, an outfit not designed for walking and guanaco hunting. I imagined that I was Charlie Chaplin with his clown shoes, baggy pants, and oversized knife following the regiment through the jungles of Vietnam. Then the blood oozing through my open saltwater sores washed all the romance and humor away.

We crossed over a glacier-fed river by climbing upside down, slothlike, along a fallen tree and dropped into the waist-deep water when the tree grew too thin to support our weight. Phillip got his tommy gun wet. I held the binoculars above my head but sacrificed the knife. We crossed over a mountain and through a swamp but saw no guanacos. Finally we returned home to a late-afternoon lunch of king crab, tomato-vegetable soup, lamb stew, and cinnamon-coated fried bananas. With the exception of storm days, it was my first respite from boating in nearly four weeks.

18

I rested at the lighthouse for a day and a half and then continued eastward. I had originally planned to turn southward into a protected strait along the west side of Isla Navarino, but I had promised the *comandante* that I would report to Puerto Williams, so I reluctantly continued straight along the Beagle Channel.

Puerto Williams is a military base. I recently read a travel article in which the author described Puerto Williams as a remote, dreary outpost, but she had flown there directly from a fancy hotel in Santiago. When I looked at the repetitive rows of pale green barracks, I thought about warm dry beds, not about exterior architecture. Coffee and doughnuts sounded great; I didn't expect cappuccino and a croissant.

The naval officers invited me to dinner and offered me a shower, a bed, and a dry shed to repair my boat. In five days of luxury, I gained weight, resupplied for the journey ahead, and patched worn gear. But at the same time I lost my contact with the land. In a sense, I had to start the trip all over. It's hard to slosh through the cold water in the morning to launch your boat, but your feet have memory and it's harder to get them wet if they remember dryness.

When it was time to go, I knew that I should paddle back upwind toward the safer passage, but I didn't want to. If I sailed downwind from Puerto Williams, I could round the east side of Isla Navarino and paddle south to Punta Guanaco. From Punta Guanaco I would have to paddle a sixteen-mile crossing to Isla Wollaston, the closest island of the Cape Horn Archipelago. Sixteen miles of open water is a long crossing in a kayak, and this crossing was complicated by the fact that the prevailing winds blew from the southwest, pushing me into the South Atlantic. The journey was dangerous but possible. Isla Herschal lay twenty miles further south; then, after four miles of open water, was Isla Hornos, Cape Horn Island.

I thought, "With favorable winds and a little luck, I can make the dangerous passage safely in a week—seven days, 168 hours. Then I can paddle back to Puerto Williams and return to Telluride before ski season ends."

Most of the moisture carried by the westerly winds falls in the islands to the north and west, so the sun shines and the climate is relatively dry in the passages east of Puerto Williams. I paddled out of town under a blue sky with a full stomach and found real earth, not marshy muskeg, to sleep on.

In three days I paddled into Puerto Toro, which was a busy place, with perhaps fifty or one hundred soldiers and a few civilians. A bright sign greeted me. It showed a picture of a penguin with a woolen cap and read:

> BIENVENIDO A PUERTO TORO
> LA CIUDAD MAS ASTRAL DEL MUNDO

> [WELCOME TO PUERTO TORO
> THE SOUTHERNMOST CITY IN THE WORLD]

A port guard told me to check in with Heraldo, the harbormaster. Heraldo's first question was, "What do you think of the sign?"

"The sign?" I queried. I was prepared for normal questions, like "Where did you come from?" or "How far did you paddle today?" and with my marginal Spanish was disarmed by the unusual.

"Yes, the sign," repeated Heraldo. "What do you think of it?"

"Well, I guess that I haven't thought much about it."

We sat down to tea, and Heraldo laid food out on the table. "Yes, it's all wrong, Puerto Toro is not a city, it's a military base, and it's not the southernmost military base, there are many bases in Antarctica. The penguin is phony too," he continued. "There are no penguins around here."

I had to disagree on this last point. I had seen Magellanic penguins to the north and a genuine Antarctic penguin earlier in the afternoon. He discounted my recent sighting and told me that it was merely a wanderer, an adventurer, a gringo like me.

19

With the Horn only a few days away, I wanted to be on the land by myself, not in a house talking about signs and penguins. I left after lunch and paddled around a rocky point until I saw the northernmost tip of Isla Wollaston, fuzzy on the horizon. Cape Horn lay to the south, just beyond the horizon. I had been paddling for thirty-two days, and success seemed very close.

The next morning a brisk wind blew from the northeast. I stuck my head out of the tent, watched the whitecaps, and went back to sleep. A few hours later the wind subsided, so I awoke and ate breakfast. High cirrus clouds raced across the sky, announcing that the weather really hadn't settled. I told myself to wait but then refused to listen. Punta Guanaco was only a few hours to the south. From there I would need a full day to cross the sixteen miles of open water. I reasoned that I could save a day by racing the storm to Punta Guanaco. I had plenty of food and a day hardly mattered at that point, but I refused to listen to my conservative voice.

When the wind freshened, I changed my mind again and decided to make an early camp. Unfortunately, a rising sea had built an ugly surf on the rocky coast. According to my map, there was a broad valley with a river a few miles to the south, and I thought I could avoid the surf by paddling up the river. When I reached the river mouth, the tide was low and the river dropped off a small cliff and cascaded the final ten feet into the sea. No shelter here.

The storm intensified, and I began to worry. I couldn't turn northward and paddle against the wind; instead, I followed the coastline south. Perhaps if I rounded Punta Guanaco and paddled west, the point would offer a protective lee from the northeast wind. It wasn't a good plan, but it was the only one I had.

Punta Guanaco lies at the razor tip of the meteorological triple junction. Right here, at this insignificant rock outcrop, Atlantic, Pacific, and Antarctic storms all converge. I rounded the point, hoping to find a sheltered harbor, but instead the wind shifted and the northeast Atlantic Ocean storm gave way to a Pacific storm from the southwest. The shore that should have provided protection was facing directly into the gale, and I had nowhere to go. I pointed my boat offshore, into the wind, and paddled as hard as I could. My best effort resulted in a standstill, gaining nothing but losing nothing. All I could do was hope that the storm would run out of strength before I did.

I held on for two hours, rain streaking down my face. The treadmill effort carried me into a trance that seemed to lift me out of danger. Then the wind slowly intensified and pushed me toward the beach. As I fought for sea room, an acre-sized clump of kelp drifted toward my boat. The kelp wrapped around my paddle and anchored the blades to the rising sea. I took a stroke, shook the kelp free, and then tried to half-paddle, half-push my way through the entanglement. One wave rose under me, and I teetered on the breaking crest. The next one broke a few feet out to sea. For a few seconds I stared at the white wall, until it engulfed me and rolled the boat over and over, like a window shade gone amuck. I tried to reach under the cowling with my thighs and hold on, but I spilled into the foam, tumbled in the turbulent aerated breaker, and then bobbed to the surface in the green water behind the wave. I considered abandoning the boat and swimming for shore, but I needed to salvage warm clothes and a sleeping bag, so I swam to the overturned boat. Miraculously, the paddle was close by; I grabbed it, flipped the boat over, and hoisted myself crosswise over the cockpit. Even though the kayak was full of water and unstable, I was able to maneuver carefully into normal paddling position. But before I could gain sea room, another wave hit and the kayak pitchpoled, end for end, vaulting me into a graceful arc through the air. When I surfaced the second time, I looked out to sea at a long line of breakers and decided to swim ashore and pull the boat along with me. I half-swam and half-body-surfed with a sequence of smaller waves. My feet touched the sand, the undertow tugged against my body, and I lost footing. A big wave approached, and I hung on to the kayak. The wave lifted the boat over my head and effortlessly yanked my right shoulder out of its socket.

I let go and tumbled in the surf, felt a sandy bottom, and struggled to my feet, only to watch the boat coming at me, broadside, chest high. The wave slammed me up against a rock and the kayak beat down against my chest.

I had dislocated my shoulder numerous times before, and a doctor had taught me how to reduce it myself in an emergency. I closed my eyes and concentrated. I was no longer in Chile far from people, rescue, or medical attention. I was no longer underwater, in the surf, with a dislocated shoulder and a heavy boat pounding against me. The cold southern ocean wasn't in the picture. Certainly my life didn't pass before my eyes or anything romantic like that. I mentally crawled inside my body and tried to picture the positions of the bones and ligaments. The doctor's words came back to me, and I tried to unite them with my past experiences and present situation. With my left arm, I grasped my right elbow, rotated the shoulder, lined up all the parts and pieces, and shoved it back into its socket. The pain was intense. I rolled out from under the boat and staggered onto the beach.

The storm was all around me, inside me even, for the sea had filled my sinuses with kelp, plankton, and salt. The cold made me feel like a skeleton with the wind blowing through me. The loneliness was cathartic, so that my mind was clear and I felt almost content. I had one simple task: Stay alive.

As the next wave broke and the foam retreated down the beach, I ran back into the surf to retrieve my boat. Using my left hand this time, and taking care to avoid another disaster, I pulled the kayak onto the shore. Working quickly, I grabbed my sleeping bag, tent, stove, and a small bag of food. The next wave had already broken and was rolling toward me. I started to retreat, then raced back and grabbed the waterproof bag with my journal and film. The wave reached its apex, then slid down the beach, tugging at my legs and the kayak. I stood firm watching the knee-deep water rush past. It could take the boat, but not me. I let go, walked to dry land, and watched the kayak float into the water. The next breaker lifted the boat, dropped it on a rock, and broke it in two.

The narrow beach was a transient haven at low tide; in an hour or two the waves would break directly against the cliffs. Therefore, I needed to gain the grassy plain above me. I found a steep, rocky gully that was loose and slippery but climbable. I separated my possessions into three manageable bundles, filled a duffel bag with a light load, draped it over my good shoulder, and started up. My left arm did most of the work, but I clutched loose holds at face level with my injured right. After I reached the top and unloaded, I started back down immediately, before I lost my nerve or resolve. I moved more confidently on the second trip, remembering the route I had taken the first time. As I climbed the gully for the last time, I shivered so violently that I imagined my right shoulder rattling in its loose socket, like a bad bearing on an old car engine.

Once I reached the top, I curled up in the fetal position with my possessions and shivered in the rain. However, I hadn't fought so hard to give up now. I rose and tried to fit the tent poles together, but my hands were shaking too erratically. Frustrated, I pinned one pole on the ground with my knee and slid the other into place carefully with both hands. Each pole was composed of many segments, and each segment was a struggle. As a result, I was still working when the evening darkness added to the chill. When I had finally pitched the tent and tied it down—when warmth and comfort seemed only moments away—I discovered that one of my waterproof cases had ripped on the rocks and my sleeping bag was soaked. Still shivering, I lit the stove and brewed hot milk. The hot liquid warmed my insides, and the stove heated the tent. Gradually I stopped shivering and then even felt warm. I hadn't salvaged much fuel, so I turned the stove off. I wrung out my bag, crawled in, and shivered again until my body heat dried out the bag. By two in the morning, I fell asleep.

20

When I awoke, I walked out to the bluff and looked across the bay. Isla Wollaston was so close, and beyond that, Cape Horn. The wind had died, and the sea was flat and glassy. When the ocean is stormy it seems as if it has been stormy forever, from the start of time, before life appeared on the earth, when the planet boiled with volcanic eruptions and shuddered under the impact of countless meteorites. And when the sea is calm, it is life-mother herself, relaxed and soothing, secure and loving for all of eternity. It seemed impossible that such a placid surface could have been so nasty a few hours before.

The sun was warm, and wisps of steam rose from my damp clothes. The desperate moments of the day before already seemed like something that had occurred long ago or to someone else, and I was more relaxed than I had been in months. I set my things out in the sunshine to dry, rationed my remaining food, and cooked a light breakfast. Survival seemed so easy in the dry sunshine.

A dreamy image arose out of the stillness. One hundred years ago, the Yamana built canoes out of pieces of bark sewn together and caulked with straw or reeds. The bottoms were lined with clay so people could build a fire and cook dinner while they were out to sea. I imagined a pastoral scene with a family paddling off the point to visit some relatives or to seek a new shellfish bed. The woman was suckling a baby and cooking mussels in the bottom of the boat. Men hunted whales or seals nearby, hoping for the slim chance that success would bring a feast. They knew something that I didn't know. They had lived and sailed where I had nearly died.

I thought that to these people, the sea and their boats were life itself. For me this is sport. But the two views on life are interconnected. The sport keeps me sane, spiritually alive. Take away the wilderness, imprison me forever in an office in a city, and perhaps I too would succumb to "disintegrative factors."

I took a nap, and when I awoke my mood had changed. I forgot that I was happy to be alive and instead became angry and depressed that I had failed. I wrote in my journal:

I've chosen a hard master, the winds and mountains in harsh places in the world, but I can do better. It's my impetuousness sneaking in. Maybe this will finally teach me to do things slower, and do them right. I made a serious judgment error, and that's not good, but now it's history.

I am 34 years old and I have finally come to realize that I am a bit of a fool. I mean I've known it for years in an offhand sort of way, toyed with the idea now and again and rejected it, but it has stayed with me nevertheless. So, my grand realization isn't a realization at all, just a verbalization of what I have known all along.

I climbed down to the beach to search for anything of value. A few shreds of kayak were buried in the sand. My Nikonos camera lay almost concealed beneath a layer of sand and wet kelp. I rinsed it off in the stream and discovered that it still worked. I looked for another bag of food, but everything else had washed out to sea.

No, I wasn't a fool. I had been caught in a storm and crash-landed on a barren coast near Cape Horn. This wasn't the first shipwreck near Cape Horn. I should have been elated to be alive. Anyway, I argued that failure was an incongruous concept that I had imported from the outside world and pasted onto the landscape like a bright red billboard rising against the yellow-green tundra. I had successfully paddled four hundred fifty miles across harsh channels, through the rain forest, along the historic Straits of Magellan, past the glacier-capped mountains of the Cordillera Darwin. Fine, but I couldn't ignore the fifty untraveled miles. I had failed.

I thought again of that day in Telluride, sitting on the toilet seat, talking to my friend who was floating in the bathtub. She had told me that the purpose of the journey was to listen to feeling and not to reason. Okay, I had listened to the inner me and had set off, searching not for the Horn but for direction in my life to replace all the abandoned paths. I had experienced a great adventure, learned to live alone.

"Bullshit!" I told myself. "I set out to paddle around Cape Horn. When I get home, no one is going to ask me if I found spiritual contentment. People are going to ask, 'Did you get around the Horn?' And I'm going to have to say, 'No!'

49

21

The following day, I bundled my belongings into one heavy duffel bag and started walking north toward Puerto Toro. With even a rudimentary trail and a few bridges, I could have made the twenty-five-mile trek in a long day. But there was no trail. After a few hours of leisurely walking over the grassy bluff, I descended into the river bottom where I had hoped to find shelter the day before. I took off my clothes, separated my gear into three equal bundles again, swam across with one, built a fire to warm up, and then swam back and forth twice more to complete the ferry.

The coast was rocky and convoluted, so I tried to save time by shortcutting across a peninsula. But the resistant rock that formed the peninsula extended inland as a steep bluff. I clambered up, holding with my injured arm and pushing my duffel ahead of me with my good one, occasionally balancing the bag on my head when I needed both hands to climb with.

On the third day I took another shortcut through what had looked like an open meadow. However, it was a burned forest, blanketed by flowers and briars. The dead trees had fallen on top of one another to form a jumbled mat a few feet off the ground. I balanced on the tree trunks and walked a zigzag course, jumping from one to another. Travel was agonizingly slow, so I returned to the beach, only to be hindered by streams and cliffs.

On the afternoon of the fourth day, I climbed a hill and looked down on Puerto Toro. People were walking in the streets, and Heraldo's house stood in a small grove of trees. Heraldo, who had been so hospitable and eager to discuss the nuances of that silly sign, would surely offer me food and warmth. I wouldn't have to build a boat, fight hostile cannibals, and spend years making my way home. We'd simply radio Puerto Williams, and within a few days someone would whisk me off in motorized comfort. Even though I welcomed rescue, it made me feel incomplete. The moment I entered the town and knocked on Heraldo's door, the adventure would be over. Suddenly I wasn't ready to return home. The sun shone warmly, and I leaned against the heavy duffel. I felt so good, being outside in the sunshine, looking at the gale-twisted trees. Life should really be simple, but I had made it complex. Then I had crash-landed. I watched the daily routine of the village for an hour and then walked down to say hello.

Part 2

THE NORTHWEST PASSAGE

The ice seems almost human in the variety of methods it uses to repel the explorers who would invade the secret places it guards. Sometimes it is like a wary general who stages a shameful retreat in order to ambush the intruder; or it is like an enchantress, a grim, golden Circe, whose song ensnares. It became the too eager grave for a host of gallant men. . . . From these tragedies and defeats it has been learned that this stunning force is not ruled by local evil deities, but is governed by the flow of waters around the whole earth.

—Jeannette Mirsky,
To the Arctic!

1

I flew home to Telluride and, three weeks later, dislocated my shoulder again in a ski wreck. The doctor told me that I would need reconstructive surgery after the swelling subsided, and he ordered me to rest for several months. Bored and impatient, and still dazed and unsettled from the trip to Chile, I decided that I no longer wanted to live in a ski town, so I traveled north to buy rural land in Montana. Between visits to real estate agents I met an old friend, Tom, in a grocery store in Bozeman. He invited me to dinner to meet his wife, Karen, and their new baby. His wife's sister, Chris, was at the house, helping with the newborn. Karen greeted me warmly; Chris acknowledged my existence and went about her business. She wasn't shy or rude, but if she didn't know me she wasn't going to pretend that she was happy to see me. I started to watch her more carefully. She was short—about five feet, three inches—and square shouldered, and she wore her sandy blond hair in braids. I talked of my recent journey; Chris listened for a while, then wandered into the back room to change the baby's diapers.

By the time Chris returned, I had lost interest in telling the Cape Horn story and tried, instead, to draw her into the conversation. I explained that I was thinking about leaving Telluride and asked about the skiing near Bozeman. I had posed the question equally to all three people but was disappointed to hear Tom answer. I didn't want information; I wanted Chris to speak to me. After listening patiently to his descriptions of the local ski area and surrounding backcountry terrain, I looked at Chris directly and asked, "Chris, do you ski?"

She had to say something so she responded, "Yes."

I wanted to yell, "What the hell does that mean, 'yes'? Yes, you skied once in high school when your mother bought you a lesson, or yes, you can ski in any type of snow, on any skis, in virtually any terrain, with grace and beauty?"

I looked into her tan face. Only skiers and vacationers recently back from Mazatlán are tan in the early spring in Montana. Then I focused on the weather wrinkles crawling from the corners of her

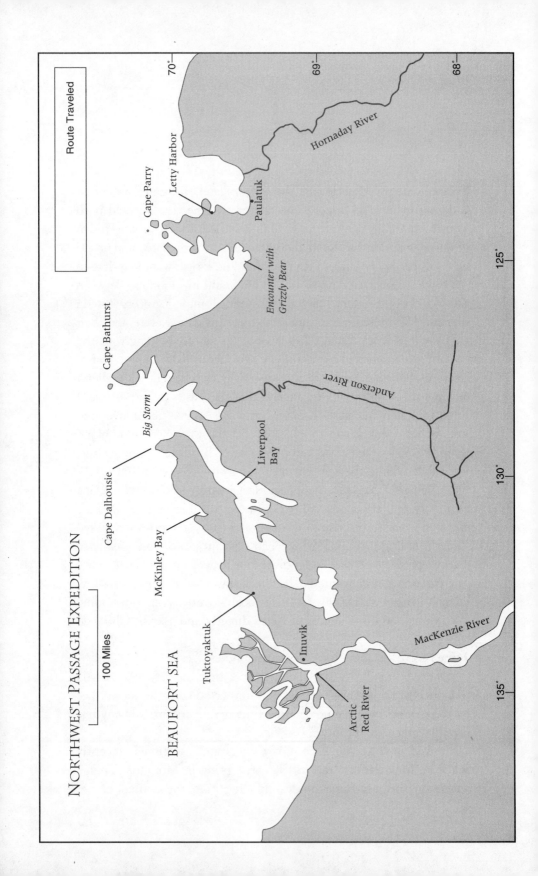

NORTHWEST PASSAGE EXPEDITION

100 Miles

Route Traveled

BEAUFORT SEA

Tuktoyaktuk

McKinley Bay

Cape Dalhousie

Big Storm

Cape Bathurst

Cape Parry

Letty Harbor

Paulatuk

Encounter with
Grizzly Bear

Liverpool Bay

Inuvik

Arctic
Red River

MacKenzie River

Anderson River

Hornaday River

135°

130°

125°

70°

69°

68°

eyes. She had stories to tell me, and I would have to be patient if I wanted to hear them.

Over the following few days, Chris gradually told me about herself. She had dropped out of college to ski at Alta, spent a year in Norway learning the telemark turn, was a ski instructor at Steamboat Springs Resort, and returned to school to study nursing. She drifted out of nursing to guide for a helicopter ski operation in the Pintlar Mountains in Montana, then went back to school when the guide business went bankrupt before entertaining its first client. She was now studying soil science. When I asked her why she was interested in soil science, she explained that she was really interested in forestry but the school of forestry was in Missoula and the air was polluted in Missoula in the winter.

"Winter is too beautiful to be ruined by breathing bad air."

After a week of casual encounters at her sister's house, I visited Chris in her own apartment. We chatted and I told her the story about the dolphins and their playful visitation on the dark waves in southern Chile. For the first time, she listened to me intently. As she told me later, she thought that if the dolphins had come to play with me, I might be okay.

I was headed south to take Nathan and Noey rafting on the Dolores River in southern Utah. I asked Chris if she would like to join us. She answered, "Yes."

I could have interpreted her answer as "ho, hum, yes, I guess so" or "yes" as in "yes, I am a skier." I hoped it was the latter and made arrangements to meet her in Utah after she finished her final exams.

We drove to the river, blew up the rubber raft, ate dinner, put the kids to bed, and then walked through moon shadows cast by pink sandstone spires. Later that night, lying in our separate sleeping bags, we stared up at the canyon walls, and Chris pointed out a rock outcrop that looked like a Buddhist guru watching us from above.

"Look at him," Chris whispered. "He's watching us."

I reached out tentatively and put my arm around her shoulder; she snuggled up against me.

After the river trip and before Chris headed back to Montana, she suggested that we spend the summer together in her cabin, which was perched at seven thousand feet near Butte, Montana.

I said, "Yes."

2

I returned home, loaded my car with enough possessions to stay the summer, and drove north. I had been driving for twelve hours, and when I stepped out of the car my inner ears were still moving and my hands felt useless without a steering wheel. It was July 7, and wet, fluffy snowflakes softened the air. The snow stuck to my hair and caressed my eyelids, restoring my equilibrium.

Old mine buildings littered the mountainside and spoke of a bustling community half a century ago. The rust-covered boarding house, delicately offset by the new snow, cut a dark square out of the white mountains, while the skeleton of the ore crusher sliced the sky. Hops plants grew through the windows and doorways of most of the smaller buildings, and old tin roofing rattled as the storm passed through the mountains. Paths crisscrossed the meadow, leading toward a few restored cabins and outhouses.

The slip of paper with directions was soggy and smeared when I read it for the last time. "Follow the trail down the hill toward a cabin with a green roof and cedar shake siding. I'll be home from work at 5:00." It was four-thirty. The electric power line that ran along the road offered no spur toward her cabin. The omission was not obvious at first, but once I noticed it, the cabin below seemed to snuggle deeper into the summer snow. I walked down the path and peered into the window for more clues about this stranger who had chosen to share her summer with me.

A gruff voice called from the hillside above. "What hell kind of guy you are 'nooping 'round Wanapeka's house?"

I can't remember what I saw first, the cane waving in the air, the white-whiskered face, the fat belly, or the skinny legs that swung to the side as he ran, like wheels with bent rims and a twisted axle. I recognized him immediately as the troll who lived beneath the drawbridge to the princess's castle. But I didn't know whether the troll had charmed himself into the princess's heart or had survived because he was too terrible to kill. I had only a few moments to speculate because despite his awkward movement he was approaching rapidly with the brandished cane. Should I grab a shovel and make quick work of this menace once and for all, or should I offer him a lump of sugar and an apple? I tried the sweets, and by the time Chris came home I was in his warm kitchen drinking strong coffee and eating yesterday's stew.

3

We spent that summer in love. Chris worked as a timber cruiser for the U.S. Forest Service, and I started a revision of one of my environmental science texts. In the fall, an orthopedic surgeon repaired my shoulder, and we moved to Bozeman so Chris could continue school. Nathan and Noey spent the year with us, and we rented a small house close to town. I finished my book, went to PTA and Boy Scout meetings, and took the children hiking and skiing. Chris tried to teach me backcountry skiing, and I struggled to keep up with her. We faced the normal adventures of any suburban family. A dog bit Noey. Chris crashed on her bicycle and broke a bone in her face. Nathan refused to follow a few simple rules imposed by his fifth-grade teacher, and she threatened to flunk him.

Early that spring, a large corporation swallowed my publishing house. I disagreed with the liaison officer, we argued, and I pushed him too hard. He told me that he would talk to my agent or my lawyer, but not to me. I told him I didn't need an agent or a lawyer; I didn't even need this stupid job. I could make a living as a fisherman in Alaska. He laughed and hung up the phone.

"Great," I thought to myself. "For the past nine months I've lived in a relaxed family again, surrounded by two of my children, a loving woman, and a high-paying job that has left adequate time for skiing and climbing. Now what did I just do? I insulted my boss and then quit. For what? A dirty, dangerous job—that I don't have."

Yet the adventure intrigued me. Chris came home from school, and I told her what had happened. She didn't say much.

Nathan and Noey returned to California to stay with Debby, Chris finished school and returned to her Forest Service job, and I flew to Naknek on the shores of Bristol Bay, Alaska. Tundra spread out to the north, the sun hung on the horizon providing twenty hours of daylight, and I walked the docks looking for work. Eventually, I found a job on an older thirty-two-foot gillnetter with cramped crew quarters, slow hydraulics, and small fish holds. Chrome captain's chairs, spacious bunks, and comfortable galleys don't catch fish. With a madman skipper, a superb mechanic, and me as deckhand, we pulled tons of sockeye salmon over the stern roller. Whenever we tired and started to slow down, the skipper reminded us of his mantra: "Piss in September, sleep when you're dead."

Jack London had been a cod fisherman in the Bering Sea. But Jack London fished from an open dory, while I saw adventure through diesel fumes. The motor, winches, and electronics on a modern fishing boat diminished my concept of a romantic adventure. During still mornings near the end of the season, when I stood on deck alone while the others slept, I dreamed of more-distant oceans. There are two sea routes around the Western Hemisphere, one to the south and one to the north. I had kayaked in the southern oceans; now I would try the Northwest Passage.

The route around Cape Horn or through the Straits of Magellan was dangerous and arduous, but sailors routinely followed these passages in the sixteenth and seventeenth centuries. By the 1800s, clipper ships loaded with tea and spices raced each other from China to England, and others sailed from New York or Boston around the Horn to supply the west coast of North America.

In contrast, attempts on the Northwest Passage had produced failure and death. The major obstacle is ice. Towering icebergs calve from tidewater glaciers in Greenland and drift southward into commercial shipping lanes. The *Titanic* sank after striking a Greenland berg in the North Atlantic, but that accident was brought on by hubris and poor seamanship. The battle against ice in the Northwest Passage is more insidious. There are no tidewater glaciers in the central and western Arctic and therefore no icebergs. However, in winter, the entire ocean freezes from the North American coast across the Pole to Asia. When this ice is warmed by the returning sun, it breaks into low-lying floes, called *pan ice*. A single floe rises a foot or less above the surface and is benign, but when millions jam together in groups the size of Texas, and the whole pack is blown back and forth by the wind and pulled by the tides, the ice forms an impenetrable barrier or a deadly trap.

4

Marco Polo wrote about wealth and opulence unimaginable in the cold, damp castles and filthy cities of medieval Europe. Some called him a liar or a madman, but others began the journey to Cathay. Portuguese sailors pioneered trade routes eastward around the Cape of Good Hope on the southern tip of Africa, while the Spanish, led by Columbus, headed westward. Almost immediately after Columbus returned to Spain from what he claimed was the Orient, tension arose between the two great maritime powers. To maintain the peace and to bestow favors on his religious and political allies, the pope divided the world into two halves. All passages to the Orient via the Cape of Good Hope belonged to the Portuguese, and all routes southwest belonged to Spain. Other European nations were excluded. But the halves envisioned in the pope's limited geography included only the southeastern and southwestern passages. If trade routes existed around the southern boundaries of Africa and South America, perhaps other routes existed to the north. Thus the pope's proclamation launched the search for northern passages.

John Cabot left England in 1497, five years after Columbus's first journey, and steered a northwest course for China. He explored the east coast of North America from New England to Labrador and, like Columbus, returned home claiming he had reached Asia. King Henry VII awarded him a pension and supplied five ships and 300 men for a second voyage. The following year, Cabot again sailed northwest, searching for spices, tea, and gilded palaces. However, he steered so far north that he landed on the east coast of Greenland. Lost in a frigid, barren land, the crew mutinied. Cabot was lucky to return home, but weakened by disease and discouraged by failure, he died a few years later.

By the mid-1500s, both Spain and Portugal were enriched by trade and pillage, and the pope's edict was enforced by the world's largest navies. In 1576 a British adventurer, Martin Frobisher, concluded that the Northwest Passage was "the only thing of the world that was left yet undone, whereby a notable mind might be made famous and fortunate."* Private investors supplied him with a ship and crew, and Queen Elizabeth waved from her palace window as he sailed down the Thames. Besieged by gales, Frobisher finally landed on the southern edge of Baffin Island, where he found a waterway that he believed led through to China. He named the opening Frobisher Straits, after himself, but never explored it. When the crew put ashore to fill the water casks, one of the sailors picked up a black stone that "glistened like a bright marquesset of gold."

Frobisher raced back to England to bring the news. The investors and even the assayers agreed that the shiny black stone was speckled with gold. The next year the queen offered her hand for a kiss when Frobisher embarked with more ships, more men, and shovels. He returned to Baffin Island, and even though he couldn't find another shiny rock "so bigge as a walnut," he found a beach where "all the sands and cliffs did so glister and had so bright a marquesite that all seemed to be gold." The ships returned home with two hundred tons of the stuff, and again both the investors and assayers agreed that the ore was rich in gold. On his third voyage Frobisher left with fifteen ships, and the queen set a golden chain around his neck. They had a rough crossing, lost ships and gear, and returned home to find that the sparkling grains in the ore were bits of iron pyrite, commonly called "fool's gold."

If the Arctic couldn't be conquered by swashbuckling melodrama, perhaps it could be ground down by persistence. But after thirty years of failure by Davis, Hudson, Button, Bylot, and Baffin, people realized that even if a Northwest Passage did exist, it was a tortuous route through ice-choked straits. Private investors abandoned the quest and became rich instead from whaling, fishing, and trapping. However, the quest survived negative economics. Scientific mysteries were

*Sir John Barrow, *Chronological History of Voyages into the Arctic Regions* (London: J. Murray, 1818), quoted in Jeannette Mirsky, *To the Arctic!* (Chicago: University of Chicago Press, 1948), p. 29.

enshrouded by the fog, and national honor was waiting at the other edge of the ice. During peacetime, naval officers headed north to prove themselves against the only enemy with real mettle.

The strategy that developed was dogged. Crews inched westward into the pack ice through small passages, called *leads*. But leads open and close. We can imagine the fear when the ice entombed a ship and the men listened as the hull creaked under the strain. Despite the fear and the danger, they pushed on when the leads opened again. When fall approached and the numbing cold formed a film of new ice, the crews sailed into a protected bay, dropped anchor, and watched the entire ocean freeze over. They waited in darkness and fifty-below-zero temperatures for nine months until the sun melted the ocean once again by July or August. Then many proceeded, again westward. Some adventurers discovered new channels and islands and returned home as triumphant heroes, but many were maimed by scurvy or died of cold and hunger. A few went mad and ate their companions. Centuries passed and no one completed the Northwest Passage.

By the 1840s, explorers had mapped most of the passage from the east, west, and south, and all that remained was for one crew on one expedition to link all the components. In 1845 the British outfitted two of its stoutest ships, the *Erebus* and the *Terror*, with supplies for three years and put 134 men under the command of Sir John Franklin, a veteran of twenty years in the Arctic. It was perhaps the most lavishly outfitted expedition in Arctic history. Planners believed that the men had everything they needed to remain comfortable during the long journey. They even carried twelve hundred books. One, written by explorer John Ross, proposed that Arctic expeditions should be small and travel light, and that scurvy could be avoided by eating fresh meat rather than salt rations packed in England. Ross's advice was lost in all the words and enthusiasm of the undertaking. When the *Erebus* and the *Terror* left England, confidence was so high that relatives were advised to address letters to Petropavlovsk, a Russian town on the western side of the Bering Straits.

The first summer the ships penetrated the pack and proceeded westward. As planned, they found anchorage in the fall and waited out the winter. They read, they were warm, and they entertained themselves with plays, but no one ventured onto the ice to hunt. That winter three men died. The following year, the crews laboriously sawed a passage through the harbor ice and set their ships free in the open channels. Swinging southward, they sighted the northern point of King William Island.

Although the coastline to the south was unexplored, British cartographers had assumed that the land was a peninsula, not an island. The ice to the west was dark, thick, old ice from the polar seas that had survived many summers. Polar ice is transported southward by a current that continuously presses against the west shore of King William Island. The whiter, snow-covered ice to the east was new ice that forms every winter and melts again in summer. Although the new ice was clearly less threatening, Franklin believed that the route to the east was a dead end, so he bravely sailed into the pack.

The events of the next few years are summed up in a short note that was left in a cairn by dying men and later retrieved by a search party that came too late to find any survivors:

April 25, 1848—HM's Ships Terror and Erebus were deserted on 22 April, 5 leagues N.N.W. of this, having been beset since 12th September, 1846. The officers and crews, consisting of 105 souls, under the command of Captain F. R. M. Crozier, landed here at Lat. 69° 37' 42" N, Long. 98° 41' W. . . . Sir John Franklin died on 11 June 1847; and the total loss by deaths in the expedition had been to this date 9 officers and 15 men.*

James Fitzjames, Captain HMS Erebus and F. R. M. Crozier, Captain and Senior Officer start on tomorrow, 26th, for Back's Fish River.

The explorers had watched shipmates die as they waited over a year and a half for a lucky combination of wind and tide to set them free. But the currents pressed an infinity of ice around the wooden ships. Starving and racked with scurvy, the men tried to walk to the nearest civilization, a trading post four hundred miles away on the Fish River. They pulled twelve-hundred-pound sledges laden, incredibly, with pewter dishes, silk handkerchiefs, bedroom slippers, and combs. Weakened by scurvy, they moved slowly with the overloaded sleds, and one by one they died.

The passage was finally completed by Roald Amundsen with a small crew in a forty-seven-ton herring boat, the *Gjoa*. He was frozen in the ice for two consecutive winters in a small bay on the east side

*Five men took sick the first year and returned to England on a whaling ship.

of King William Island. He and his crew supplemented their diet with seal and caribou. Finally Amundsen sailed through the Bering Straits in the summer of 1906.

You might think that Amundsen's success would have ended the quest, but it didn't. In modern times the banner has been taken up by two different groups of people. Oil and minerals have been found in the Arctic, and with these discoveries, machinery must be transported north and riches shipped back south. In addition, during the Cold War, the United States and Canadian governments feared that the Soviet Union would attack North America from across the Arctic. Thus, after World War II, corporations and governments penetrated the ice with modern technology. In 1954 the Canadian icebreaker H.M.C.S. *Labrador* became the first deep-draft vessel to navigate the Northwest Passage. From time to time since then, someone sends up a bigger, meaner, diesel or nuclear-powered monster to crunch its way through the ice and bring the industrial age one step closer to the frozen North.

A second group of twentieth-century explorers have no new lands to discover, no riches to gain, and no enemies to defeat. They have little money and little support and are largely impoverished by their passions. Most have no significant geographical starting places or destinations. They wander around in sailboats, walrus-skinned *umiaks*, rowboats, catamarans, and kayaks. Modern adventurers create seemingly arbitrary goals and then strive hard to achieve them. In 1981, when I started to plan my journey, no one had completed the Northwest Passage in a single season in a nonmotorized boat.

5

At the end of the fishing season, I flew back to Anchorage and asked a friend if he would join me on the Northwest Passage the following summer. He asked how I could consider the journey when so many competent people had failed and died.

I told him of a remarkable drawing that chronicled an encounter off the west coast of Greenland between British naval officers and a band of Inuit on August 10, 1818. The officers were dressed in ceremonial uniforms with tails and gold epaulets. They walked across the slushy, summer snow in shiny, buckled shoes. The Inuit were dressed in fur-hooded anoraks (jackets) with sealskin *kamiks* (boots). The British ships lay moored against the ice with proud flags flying, while two fragile dogsleds appeared behind the Inuit. As the two parties stared at each other, the startled stone age hunters asked, "Where do you come from, the sun or the moon?"

Many early explorers died because they relied on unsuitable European clothing and food. Nearby, Inuit raised their babies through cold, dark winters. I would mimic explorers like Peary, Amundsen, and Stefansson, who blended European and Inuit technology. I would use a small boat that could be sailed when the wind was behind me and dragged or rowed when it was not. Moreover, my boat would displace less than a foot of water. In early season, shore leads open in shallow water adjacent to the beach as ice is melted by radiant energy from land. A large ship can't follow the shore leads, but a small boat can, and thus I would be able to move when the early explorers couldn't.

I had the luxury of adopting this strategy because I never intended to complete a commercial Northwest Passage; I wouldn't cross the North Atlantic from Europe, and I never contemplated freighting spices from China. My proposed route extended from the Mackenzie Delta to Pond Inlet on Baffin Island, and it would traverse the most difficult portion of the original route.

In addition to skipping part of the journey, I planned to go the wrong way. The western Arctic is warmer than the eastern Arctic. Therefore, I could start earlier and experience a longer season if I traveled west to east than if I followed the traditional direction. I decided to drive to the headwaters of the Mackenzie River, float northward to the Beaufort Sea, and then start the journey. The total expedition would cover eight hundred miles of river and two thousand miles along the ocean coast. If the plan worked, the ice would melt before me like a red carpet being rolled out in front of royalty.

My friend is a large man, over six feet tall, with unkempt, shoulder-length hair. He leans forward from the waist when he walks, as if he is always intent on moving toward the next destination. Even though he was still in his thirties, his face was etched from a lifetime of living outdoors. He listened quietly to my story and then said, "What happens when the wind shifts and the ice closes in on you? Many of the early explorers lost stout oak ships in the ice. What's it going to do to your little plastic rowboat? You're going to die on this one, Jon."

I explained that when the ice moved, I would row to shore and drag my boat up on the beach, an option unavailable to people on a ship. Even if disaster struck and I lost my boat, I had avenues of escape. Franklin was a dot on the landscape, alone, with incomplete maps and no communication or resupply. After he was feared lost, thirty-five rescue expeditions were dispatched before anyone found evidence of his fate. Today, failure does not condemn one to a slow death from hunger and scurvy. There are airports in the modern Arctic, and when the ice is too thick, you buy a ticket and fly home. I told him that I could foresee failure but not death.

He was unconvinced.

I returned to Montana but didn't tell Chris about the Northwest Passage for a few days. Finally, after the initial excitement of our reunion had passed and I could no longer restrain my enthusiasm, I told her of my plans. I expected an argument, a confrontation, anger. This wasn't going to be pleasant, I told myself, but we had to face it.

Chris thought for a while and then asked, "Who are you going with?"

"Myself, I guess."

"May I come?"

Chris had never been to sea in anything smaller than a passenger liner, had never rowed a boat even on a lake, and had never been on an expedition. I thought about my friend's words, "You are going to die on this one, Jon." Then I mentally redrew the map of the route. The passage toward Cape Horn had been mostly protected by islands, but long stretches of the Northwest Passage followed exposed coastlines. The ice in the Beaufort Sea poses a unique danger, one that I knew nothing about. With all my rationalizations that I would think and act like an Inuit, I had no experience in the North.

I asked Chris why she wanted to come on the expedition. She answered, "I've been to Norway and I like the North. That low-angle sun bounces off the sea and earth and produces a special soft glow; it makes everything seem so peaceful. I've always wanted to go back."

I asked myself, "How well do I know this woman?" We'd hiked in the desert, Nathan and Noey adored her, we'd skied and dodged a few avalanches together, we'd been lovers for a year. She wanted to go because she liked the North.

I thought, "That's a fine philosophy in normal life when the dangers are subdued, but how well will it work with blistered hands, a few thousand miles of rowing behind us, and another thousand in front? How will she like the 'peaceful lighting' when a gale rages against us, crashing ice and spume across the gunnels? Should I tell her that my friend—a veteran of expeditions on Mount Denali and the Brooks Range, a sailboat racer, and a professional fisherman—had refused my invitation because he thought it was too dangerous?"

I looked at her carefully. She weighed only 120 pounds. Was she strong enough? Dedicated enough? I didn't think so. But I loved her. Did I always want to be lonely? Then I thought about the past winter. Chris broke trail as much as I did and I often struggled to keep up with her on ski tours.

Chris waited patiently. "Okay," I said quietly. "Let's go to Seattle together and buy a boat."

Chris went into another room to do her homework as if we had just made a plan to go to the movies after dinner; I went outside for a walk. She hadn't asked me why I wanted to go to the North and she never would ask me. So I would have to ask myself. Had I forgotten the cold dampness, loneliness, and fatigue that I endured on the Cape Horn expedition? Had I forgotten all those despairing times when I wished I were somewhere else? No. So why did I want to go? Instead of trying to answer the question, I got angry at Chris, even though she was in the house reading her soil science text.

"How the hell can that pip-squeak woman sign on to a major Arctic expedition because she 'likes Northern lighting'? We're not going up there to appreciate the sunsets, we're going to challenge the same elements that subdued all those great explorers; only we're going to succeed. I failed at Cape Horn; I'm not going to fail here. I hope she doesn't think we're on a sunset cruise."

The silent hostility surprised me. I left for Cape Horn on a spiritual quest. I failed. But now I was tense and irritable just thinking about the expedition from a comfortable house in Montana. Maybe the purpose of the journey was to appreciate the lighting. No, I couldn't accept that. The purpose was to complete the Northwest Passage.

6

Although I wanted a small, light boat, I thought that a collapsible kayak was too flimsy and would be destroyed by ice. Perhaps a rowboat would best balance size, cargo capacity, and durability. We drove to Seattle and found a mold for a sixteen-foot fiberglass wherry. A wherry is double-ended, with the bow and stern rising gracefully to lift the boat in heavy seas. At the same time, it carries a flat keel, so it can be pulled up on the beach. Wherries were often used as lifeboats on ships that rounded Cape Horn or attempted the Northwest Passage.

The man who owned the mold told me that a completed sixteen-foot hull would weigh 100 pounds. He laid up the fiberglass; we fashioned teak gunnels for strength, hoisted it on the roof rack of my 1964 Plymouth Valiant, and drove back to Montana. During the winter Chris continued at the university, and I reunited with my publisher and started a new book. In our spare time we sewed spray dodgers and rigged sails.

7

In the middle of May, the Royal Canadian Mounted Police (RCMP) reported that the Mackenzie River was beginning to break up. The current, aided by the twenty-four-hour Arctic sunlight, had ripped the ice apart. Chris and I loaded the wherry on the car, filled the trunk and back seat with food and gear, and drove north.

I had left for Cape Horn in the dark of winter, alone. When I launched in Puerto Natales, rain and sea mists had carried chills through my heavy clothing. In contrast, Chris and I left home under a bright sun, together, chatting and giggling like any couple who had left their cares behind at the beginning of a long vacation. We treated ourselves to a fancy dinner in Edmonton and then followed the roads as the pavement became narrower, as the white and yellow lines became dimmer, as the blacktop faded into gravel, and then, finally, as the road ended at the river.

The snow had melted off the ground weeks ago, but the riverbanks were still piled high with ice. Floes paraded downstream, riding the current northward. Sunlight reflected off the whiteness, and a breeze held the mosquitoes off, so we unfolded a sleeping pad on a grounded ice floe and sat to watch the river. Chris asked me to close my eyes and listen. We heard the dripping of ice melting, ripples made by currents flowing past beached floes, wind-chime tinkles of crystals dropping, the mashing of floes bumping into each other, and the crashes of ice falling off the bank.

"I knew I wanted to come here," Chris told me. "I knew it would be this beautiful." A particularly large floe slid off the bank into the current, submerged briefly, then bobbed slowly to the surface. We watched it as it started its journey northward, and then Chris said quietly, "There goes another alligator sliding into the river."

Because the Mackenzie flows from south to north, breakup starts at the warmer headwaters and progresses toward the sea. Not far downstream, the ice still formed a solid barrier six feet thick, from shore to shore and north to the ocean. Caution dictated that we wait until breakup was complete, but if we could follow the ice barrier downstream, just far enough behind to avoid running into it, we would be that many miles ahead and that many days closer to Pond Inlet.

We rested for a day, packed the boat, muscled it over the shattered ice, and slipped into the current. We hadn't been able to practice rowing in Montana in winter and the long drive had disrupted our normal body rhythms, so we were awkward and uncoordinated. I rowed in the stern seat and Chris was directly in front of me. Because we both faced the stern, Chris was staring directly at my back. Whenever our cadence was off, she jabbed me in the kidneys with her oars. When the accumulated pain of repeated collisions became acute, I suggested that we sit for a moment and float with the current. We had twenty-eight hundred miles ahead of us, and frantic rushing on the first day wouldn't get us there. The boat rotated and bumped into an ice floe, shearing clear crystals into the dark water. The crystals bobbed, drifted, and melted as they floated toward the Beaufort Sea.

The Mackenzie is a Mississippi-sized river that drains the center of North America from the northern Rockies to the central Canadian Great Plains to the Arctic Ocean. If you photograph the shore from the middle of the river, the picture outlines a large blue foreground, a thin hairline of green, and half a frame of blue sky above. River and sky are an almost indistinguishable shade of blue, and clouds and ice floes seem remarkably similar. If you turned the picture upside down, you could barely tell the difference.

As the current swept us closer to shore, we floated past walls of floes that had been tossed on top of one another during breakup. In places, the ice had broken trees in half and scattered the shattered trunks. The ice seemed like layers of shale, and the trees appeared as fallen ferns in a Cretaceous swamp.

8

The Mackenzie River doesn't have any technical rapids, so white-water enthusiasts would find it dull. There are no lofty peaks or tumbling glaciers along its banks. It is simply a huge waterway through one of the most sparsely inhabited places on earth. Hundreds of thousands of ducks, geese, swans, and cranes come here every year to nest. But for me, the great thrill was feeling the power of all that unfettered water. If the river wants to swing wide, grab a few acres of dirt, throw a couple of hundred trees into the water, and smash the banks up with ice, no one is going to design some engineering marvel to show it who's boss.

On the fourth day we reached the town of Wrigley, pulled the boat ashore, and went to the store to buy Cheez Whiz, white bread, and cookies. Wrigley has a population of one hundred, a store, a few government buildings, an airstrip, and a dirt road that extends for a mile from forest edge to forest edge. We sat on the steps of the store and ate our lunch. A pickup drove by, then a three-wheeler skidded around the corner in a cloud of dust. An old man was fixing his boat across the street. A few children poured from the store hyped up on candy bars and soda pop. No one talked to us or acknowledged our existence.

The largest wilderness area in the United States (excluding Alaska) is the Frank Church Wilderness in Idaho, which covers thirty-three hundred square miles. But the Northwest Territories cover 1.3 million square miles, one-third the surface area of the United States. Legislators don't have to designate it a roadless area, it just is. If we finished our sandwiches and started walking eastward, we could travel one thousand miles to Hudson Bay without crossing a road and probably without meeting another human. So the land defines itself.

I watched the ice flowing by. The forest smelled of pines and of the return of decay with the warming sun. I looked at the almost fluorescent Cheez Whiz lying on the snowy white bread in my hand and wondered if the soil mites would shun it even though they were voracious after their winter fast.

Our proposed expedition was an ocean voyage, from the Mackenzie Delta to Pond Inlet. The eight hundred miles down the Mackenzie was the approach to the start. In 1908 ethnologist Vilhjalmur Stefansson floated down the Mackenzie toward the central Arctic; he had expressed feelings similar to mine:

> *From the point of view of the city dweller and the farmer, the trappers and traders on the Mackenzie are living in the wilderness, although I must confess that from the point of view of the Arctic explorer they seem to be dwelling in the heart of civilization.**

*Vilhjalmur Stefansson, *My Life with the Eskimo* (New York: Macmillan, 1913), p. 34.

I explained to Chris that I felt as if the expedition hadn't yet begun. She looked at me incredulously. "What are you talking about? Of course this is the trip!"

9

As we rounded the bend to Norman Wells a few days later, we saw a black plume of smoke and heard the buzz of machinery. The wells of the town's name aren't springs of crystal-clear water but bore holes for oil. In addition to the wells, the town boasts the northernmost oil refinery in the world. The refinery rose starkly above the dark spruce and the smoke drifted across the taiga, announcing, "I am civilization and I am here." But it's a puny affair; if everyone in North America drove a quarter of a mile less a year or turned their thermostat down one-tenth of a degree, we wouldn't need it and a hundred like it.

The RCMP officer told us that the river was ice-free to the next town, Fort Good Hope, but was frozen farther on. I calculated that breakup was progressing faster than we were traveling, so that we could expect clear passage to the delta. Then we asked about the ice around Tuktoyaktuk, the first village on the Beaufort Sea.

He laughed. "This is a bad year for ice—Tuk will be frozen solid. Trade your boat in at Inuvik for a snowmobile. Hell, the ice can jam up against the shore and hold you down for a month."

A long, thin island splits the river downstream from Norman Wells, and the main channel runs along the left bank. Always eager to save energy, we took the shorter route through the right channel. Chris remarked that she heard a strange sound downstream as if the floes were grinding into each other rather than swishing past one another. We stopped rowing to listen but agreed that the harsh sound was only the echo of metal rubbing against metal at the refinery. A hair-width white line interrupted the horizon between blue river and blue sky. Again we stopped to think, but we decided to ignore our senses because the man in the clean office with the uniform and radio had told us that the passage was safe downstream.

Messages hardwired into our genes tell us that howling winds and crashing waves bring danger. The storms at Cape Horn had sometimes arisen unpredictably, but once I felt the windblast on my body and saw the whitecaps grinning at me like so many Cheshire cats, I understood my peril. In contrast, the North doesn't always send palpable warnings to the Arctic novice. We were drifting slowly at two miles an hour. The sun was shining; the wind was still. We swatted the last of the mosquitoes that had followed our boat from the shore and ate a kiwi shipped to the company store from New Zealand.

The ice on the Mackenzie doesn't melt passively like the snow in your backyard that recedes inch by inch, exposing the greening grass beneath. Upstream, to the south, the ice melts in Great Slave Lake and breaks into pans. The Mackenzie then carries these ice pans northward. Downstream, winter holds out against the summer sun, and the six-foot-thick ice floats immobile on the flowing water beneath. Then the river current presses the floating ice against the stationary ice until the solid barrier splinters catastrophically, flinging car-sized, or even house-sized, chunks of ice into the air.

The ice report from Norman Wells had focused on the main river, not the side channels. As we drifted with the current, I heard a loud pop and turned to watch a tractor-trailer-sized floe fly into the sky. Near it, a mature spruce stood upside down in the middle of the river, waving its roots in the air. The solid ice held fast in the shaded constricted channel but was breaking up quickly under the pressure of current and floating ice. If we were caught in the junction, we would be crushed, sheared, thrown skyward, or dragged beneath the solid ice.

I was both terrified and angry at myself for not anticipating the danger. Chris realized our predicament at about the same time and whispered quietly, "Oh, shit." I didn't turn to look at her face but sculled the boat around and started to row upstream. We were moving quickly relative to the floating floes, but that wasn't good enough; we had to move upstream relative to the land, toward the head of the island.

"Row harder, Chris!" I urged.

"I'm rowing as hard as I can!"

Talking wasn't going to help. I tried to think about bending the oar with every stroke, and told myself, push hard with your legs, pull with your back, and follow up with your arms. The bank retreated behind us. We cleared the island within an hour, turned with the current, and drifted into the wider, ice-free channel.

I opened a bag of cookies that we had bought and handed one to Chris. She ate a cookie, said nothing, and reached for another. I spoke first. "That was close."

"Yeah," she responded, "Did you see that tree root waving in the air? What power!"

"Let's try to be more careful."

She nodded, munching her third cookie, "We don't really know what's going on here; it's a new world for both of us."

I felt relieved that we had both reacted calmly to our first danger. We resolved to observe the river and the ice more carefully and to anticipate danger. We realized that we could depend on one another, and the transition brought a deeper closeness.

10

Two days later we arrived at Fort Good Hope and made our usual pilgrimage to the store. As we sat outside to eat, a young man approached, eager for conversation. Bruno had been born here and then had spent time "outside" in Inuvik, Hay River, Yellowknife, and even as far south as Calgary. He spoke of a job and a girlfriend, then an urge to return home to the forest and the river that now imprisoned him.

What new songs was Bob Seger singing? he wanted to know. Have you ever been to New York City? Do people in the city really throw televisions out of skyscrapers like I saw in the movies?

We walked a mile out of town to his parents' summer camp. His mother, Elisha, was scraping a moose hide stretched on the ground. Bruno's father, Ben, was drying meat over a smoky fire. The smoke and the meat smell mingled with the pungent sweetness of the green hide. We sat cross-legged in the soft moss at the doorway to their white canvas wall tent. Inside, caribou skins were spread out to make a floor, and the bedding consisted of an old Sears sleeping bag with pictures of ducks on the red flannel interior. Elisha rose from her work, lit a Coleman stove, brewed tea, and served it with bannock: fresh pan bread cooked on the Coleman. Ben passed us a plate of dried meat and a can of lard. We dipped a strip of meat in the lard, tore it apart with our teeth, held the greasy mixture in our mouths to let it rehydrate, and then washed it down with hot tea.

After the meal, Elisha asked Chris to help her tan the hide, and I drank more tea with the men. Ben talked about his recent hunt, naming creeks and landmarks in his native tongue. Bruno relaxed against a tent pole and announced that this was the good life, that this was why he had left the cities: "People in town are lazy and fight too much." But when his father asked him to hunt tomorrow, he refused because he was the evening disk jockey for the village radio station. His father said nothing but stared into the forest.

Chris was on her knees scraping the hide, shoulder to shoulder with Elisha. I told her we should probably head back to town so we could leave again early in the morning. She looked up. "Oh, Jon, we should stay here for a few days. We've only seen the forest drift by from the boat. We could learn to tan hides and dry meat, learn how people live, see something other than miles floating by."

Chris had studied knitting and weaving in Norway. Many of the ski patrollers and ski bums in Utah wore her colorful, hand-knitted hats. The moose hide was another expression of a long fascination with warm fabrics. But my fascination was to complete the Northwest Passage in an open boat and to become well known in the world of adventure.

Elisha graciously invited us to be their guests. I urged Chris to return to town with me. "We're not here to sightsee but to reach Pond Inlet. This is an expedition, not a tour."

Chris held her ground. "Jon, we don't have to go all the way to Pond Inlet. It's just a point on a map; maybe we're here to experience the North."

I exploded. "What do you mean 'we don't have to go all the way to Pond Inlet'! This is an expedition, not a vacation. On a vacation, you do whatever is the most fun; on an expedition you try as hard as you can to succeed. We're going to Pond Inlet."

I stopped talking and left for town; Chris followed. Bruno couldn't find the key to the radio station, so we went to a friend's house for a duplicate. The friend couldn't find his key either, but he knew someone who had bought a few cases of beer. Bruno got drunk and passed out on the floor, and Chris and I slipped back into the forest to sleep.

The next morning, we spoke to each other only when necessary as we made breakfast and launched back into the current. In normal life, if you have an argument with your lover, you can create space between the two of you by going to work or taking a walk. But there is no space on an expedition. I sat in the stern seat, as usual, and Chris took the bow oars. We were three feet apart. Chris stared at my back; I stared at the upstream current. Chris had to pull her oars in cadence with mine. If I wanted to scratch my nose, I'd say, "Hold it a second, let's miss a stroke. I have an itch on my nose." We'd both stop while I attacked the offending itch. Then I'd say, "Okay, let's go again," and we'd row together, in cadence, still three feet apart.

We rowed against a headwind that pushed us upstream almost as fast as the current carried us downstream. Boredom set in. I thought of provocative things I could say to continue the argument: "I didn't ask you to come on this expedition; you asked to come. I'm going to Pond Inlet. If you don't want to go to Pond Inlet, I'll drop you off in Inuvik and I'll continue on by myself. Then you can hang out and learn to tan hides and fly home when you're done."

But I kept silent. Why was I transporting all this anger? I thought of that day, after my shipwreck, when I sat on the hillside above Puerto Toro, happy to laze in the sunshine, free of my obsession to round the Horn. Why couldn't I domesticate that happiness? It lived inside me somewhere. Where did the anger, ambition, and frustration reside? Maybe I could lure those pesky emotions into a hidden crevice and then roll a rock over the entrance so they'd die slowly of thirst and hunger.

I relaxed, and the bad feelings left silently. Then I felt annoyed at myself for being inconsiderate the previous afternoon. One day would have been so little, and this was Chris's trip as well as mine. I couldn't see Chris, but I could feel the power of her rowing stroke. I broke the silence with a comment about something inconsequential. She responded cheerily. We let the incident pass.

11

We reached Arctic Red River on June 2, after traveling for two weeks. The Mackenzie carries enough heat northward to support a strip of forest protruding into an otherwise treeless tundra. But here, about two hundred river miles north of the Arctic Circle, latitude finally prevails and the forest becomes stunted and sparse. People who live here can't gather firewood by felling trees close to home, so they lasso drift logs from the river. Downstream, the Mackenzie broadens into its delta, a geological and ecological border between continent and coast. The head of the delta also marks a cultural border between the forest Déné people and the coastal Inuit. The town of Arctic Red River derived its name from blood that flowed frequently between warring neighbors.

So far our plan had worked. Except for the mistake below Fort Good Hope, we followed the melting ice. However, ice dams had formed in the delta, and villages and hunting camps were flooded. We would have to wait.

We wrote letters and walked to the post office for stamps. The weekly mail had arrived. There were no postal boxes, so someone dumped the bags of letters and packages onto the floor. People drifted in and out and shuffled through the pile. The scene reminded me of a game of concentration in which both the cards and players were in constant flux. "Joey, oh Joey, I saw a letter from Vancouver for you somewhere. I think it's over here. . . . No, I think Billy took it for you. . . . Oh look, here's a letter for Mary, wasn't she just here? Jimmy, go get her; I think she left for her aunt's house."

A short, elderly Caucasian woman in a clean, pressed dress found a heavy package. I offered to carry it home for her. "Can you do carpentry as well?" she asked. The question seemed no stranger than the scene in front of me, so I answered that I could and she nodded. "Good. You two will stay with me. I need some doors fixed and I will feed you well and there is a warm place to sleep in the basement." Our hostess, or employer, Sister Mattee, was fifty-nine years old and had come from France to the Arctic thirty-one years before to bring her God to the North.

As we neared her home, Sister Mattee started talking about her garden. "I have a routine. I make myself take ten trips a day, with a pail in each hand, and I go over the hill beyond the graveyard where the earth is rich, and I fill the pails with soil and carry them back to my garden, so I can have a nice garden by my house. I love to plant tomatoes. It is hard to grow tomatoes in the Arctic. They failed last year, and the year before, but before that"—her eyes lit up—"we had a good tomato year in 1979."

We ate lunch and I rehung the porch door. Sister Mattee told me to stop work in time for catechism class. Maybe we would like to come.

Chris and I accompanied her to the church, but no students arrived, so we waited for evening mass. I wanted to say something cheery, but the room was too hollow. I walked to the window, treading softly so my footsteps wouldn't echo in the large deserted building. The window caught my attention, not as a view to the outside world but as an object worthy of examination in itself. The bubbles in the pane told me it was old glass, which meant that someone, probably a parish priest, had transported it overland by dog team and then floated it downriver.

The schoolteacher, who was from Toronto, and her son arrived for mass. As the ceremony droned on, I stared at the window again, but this time to see outside. A band of teenagers, surrounded by a swarming mass of children, were coaxing a steel-wheeled wheelbarrow through the mud. A vintage outboard motor tilted precariously in the wheelbarrow, and the troop headed to the river to shoot beavers. I wondered whether the pelts would be sewn into a child's parka here in the North or into a fur coat to be worn in Paris.

12

The ice in the delta receded after three days, and we loaded our boat. When everything was ready, Chris and I walked back up the hill to say good-bye. Sister Mattee was working in her garden.

"Well, Sister, I think we will be off now."

"This is where I will plant my peas. It's a good place for peas, up here on the hill where it gets a lot of sunshine. Feel the sun warming the earth. Last year I planted peas the 19th of May. It was so cold, but the peas were smart, they slept in the ground, and when it warmed up in June they shot right up. So smart for just a pea seed."

"It's time for us to go now; I want to thank you."

"Did I show you my rhubarb? My rhubarb does so well."

So we looked at and admired her rhubarb.

"Sister, we really must be off now. I'd like to thank you. . . ."

She looked up suddenly. "You are going? Today? There is no rush, you haven't been in my way, I don't think I have been in yours. It will be lunchtime soon."

"We ate our breakfast. Our boat is loaded. We want to thank you."

"This morning? Right now? I didn't know. Well, you have been so much help, you fixed the back door, and . . . you did something else, something special. . . . I can't remember. What was it, it was so nice, do you remember what you did?"

"I sharpened your grass shears."

"Oooh, oooh, yes, they were so sharp. I have never used scissors that were so sharp, never in my life. When I was a sister in Fort Rae the brothers cut the yard; I worked in the hospital. You know when I came here the first time I was alone so I cut the yard, but the scissors were never this sharp, not ever, oh maybe when they were new. That was a long time ago. It is so nice to know how to do things. You are going? This morning? Right now?"

"Yes, thanks for everything. Good luck on your garden, and may your God watch over you."

We swung into the current and floated out of the forest into the Arctic.

13

At the delta, the current slows down and river breaks into hundreds of narrow distributaries. You have the feeling that you have left a freeway for a quiet country road. Just as you can't readily stop on a freeway because the trucks are whizzing by, it's hard to stop on the Mackenzie, where you may be half a mile from either shore, with huge sandbars blocking access to the riverbank and the current speeding you along. But in the delta, the shore is so close that you can smell the rich silt and the fresh spruce. Clearings, like roadside attractions, advertise their special qualities: STOP HERE for FREE sunlight filtering through the spruce, SOFT moss, a COMFORTABLE half-rotten log for a backrest. READ A BOOK, RELAX.

We pushed on.

About twenty species of ducks breed in the Mackenzie Delta; eiders, mergansers, harlequins, scooters, mallards, teals, and pintails are common. If you round a bend quietly, a mallard hen is likely to quack in alarm, feign a broken wing, and splash downstream, while her bewildered yellow chicks swim nervously into the weeds along the undercut bank, bumping into each other like billiard balls. Sandhill cranes paraded on their absurdly skinny legs. Swans, which mate for life, nuzzled each other, then lifted off gracefully at our intrusion. The white snow geese with the black wing tips had probably wintered in salt marshes of the Imperial Valley of California, fed briefly in marshes near the Oregon-California border, and then headed across vast forests and prairies to make love and raise their families amid the silt of this delta.

Gradually the stunted spruce of the northern forest succumbed to the frigid winter sea breezes. At river speed, the forest in front of us was nearly identical to that behind, but not quite. Behind us, a few hours ago, stunted spruce dominated even the exposed ridge tops, while to the north, on the next ridge, willows pushed some of the spruce aside; by late in the afternoon, only one or two scraggly spruce held onto the windswept high points. Then, as the week progressed, willows succumbed to tundra grasses and sedges on the high ground.

Once tundra dominated the ridges, the spruce gave way to willows even along the riverbanks and in the protected gullies. We were crossing into the Arctic. The change from forest to tundra is measured in miles or days, but it feels as if you are changing time frames, moving back twenty thousand years into the Pleistocene, when the great glaciers pushed their chilly winds across the planet.

One evening we pulled ashore late, tired and ready for camp. The clay-rich soil was crisscrossed with trails made by large animals, but the tracks had been obliterated by last week's flood. I thought that a herd of caribou might have migrated past. As I searched for a tent site, I saw a dead rabbit hanging, shoulder high, from a willow. It was folded in the middle, with its long ears rubbing against the green buds that would soon explode into leaves. How had a rabbit died in a willow branch, five feet above the ground? Chris suggested that it had drowned and was deposited by the flood. I had no alternative explanation but was not convinced. Then we saw three more dead rabbits hanging in the trees like shrunken heads left as hex signs by hostile warriors. I examined the area for additional clues and found a rabbit hole under the willow roots. Deep parallel scratches furrowed the clay around the entrance. I stretched my fingers as far apart as I could and was just able to place one finger in each groove.

Only one animal could have made these marks. I scanned the tundra, and even though I suspected it might be near, I was surprised to see a silver-blond grizzly watching us from the adjacent hillside. The bear was far enough away to appear small against the yellow-green vegetation. With no buildings or trees to provide scale, it could have been a puppy sitting close by on a neighbor's lawn. It raised its nose and twisted its head as if to say, "Are you going to throw me a ball or what?" Then it lowered its nose, stretched its long neck, and stared straight at me.

Carnivores have both eyes positioned on the front of their skull to provide accurate depth perception. Over eons of evolution, our genes have been programmed to recognize that the closely spaced triangle of eyes and nose on a streamlined face represents danger. I reasoned that evolution had also programmed the bear's senses. My eyes are also pinched ominously over my nose, so I stared straight back at the bear. The bear's neck and shoulder muscles relaxed, and it looked away to feign indifference. It had no way of knowing that my shotgun was in the boat and that without it I was no more of a threat than the bunnies. As the bear fidgeted, I glanced back to locate Chris, who was already retreating with her back to the river and her face toward danger. I followed her example until we reached the boat. As we slid into the current, I caught one last image of the bunnies hanging like laundry on the line and the wind ruffling the bear's golden fur like a field of wheat in August.

14

On June 12 we camped on the northernmost reaches of the delta, where the North American continent surrenders to the icy Arctic Ocean. There were no rocks, hills, or trees—just a thin line of silt held together by tundra and beaten by the incessant wind. The ocean was close, and at high tide the river was salty. A steady headwind blew in from the north. We fell asleep at nine in the evening, but I woke at eleven and walked down to the boat. The wind had dropped; the ocean tide, which was now more powerful than the river current, was near its high point. I reasoned that because we had twenty-four-hour sunlight and no reason to follow an urban nine-to-five schedule, we may as well travel when the wind was down and an ebb current flowed toward the ocean. I woke Chris and suggested that we pack and go.

She looked up, her faced framed by the hood of her warm sleeping bag. "You mean that we are in such a hurry that we have to break camp after two hours of sleep?"

"But it's easier now." I tried to sound logical. "We can nap this afternoon. It's not a matter of being in a rush, it's a matter of being efficient."

She retreated deeper into her bag and mumbled that she needed four or five more hours of sleep. By the time we launched at four in the morning, the ebb tide was weakening and a north wind drove a freezing rain into our bow. Chris was annoyed that I woke her so early to row in miserable conditions; I was annoyed that we slept through favorable winds and tide.

We stopped for breakfast in an abandoned hunting cabin—wet, cold, sleepy, and grumpy. I climbed to the roof and looked out to the faint line where the green-covered silt broke to a white haze, or fog— the ocean. The rain stopped, the wind subsided, and the sun came out. By midmorning we were in the Beaufort Sea—the Arctic Ocean—and it was flat calm. To the north, a hundred yards or a thousand miles away, ocean ended and the ice began. Light rico- cheted off the mirrored sea, turning the ice into a shimmering fan- tasy. The dip of our oars and our bow wake created the only distur- bance in the sea, and the squeak of the oarlocks was the loudest sound in the universe. We had floated eight hundred miles down the Mackenzie River. We had two thousand miles to go.

The sun was so intense we stripped down to short-sleeved cotton shirts. Water evaporating off the sea condensed to form a fog that hung over the sea like a layered wedding cake. A few islands poked through the top of the fog. Their edges were blurred, but the images were real. Behind them, towering ice cliffs appeared to rise and fall. They were nothing more tangible than changing, bending rays of light, but they convincingly grew taller than the islands, danced, dis- appeared, and rose again.

As we sat in the water watching, we began to wonder, "Is every- thing a mirage? Is there even any ice out there at all?" We rowed all afternoon through a landscape that couldn't exist until, like blind wanderers in a fun house, we bumped into the barrier of white-blue ice. The crunching sound jolted us out of the dream. The ice was firm and thick and only a foot above the water, so we climbed onto it. The mirages disappeared; form, shape, and reality became tangible again.

As we expected, the ocean was almost entirely frozen. But as we hoped, a narrow shore lead had melted along the beach. I was relieved because, as planned, we could continue eastward even before the main pack had broken up. We pulled to shore to make camp.

Although ice ruled the ocean, the meager Arctic snow had melted off the land and the earth was warm. We had thought that the delta was desolate, but the flora was even lower here, introducing us to the endless, stunted, marshy, duck-haven tundra of the end of the earth.

Mounds, called pingos, rose above the otherwise flat plain. A typi-cal pingo is about twenty-five to one hundred fifty feet high and looks like a volcano on the Little Prince's planet. Paradoxically, pin-gos, which are the tallest features on this otherwise planar landscape, are the frozen remains of extinct lakes. Arctic tundra is underlain by a huge ice sheet, called permafrost, which lies a few feet below the surface. Imagine a lake bed, lying on a thin layer of soil over the ice, surrounded by peaty soil, grasses, and sedges. In summer some of the lake water percolates through the soil and collects on the ice. This water then freezes as winter approaches. The ice bulges up, pushing the lake bottom higher. One would think that the following summer, water would drain away from the high point, but every year enough water freezes before it drains away, so the ice bulge grows. A pingo, then, is a lake bottom that is no longer a lake because it is the top of a hill, resting on an ice core.

We climbed the closest pingo and sat shoulder to shoulder as the sun, instead of setting, veered toward the North Pole. We had forgot-ten our unpleasant morning and its argument. Chris laughed and said that we must be in an octopus's garden for we were sitting on the bot-tom of a lake.

You can describe the tundra by listing the things you see—low plants, pingos, waterfowl, swamps, the distant ocean—but if you sit on a pingo and look across the tundra, the overwhelming sensation is that there is nothing out there. When tourists get off the plane in Tuktoyaktuk and stare across the landscape, they often look at one another and wonder, "What are we doing here? What can we photo-graph for the folks back home?" The problem is that they are asking the wrong questions. The tundra is about things you don't see: fences, roads, buildings, trees, mountains, glaciers.

Ask someone if they like to be crowded and they invariably say they like open space. No one likes to be jostled on the subway; a large apartment is more desirable than a small one. But when the space becomes too big, there's nothing out there to hold you in. Emotions flow out, thoughts escape, words don't work so well, time dissipates. I pressed against Chris. My mind glanced off the tundra like a light ray refracting toward a mirage.

15

By morning the shore lead had widened and the wind was at our backs. I felt like such a clever fellow; the lead would retreat before us as the ice on the Mackenzie had. We could see Tuktoyaktuk in the distance, weaving back and forth in the shimmering light, and I assured Chris that we would be there in time for a late lunch.

As the Mackenzie fans out, it fills the adjacent ocean with sediment, creating a shallow sea. The shore lead was so shallow that the boat scraped against the mud and oozed to a halt. It floated a little higher if we stepped out, so we tied a line to the bow and walked along the ice towing our craft. After a few miles, the lead became clogged with so many small floes and chunks of broken ice that it seemed like we were dragging the boat through a frozen daiquiri. Progress slowed. The concept of reaching a goal on the other side of the continent was so ludicrous that periodically one or the other of us announced, "Pond Inlet, here we come."

By late afternoon, we reached the end of this miserable lead. There was no more water. After following breakup for about a month, we had reached solid ice and could proceed no farther. It was satisfying to know that we had traveled successfully from the forest to the Arctic. But in my mind, the trip down the Mackenzie was merely the approach, and we had only traveled a few miles in the ocean. The Northwest Passage seemed an impossible dream.

We camped and climbed a bluff. A few leads crisscrossed the bay, but they didn't connect to form a passage. We were trapped. We returned to camp, cooked dinner, then retreated to the tent to read and write in our journals. As we were preparing for bed, we heard a motor. We unzipped the tent door and watched a snowmobile approach. It veered to the north, showing, in profile, a sled in tow. A boat was lashed to the sled and two people were sitting calmly in the boat as anyone would sit for an evening cruise across a frozen ocean in the bright 11:00 P.M. sunshine of a June evening. Everyone waved, and the driver gunned his machine to bounce over a pressure ridge. A few hundred yards away, the snowmachine stopped in front of a lead.

The passengers climbed out and helped the driver unfasten the lashings, load the sled and snowmachine in the boat, and float across the water to solid ice. Then they reloaded the boat onto the sled and sped off into the sunlit night. So that's how you do it! I felt as if I had been wading through waist-deep snow and had just seen my first set of skis.

We didn't have a sled, but we reasoned that the fiberglass would slide smoothly, so the next morning we dragged the boat onto the ice, tied lines and harnesses to ourselves, and started pulling. The boat burrowed into a thin layer of slushy snow that covered the ice. We jerked against the traces, and the boat started to move at a slow walk.

The Mackenzie Delta lies on a line of longitude several hundred miles west of Seattle, Washington; our goal, Pond Inlet, is due north of Harrisburg, Pennsylvania. To put the journey in perspective, I imagined dragging this loaded boat through ankle-deep slush across Washington, Montana, and North Dakota, and then through the entire Midwest to central Pennsylvania. I played mind games with myself: "They probably wouldn't let us on the freeway. At this speed, I wonder how long it would be between burger stands? We'd probably get robbed in Chicago."

My spirit had soared into empty space the night before, but today the harness held me inside. I wanted to space-travel to the moon and back, as the ancient Inuit shamans did. Even a quick jaunt to Tuktoyaktuk would have been fine. But all I could do was muster one step at a time into the slush.

Chris was leaning forward into her harness staring down at the ice as it passed. Chris is nearly a foot shorter and sixty pounds lighter than I am, and I tried to imagine the strain on her body. I was dedicated to reaching Pond Inlet, but clearly she wasn't. Yet she was pulling gamely beside me.

"We're so close," I thought, "but we haven't spoken for a long time. I wonder if she's also getting discouraged?"

I didn't want to ask the question in a manner that would prejudice a specific reply, so I broke the silence with a simple "What are you thinking about, Chrissy?"

We walked on for a few sloshy steps and listened to the boat swishing through the watery snow. I slacked my pace for an instant and felt the power of her pull. Someone in town was jockeying a forklift, clashing metal against metal.

"Oh, I was looking at the different shades of blueness in the snow and watching the little wind ridges melt."

Was she lying to me? Wasn't she discouraged, as I was? Hadn't she become depressed when she realized how slowly we were moving?

I focused several steps in front of me and watched the wet, blue, water-saturated snow attack the dry white tops of the snow ridges. Crystal by crystal, white turned to blue. I walked along watching the wind ridges melt.

Then I worded a question silently to myself: "Chris, what are you asking from this expedition?" I was afraid to ask because I knew that she would make me feel silly by giving me a simple answer.

Was she having fun dragging this dumb boat through this dumb slush? That was my problem. I had dreamed up this expedition to cross a continent, but right now Pond Inlet and the success theme seemed ludicrous.

The boat caught against a chunk of ice; Chris momentarily lost her balance and veered to the right while I staggered to the left. We bumped shoulders. The contact broke the reverie.

"Let's take a break and have a snack," I suggested.

We munched some nuts and then continued across the Arctic.

16

We dragged the boat seven miles in two and a half days before reaching Tuktoyaktuk—two and a half days to travel a distance that could be traveled in a morning under decent conditions. Breakup was late and progress was too painful; we would have to wait. We sat on the beach as mixed rain and sleet blew in from the northwest.

I had been careful not to follow "white man's ways" as Frobisher and Franklin had. My heroes and models had been those who lived with the land, and in my romantic image they had traveled under all kinds of conditions. I asked Chris: "Why can't we just keep going?"

Chris reminded me that if we really wanted to travel "in the old way" we not only had to adapt appropriate technology, we had to assume an appropriate attitude. We needed patience. Inuit migrated over generations, not weeks or months. Even my hero, Stefansson, took two years to travel from the Mackenzie Delta to Union and Dolphin Straits, a few hundred miles east. Chris pointed out that in the Arctic a week's delay was nothing more than a red light or a stop for gas.

Silently we pulled the boat above the high tide line, pitched our tent on the oil-soaked gravel amid a jumble of abandoned snowmachines, and walked to the local cafe to pay too much money for pale eggs, white toast, and diluted coffee. It would be easy to become depressed if we waited like this for long. So we followed the path laid out by many Inuit, by !Kung Bushmen, by Amazonian hunters, and by cannibals from New Guinea. We went to town and looked for a job.

Tuktoyaktuk was half village and half city, half Inuit and half white, half a charming outpost of people and culture in the North and half a garbage-ridden industrial depot. The economy was driven by petroleum exploration in the Beaufort Sea and a military surveillance base that was located on an adjacent hill.

We soon learned that the industrial czar of this throbbing eyesore was a man named Joe Pidborochynski, known as Joe Pitts. We found him in his garage washing a taxi. He said there was no work but chatted as he squirted hot high-pressure water against the windshield. The most hot water we had seen since Arctic Red River was in a cup of tea or coffee, and Chris chided, "I guess you don't have to worry about wasting hot water when you're the boss."

Poker-faced, Joe continued to spray the water against an already clean portion of the taxi, until he had made it clear that he would not be influenced by a spunky woman who had traveled nearly a thousand miles through the ice. Then he hired us with an admonition: "Okay, come for dinner. You start tomorrow morning. If you are half worthless you can work for room and board; if you actually do anything, you'll get paid."

And so we became part of the military-industrial invasion of the North.

At the time, there were no municipal water mains or sewers in Tuktoyaktuk because it is difficult to prevent liquids from freezing when the air temperature is sixty below zero in winter and the earth is solid ice even in the hottest part of summer. Instead, Joe's trucks delivered drinking water and picked up sewage from every house in town. He also delivered heating oil, ran the only reliable taxi service, and owned the only gas station, garage, and car wash.

Joe owned three new Cadillacs. If he fired one of them up, he could drive a mile to the spit, two miles to the Arctic Transportation docks, or three miles to the sewer lagoon. Beyond these dead ends lay the tundra, which surrounded the city and left it as a virtual island, connected to the outside world only by air, by sea for a short time in the summer, and by an ice road in the winter.

Joe assigned Chris the jobs of cook and taxi dispatcher and gave me work as a carpenter. My job was to help finish a three-story command center for Joe's enterprise. Half of the bottom floor was the garage, which was big enough to hold a tractor trailer and a few pickup trucks simultaneously. The other half was reserved for his offices. According to his plan, the second story would be his own living space, and the third would be a dormitory and a cafeteria for his employees, complete with a spacious game room and pool hall. In a land where everything that is shipped from the south is expensive, where there are no trees bigger around than your little finger or taller than a paper clip, Joe's castle was built entirely of wood and he didn't pay a penny for any of it. For years, he had collected old packing crates and pallets from the military base and from the dumps behind warehouses scattered around the city. For years he had hired peons to pull nails and carefully stack his treasures in piles, and then last fall, in a burst of activity, they had built Tuk's first skyscraper. There was only one problem. The whole building was hopelessly out of square and out of plumb. The concern wasn't that a trained eye or a skilled cabinetmaker would notice that the framers had made a few errors; it was that even from a distance it seemed certain that the whole pile of trash was about to topple over. My job was to help straighten and strengthen it.

The foreman was a French Canadian from Yugoslavia. I never learned how or why he came to Tuktoyaktuk; in the North, as in the old American West, you don't ask about a person's background. The crew consisted of myself and another carpenter. We were each issued a chain saw, but there was only one hammer for the two of us, so we had to trade back and forth when we needed to drive nails. No matter; it was mostly a chainsaw job. The Yugoslav ran around yelling in English, French, and Yugoslavian, and on the rare moments that I understood what he was saying, I heard commands like "slash that wall, cut through this framing, chew up this floor, hack these joists." The sawdust flew, sparks jumped when we hit nails, and the noise in the enclosed space was deafening.

When the building was just about chainsawed to death, when I was almost ready to toss my tools and leap out of a window for safety, the Yugoslav raced outside and started the engine on a huge loader, one of those machines with wheels bigger around than a man is tall. With a short, thick wooden shaft chained to the raised bucket, he backed up about twenty yards, threw the machine into forward, hit the throttle, and *kaboom*, rammed Joe's castle. Creak, groan, shake—*vroom, vroom* of the diesel—a puff of black smoke and *kaboom*, he rammed it again. Creak, groan, shake, and bit by bit, smash by smash, the building started to straighten. The Yugoslav then leaned out the window of the loader, waved his arms and yelled, "Truss it and nail it!" We grabbed bits of old plywood, color coded and addressed (from Toronto to Dome Petroleum, Tuktoyaktuk), found the biggest nails we had, and raced around connecting the building back together, furiously passing the hammer back and forth between us. Then there was another evaluation, more chainsaw work, and more ramming. In a few days the building was square and plumb, more or less, and ready for the sheetrock that would arrive when the barge could navigate the ice and bring the year's supplies to the city.

17

As taxi dispatcher, Chris became enmeshed in the sordid side of Tuktoyaktuk. If people feel healthy and happy, they are content to walk the few blocks across town, but if they are drunk or sick, or if they have fought with their husband or wife, they call a taxi.

Chris's daily telephone encounters were depressing, but I reminded myself that a traveler is neither a scientist nor a social worker and that value judgments are not good passports across harsh lands.

On my way home from work I passed a sculptor who sat outside carving caribou antler and walrus ivory. One day I asked if I could watch him work. He grunted assent and then ignored me. The next day I nodded hello and squatted on my heels, watching again and occasionally admiring. By the fourth day he greeted me and held up a finished piece. Six ivory swans were supported by antler tines as they approached a lake formed by the broad shovel of the antler. I held it and turned it slowly in my hands.

"One hundred dollars," he announced.

"That is a gift," I responded. "This piece is worth much more than that."

He smiled.

"I am a traveler; I have no room for this in my boat. I will take it home in my mind."

The old man invited me in for tea. The house was cluttered with half-decayed skins, snowmachine carburetors, dead Coleman stoves, and pieces of whalebone, antler, and ivory.

"You are traveling east when the ice moves out," he affirmed.

News spreads rapidly in a village. I nodded.

"I was born in an igloo near the Anderson River. Very good fishing there, be sure to set your net. In those days we didn't live in towns. You couldn't build a town because maybe the game wouldn't come there next year. We hunted whales near the Mackenzie in early summer, then moved inland to hunt caribou and sometimes came back to the coast to catch fish when the char start to swim upstream in August. We always lived on the coast in winter when the caribou went south. In the winter you must hunt seal to survive. But the white men came and built these houses; they are warm in winter you know. We have doctors now and schools. The young people need schools to get jobs. People go out and work on the drill rigs maybe two weeks on and two weeks off. When they are in town they have plenty of money and nothing to do. Sometimes they drink a lot. This summer you will be having all the fun traveling across the land in your boat. This living in town is not so much fun."

"Yes," I said, "it is fun to travel, but I always have plenty of food in my boat, and when winter comes I will go home to a warm house like yours. Maybe it wasn't so much fun in the old days when people hunted seals in the winter darkness and then sent the old people out in the snow to freeze to death if the seals didn't come."

He was undaunted. "You are having all the fun."

I let silence rule before rising. He held me for one more moment with a raised hand. "Maybe you will be hungrier than you think; don't forget to set your net near the Anderson River."

18

By the end of the week, open water extended as far as we could see around the headland to the northeast, so Chris and I drew our paychecks and bought more supplies for our journey into the central Arctic. The next village was almost five hundred miles away, although in an emergency we could expect help from a drill rig only fifty miles away or from one of the two DEW line radar installations along the coast.*

The central Arctic, guarded by the barren lands of north-central Canada to the south and ice to the north, east, and west, was the last region in North America to be explored by Europeans. Greenland was settled by Eric the Red in A.D. 982, and Baffin Island was visited by Frobisher in 1576. On the other side of the continent, Vitus Bering left Saint Petersburg, Russia, in 1725 to map the western Arctic and was followed by trappers, traders, and settlers. Alexander Mackenzie canoed to the Mackenzie Delta in 1789, and fur traders followed close behind. By the 1800s Alaskan Inuit held seasonal jobs and traded extensively, and many had been Christianized. Although

The DEW line was the Distant Early Warning system designed to detect an air attack launched from Russia, over the Pole, against North America. It consisted of a string of radar bases spread across the North from Alaska to eastern Canada. In the late 1980s and early 1990s the DEW line installations were upgraded and renamed the North Warning System.

the pincers of civilization had been drawing inward for several centuries, they had not intruded on the central Arctic.

Seventy-five years prior to our journey—only one lifetime before—the central Arctic remained primeval. The Alaskan Inuit had heard of ferocious bands in the central Arctic called the Nagyuktogmiut, "those who killed all strangers," but they hadn't made any contact.

Vilhjalmur Stefansson floated down the Mackenzie in 1908 with a plan to head east, as we were doing. However, his goal was not to cross the Arctic but to live in it as an Inuit and to study its land and its people. Traders warned him that there were no caribou or seals east of the Mackenzie and it was suicidal to proceed. He ignored all admonitions and headed into the unknown.

19

We left Tuktoyaktuk on June 23, two days after the solstice. We had launched on the Mackenzie headwaters a little over a month previously and had traveled for three weeks and worked for one. I was excited and glad to be headed onto the land again. I wrote in my journal:

I'm leaving Tuk feeling fat, strong, well showered, and ready for the next two months. In a sense this is the beginning for us; the start of our journey east. We could have flown here and still done the Northwest Passage. Well, we are a bit harder and more experienced, our gear is a little more broken in and broken down, and we are an entire chapter of our lives richer for the trip so far.

We encountered bad ice only a few miles from town, but even the hard going didn't quell my enthusiasm. I continued writing that evening:

Finally left town at 5:00 P.M. for a sandbar slog, an over the ice slog, and then an around the bay slog. It's good to be on the road again, Pretty Mama.

On the third day after leaving town, our already pitifully narrow and distorted shore lead constricted, and we inched closer to the beach until the keel crunched into the sand. We sat silently with our left oars touching the beach and the right oars banging against the ice. The boat floated without our weight, so we fixed lines and continued by walking along the shore and pulling the boat through the water. After an hour, a single chunk of ice blocked our lead. Chris is normally patient when confronted by obstacles, and I assumed we would drag the boat around the rogue floe and proceed. But as I coiled my towline, she splashed into the water and tried to roll the ice out of the way. It was too heavy, so I walked into the water and helped. Even together we couldn't roll it free. It looked rotten, so I lifted the heaviest rock I could muster, held it over my head, and with a caveman grunt, hurled it against the ice. It impacted with a dull thud and left a small crater in the offending berg. At Chris's suggestion, we both climbed onto the ice and jumped up and down. Waves soaked our pants but the wetness was irrelevant; everything was irrelevant except this childish confrontation with one piece of ice amid a continent of ice. When the floe finally broke, I lost my footing and fell into six inches of icy water. Chris laughed, and the soot smudge from last night's driftwood fire stood out sharply across her cheek and nose. I ceremoniously stood up and pushed the boat another few feet toward Pond Inlet.

We walked up the beach to a south-facing bluff that collected sunlight like a reflector oven. I undressed, spread my wet clothes out to dry, and sat down to eat lunch.

"Let's sit here this afternoon and watch the ice melt," Chris suggested.

"Sure, sounds good," I responded. "Is that like when we were teenagers and parked the car on a lonely back road to watch the submarine races?"

Chris giggled and put her arm around me. Arctic mirages created imaginary pulsating, dancing ice cliffs. Pingos formed the only true relief, but they too joined the dance and in doing so lost all sense of reality. One conical top was so flattened that it looked as if a dinner plate was balanced on the summit. Then the hill inverted over itself to become an hourglass that soon disappeared behind a rising ice fog.

We made love. The ice didn't melt much, but regardless we dressed, walked back to the sea, and continued dragging the boat eastward.

20

June 27 was windless, and the hot sun reflected strongly off the sparkling snow. We both stripped down to our underpants as we abandoned the fickle leads and pulled across the ice. We saw green grass for the first time. Had we been unobservant the day before, or had the grass turned green that day? A small herd of caribou passed, and the first mosquitoes since the forest along the Mackenzie drove us back into our clothes when we neared land.

A frozen ocean is a monumental landscape, like a mountain range. The difference is that ice changes in weeks or days, not millennia, so when you watch the ice melt you can imagine watching the Himalayas rising from the sea or the Colorado River eroding through a vertical mile of rock to form the Grand Canyon. Time distorts just as distance and space distort in the treeless plain bounded by curtainlike mirages.

The softening ice and widening leads made travel easier in some places and harder in others. At times we found a lead and rowed. Even though our oars sometimes banged the ice or the beach, and even though we weren't always heading exactly where we wanted to go, at least we were moving eastward, and rowing was immensely preferable to dragging the boat. When we couldn't find a suitable lead, however, dragging was our only option. Our progress became increasingly erratic. One day we had open water and rowed seventeen miles, and the next day we made only two miles dragging across slushy ice. On June 30 we rounded the point into McKinley Bay. We had traveled fifty-four miles in a week; at that rate we would arrive in

Pond Inlet in thirty-seven weeks, sometime the following March. If we didn't speed up soon, we would certainly fail.

Both Chris and I understood the arithmetic, but we reacted to it differently. After one particularly slow day, I wrote:

> If the navigation season doesn't improve, we'll be lucky to make it to Paulatuk. How will I feel to return home after failing again? Was the plan a failure, or are we doing something wrong?

In contrast, Chris had never shared my ambition, so she never shared my sense of failure. She saw the daily movement as an existential exercise superimposed on a wondrous landscape. On the same day that I wrote of failure, she also wrote that we would be lucky to make Paulatuk, but her tone was different. I quote from her journal:

> The day has been deceiving, we've gone in and out of many bays and around points. We are travelling along but gaining little. There is fog on and off and if you add the ice mirages, it makes it hard to know what is real land and where it is. At one point while pushing the boat, we realized how close our endeavor comes to theater of the absurd. Maybe we should just Wait for Godot. At our present rate, we will be pressed to make Paulatuk. Things should improve though as July is navigation season. The last couple of days have been sunny but if there is any wind it is cool. Today started out warm with no breeze. Now it is breezy and cool, we sit in the tent to sip after-dinner coffee.

21

As we entered McKinley Bay, fog cut our vision to a few yards, but we heard the clash of cable against steel, the whir of winches, and the mechanical voice of a loudspeaker barking orders.

Somewhere out there in the middle of the bay, a drill rig was grinding into the sediment and rock beneath the sea, looking for oil. Late in the afternoon, the sun burned a hole in the fog, highlighting the red, white, and black machinery. We wanted to make the rig disappear, but it remained, bathed in a ray of sunlight like a Madonna and Child in a medieval painting.

Oil rigs occupy a few specks in the 1.3-million-square-mile Northwest Territory. As long as they mind their business and don't break a pipe, don't tip over in the ice, don't find so much oil that they call their friends, don't induce people to build roads and pipelines, don't encourage tankers into the ice, and don't bring workers north to shoot the caribou—the rigs in the central Arctic will remain nothing more than an annoyance to the few travelers on this desolate land. The problem is that the oil extraction industry isn't that well behaved. A few rigs on the Alaskan north slope grew into small industrial cities like Prudhoe Bay; a plan on someone's map evolved into a long, thin scratch called the Alaska Pipeline; a floating chunk of steel named the *Exxon Valdez* that was entrusted to an inexperienced seaman and a drunken captain ran aground on a rock, spilling eleven million gallons of crude oil into the fragile waters of Prince William Sound. Today the Canadian-Alaskan Arctic is one of the last great wilderness areas left on earth. The caribou migrate in the biggest herds of ungulates outside of Africa. Globally, the taiga rivals the tropical rain forest in size. Perhaps we should let the North stay wild.

When the great Sioux warrior and visionary Crazy Horse lay dying in the dirt, a cavalry officer offered him a bed to make his last moments more comfortable. He said that he had never slept on a white man's bed and he wasn't going to die on one. Few of us have Crazy Horse's strength. I wished that the rig didn't exist, but as long as it stood in front of us, I suggested that we row over and beg a Wonder Bread, Miracle Whip, and bologna sandwich and a cup of muddy-brown, lukewarm coffee.

But the ice in the middle of the bay was broken, rotten, and disintegrating, too thick to row through and too treacherous to walk on. We continued on, around the bay and around the rig, hugging the shore.

22

The next day was so windy that we couldn't travel even in protected waters. I sat in the tent and read *Doctor Zhivago*, but I couldn't relate to love, tragedy, and the Russian Revolution. I tried to nap but instead lay awake, frustrated that it was the first of July and we were only sixty miles from Tuktoyaktuk.

Chris thought that the day was perfect for a change in routine and a walk. For the past few days we had noticed piles of driftwood along the low hills above the beaches. They were too ordered and far from shore to be natural, and I thought they were blinds for the fall waterfowl hunt. Chris had disagreed, arguing that they weren't placed strategically in natural flyways. Now she suggested that we climb a hill above camp and examine one.

I responded, "Maybe the wind will die while we're up on the hill and we won't be ready to continue onward. We've already lost most of the day, and I'd hate to lose another hour. You're always holding us back."

Chris snapped, "Don't be an idiot. We're out here for the whole summer. Time is never lost. We can't lose an hour; we'll just be doing something other than rowing or dragging that stupid boat for an hour!"

I was angry at her for not sharing my focused ambition, yet envious because she was happy and I wasn't. Pond Inlet was inconceivably far away. Success on this journey was becoming increasingly improbable. I, too, was curious about the driftwood piles but chose to remain irritable. I told her that I didn't want to look at anything except miles going by, and I wasn't going to waste my strength on a hike. Chris started up the hill without me until I called up to her that I was coming.

We reached the hilltop, and Chris veered to examine one pile while I walked to the neighboring one. It was roofed and there was no entry, so it would be useless as a blind or an emergency shelter. I peered into the darkness between the logs, and when my pupils adjusted, I saw bones. I reached in and lifted one of the larger ones into the sunlight. I inspected it, and then, mesmerized, held it against my thigh to confirm that it had the right shape and size to be a human femur. Squatting there on the tundra with the leg bone against my leg, I looked over to Chris, who was watching me, nodding.

She said, "Human skulls."

Suddenly self-conscious that I was intruding, I replaced the bone in its moldy indentation in the soft earth. Then I walked over to Chris's pile. Two bronzed skulls and two sets of arms, legs, and vertebrae lay side by side, only slightly scattered by foxes. A small, shallow, soapstone dish lay next to the bones. When in use, it had been filled with seal or whale oil, wicked with a bit of moss, and lit to become the sole source of light and heat for a snug igloo during the long, dark, Arctic winter. Chris picked up a hookless ivory fish lure. Aboriginal Inuit hadn't invented fishhooks and used lures to entice fish close enough to spear them. The grave also held a metal bowl, a fragment of hide clothing with glass beads sewn into the fabric, two driftwood sled runners, and a spear point. The dead souls had light, heat, clothing, a bowl to eat out of, transportation, and a way to obtain food.

Imagine parachuting into the Arctic where you must survive with a fur coat, a dogsled, a fish lure without a hook, and a harpoon. Imagine several dark months every year when the temperature plummets to 50 below zero, and your only source of light and heat is a small soapstone dish to burn seal blubber. Yet here on these hillsides and on this frozen ocean, in a land where pingos grow a fraction of an inch every year, where imaginary ice cliffs appear on the horizon and mountains dance the afternoon away, where the sun never sets all summer and doesn't rise for several months of the winter, where a hunter must harpoon his dinner—here people survived.

No one knows when the first humans migrated across the Bering Straits from Asia to North America. We all learned in school that migrants traveled across the Bering Straits when the sea level was lower and a land bridge connected the two continents. However, Inuit commonly travel over the ice in springtime. According to early explorers, Arctic Inuit routinely made fifty-mile passages across the ice. Thus I believe that people wandered freely back and forth across the Bering Straits before and after the time of the land bridge.

Archaeologists have found crushed, chipped, and scratched animal bones and tool-like rocks from sites in North America that are between forty thousand and one hundred thousand years old. Scholars debate these findings. They could be the remains of early human habitation or they could have been formed by random natural events such as fire and rockfall. However, many reliable sites have been excavated that date from twelve to sixteen thousand years ago.

On the basis of studies of tooth structure, language, and genetics, researchers agree that the Inuit and Aleutian Island people are ethnologically different from the American Indians. Most likely the Inuit migrated later, arriving in North America nine to ten thousand years ago, roughly at the same time that agriculture and pottery began to thrive in the Middle East. The Inuit are descended from Mongolian nomads. Thus they share a common ancestry with Genghis Khan, who terrorized Asia around A.D. 1200.

By four thousand years ago, people of the Arctic Small Tool Culture had spread across Alaska and Canada to Greenland. They primarily hunted caribou and musk ox with bows similar to those used by Siberians. Bone harpoon heads tell us that they supplemented their diet with seal. They dug permanent houses into the ground and constructed roofs from wooden poles covered with animal hides and sod. Sites reveal evidence of domestic dogs, a further indication that migrations occurred over the ice with dogsleds to carry their loads.

In many regions the Arctic Small Tool Culture died out, and portions of the North were uninhabited during a cold spell from thirty-five hundred to three thousand years ago. Then, rather suddenly, the land was repopulated. These later people refined techniques for hunting sea mammals. In winter and spring they hunted seals on the ice, and in summer they ventured out in kayaks and larger *umiaks* after seals, whales, and walrus. Survival is tenuous in the North, and people must exploit as many resources as possible. By hunting different game in different seasons, by feeding off both the land and the water, Inuit flourished.

To survive on the land, one needs patience. To harpoon a seal in winter, a hunter must wait for hours above its breathing hole, or *aglu*. To turn the sealskin into warm *kamiks*, a woman must carefully scrape the hide, chew it to softness, and sew it together with an intricate, waterproof stitch. To travel across Asia, across the Bering Strait, and across the entire Northwest Passage, a tribe needs not a season, or a lifetime, or even a century, but a millennium.

Wind had been blowing ice into the continent since the time North America, riding slowly on its tectonic plate, had drifted into the Arctic. All morning I had been in a hurry to go on, but the Arctic didn't care. I could rail at the heavens, but it made no difference. So I had become irritable with Chris. She was close, convenient, and vulnerable, and she would react to my petulance; the wind and the ice would not.

During my enthusiastic planning for this voyage, I had ignored distance, ice, and wind. Now I sat amid the graves of the old people and tried to release myself from my self-imposed bondage to a goal. But then the old mantra came back: "I failed at Cape Horn; I better succeed this time."

We had been sitting in the cold wind. We stood stiffly, placed the artifacts back in the grave, and returned to camp.

23

The wind died that evening, and we continued eastward the next morning. The air held a strong musty odor, and as we rounded a small headland, we saw a large herd of caribou.* In the temperate regions, when people see a herd of deer or elk, they usually see about half a dozen animals, maybe twenty on a lucky afternoon. Occasionally, a few hundred animals feed on a sunny, south-facing hillside. But the prairie wilderness has been tamed, and the great herds of bison have been shot. Here in the Arctic, the cold has held technology to an uneasy truce and the land remains unfenced. Great

---

*Caribou are indigenous to North America, and reindeer are native to northern Europe and Asia. However, reindeer have been imported along the coast close to Tuktoyaktuk; therefore, some of the herds we saw were probably reindeer. Because it is difficult to distinguish between the two without a side-by-side comparison, for the sake of simplicity I call all these creatures caribou.

herds of caribou roam the tundra. Therefore, we saw not one, or twenty, or even one hundred, but a panorama of caribou. A few hundred had collected on an island situated close to the beach. Some were grazing while others lay in the water to escape the ubiquitous mosquitoes.

With the image of the stone age artifacts fresh in my mind, I wondered how easy it would be to hunt caribou on the open tundra with a spear. I didn't want to kill one, just to get close enough to see if it could be done.

We rowed around the herd to the far end of the island, and Chris sloshed ashore. While she hid behind some rocks, I rowed back to a sandbar that linked the island with the mainland. When I raised my oar as a signal, Chris walked down the center of the island. The strategy was to herd the caribou to the end of the island and then scare them toward land. I guessed that they would run along the sandbar; if they did, I could easily ambush them from the boat.

Halfway across the island, Chris stopped and studied the ground. She looked up, cupped her hands around her mouth and shouted, "I see tracks."

Yelling back, and talking slowly so that each word would have time to float across the distance without bumping into the one before it, I called, "Of course there are tracks; there are caribou everywhere."

"No, bear tracks, grizzly tracks, big ones."

"Don't worry about it. We always see bear tracks with caribou tracks."

There was a moment of silence. "They're fresh, real fresh."

"They are tracks, not a bear. If there were a bear here now, the caribou would be spooked. Keep herding."

There was a long wait.

"Are you sure?"

"Yes!" I said, although I must confess that a twinge of doubt crept in.

She continued to walk slowly toward the herd. One of the cows looked up at Chris, then turned her head to watch the rest of the herd. None of the other animals showed alarm, so the more vigilant cow went back to feeding. A few moments later, three animals looked up simultaneously, stared at Chris, and looked at one another. They fidgeted, but the bulk of the herd remained unperturbed, and the inertial peacefulness prevailed. Then Chris started running, waving her arms, and yelling. In one instant two animals were running, in the next one hundred had taken flight, and within a few moments they were all racing through the water, over the bar, toward land.

With a few strokes I was an oar's length—a spear's length—from the panicked animals. I could see the moisture on their noses, watch the muscles in their shoulders, feel the splash of saltwater as they ran past. In my imagination I was a Sioux riding bareback among stampeding bison; I was chasing mammoth toward a cliff with flaming torches; I was in my sealskin kayak, hunting caribou. But in reality I was a tourist, so I backed away to keep my camera dry and took pictures.

24

Cape Dalhousie lies at the tip of a narrow peninsula that protrudes above 70° north latitude. When I studied the map as we were planning the trip, I imagined breakers, rolling surf, rocky bluffs, and the wind and seagulls screaming. However, the wind was calm and the water in our narrow lead was flat as we approached the cape. Old-squaws paddled through the floating ice, searching for mussel banks. Eiders built their nests in the nearby tundra ponds. A bachelor mallard rose to search for a mate or a territory that would attract a mate. The tundra and the sea around it had an aura of domesticity. These feathered wanderers were coming together, settling down, building houses, visiting, chatting, mating, and relaxing. What a great life, to experience this short intense explosion of home and hearth, and then in a few months, take flight again to honk your way across the continents.

An uninsulated, metal-sided shelter stood on a bluff ten feet above the cape. Outside, a fifty-five-gallon drum of human excrement was decomposing in the sun. The camp was probably used only in winter when the contents of the drum would be frozen. Tin cans, a few quarts of unopened snowmachine oil, half of a wool hat, some rusted tools, and an unopened bottle of nonalcoholic malt beverage were scattered about the ground. I tried the malt, but numerous freeze-thaw cycles had rendered it undrinkable. Inside we found a wood-burning stove with one round air vent that had been cut in the factory and three more jagged ones that had been stabbed through with a screwdriver. We were far from any large river that would transport driftwood, so it seemed odd that people would be so wasteful of such a limited resource. Why didn't they insulate the shack or camp in igloos that could be heated with a few candles?

We camped early and wandered inland to find fresh water. A swan fled our approach, leaving one perfect egg vulnerable in the nest. Nearby, a dead cygnet lay rotting in a small puddle next to its smashed shell. Perhaps a fox had almost escaped with a meal before the mother returned, too late, to chase away the predator. We hurried past so that a second disaster wouldn't occur.

During dinner, a huge caribou herd grazed less than fifty yards from our tent. They were moving slowly eastward, grunting contentedly like a herd of pigs. A few sought relief from the mosquitoes by rolling in the snow beneath a cut bank. They passed us in a seemingly endless, fluid mass as we ate and wrote in our journals. When I lay down to sleep, I heard the hollow sound of hoofbeats on the peaty earth. I turned over on my back to listen to their bodies shuffling. When we awoke, they were gone, and the tundra stretched lifeless from horizon to horizon.

25

Past Cape Dalhousie the coastline doubled back toward the southwest to form Liverpool Bay. If the bay had been ice-free and the wind at our backs, we could have sailed thirty-five miles across its mouth to Cape Bathhurst in a day. With solid ice we would have dragged across rather than go tens of miles out of our way along the shore lead. But within the last few days leads had widened and interconnected, releasing the ice as a dense concentration of independent floes that ranged from a few square feet to the size of a suburban house. We could no longer walk across the ice as we had earlier in the season. We couldn't sail through it either because the floes washed back and forth so that leads opened and closed as the ice separated and collided.

We pulled the boat to shore to evaluate our new situation. The wind blew gently from the south, pushing the ice northward. If the weather held, the south end of the bay would be ice-free before the northern portion. Therefore, we inched into the bay, even though this course would steer us momentarily southwestward, away from Pond Inlet.

Chris stood in the bow and pushed floes out of the way with her oar, while I paddled or pushed from the rear. When Chris pushed too hard against a heavy chunk of ice, the boat drifted backward. Then she waited until I propelled us forward toward the next floe. If a house-sized pan blocked the way, we climbed out of the boat, dragged it over the ice, and launched back on the other side. Occasionally, we came to shore, waded into the water, pushed a few beached floes out of the way, and dragged the boat through the shallow opening. We weren't making much progress. We worked with the concentration of an old couple assembling a jigsaw puzzle. The only difference was that we were one of the pieces, and we were trying to move through the half-finished puzzle without getting locked into place.

In a typical conversation, I would say, "If you rotate that pan clockwise, you can push it out of the way and we can squeak by."

The Chris might reply, "Whoa, whoa, try to hold the boat steady."

"Okay, great, now push."

"Yeah, now, paddle a stroke on the left side."

"Good."

And then we would be another ten feet closer to Pond Inlet, which was still nineteen hundred miles away. Whenever we stopped to rest, we looked across the churning ice-choked ocean and listened to it grumble, like a bear awakened a week too early from a long, peaceful sleep.

The following day, a rising tide generated a current moving south, but at the same time the south wind pushed the water and ice northward. The wind drove the tops of the floes and the current pushed at their undersides; as a result some floes drifted north, others moved south, and many spun in place.

The previous afternoon we had paddled southward while the ice paraded north, like a flock of polar bears headed to feast on a dead whale. But now half of them turned back southward as if the party were over. The north-moving and south-moving floes swished past one another, throwing off sparkling crystals when they collided. Sitting in a boat in the midst of it all, north-south, left-right, here-there became one swirling dance.

Chris remarked that she felt dizzy from the loss of a stable reference. She pushed against a floe directly in front of us, and then with an annoyed tone in her voice told me, "Don't push us forward, Jon, until I get this floe out of the way."

"I'm not pushing," I answered.

We looked at each other, then back at the ice. A north-moving floe pressed against the bow while a south-moving floe nudged the rear. We were trapped. The fiberglass creaked, and I thought of oaken ships crushed in the ice.

Chris reacted before I did, jumping out of the boat onto a floating floe. "Move, Jon!" she shouted. "Lift the boat so the ice can slide under it!"

She shocked me out of inaction. I felt that too-familiar feeling: the exhilarating adrenaline-laced clarity mixed with a dull sickening fear.

I jumped out, lifted one gunnel while Chris lifted the other. The two floes floated under the boat and crunched together. The edges shattered, ice chunks broke loose, and I knew that if the boat had remained in the water for even a few more seconds, it would have been crushed. The two floes continued to push against one another, then one sprung loose and jumped over its neighbor, sliding up onto it as both were squeezed by the millions of floes that surrounded us. We were only a hundred yards from shore, but our path was blocked by congested ice. Nearby, floes collided and slid on top of one another, rapidly building a wobbly tower that then collapsed like an unstable stack of plates.

I wondered what would happen if we lost the boat. We were farther from help than I had been during my shipwreck in Chile, and
the water was colder. Could we make it to shore through the ice?
Could we walk back to civilization? I remembered myself clearly—
huddled in a fetal position, clutching my shoulder—at Cape Guanaco, as the winds blew over Cape Horn.

We read each other's faces, registered the tension, and then turned
our heads to watch the ice. The noise grew louder as the sun shone
brightly and the wind whispered gently on our faces. A lead opened
toward the shore. One of us said, "What do you think?" and the other
responded, "We better go for it," and we shoved back into the water.

We paddled a few yards until the ice closed in around us again,
and the fiberglass creaked. Chris and I jumped out to lift the boat
again, but Chris's pan tipped and she fell in. I wanted to help her
back into the boat and hug her for support and warmth, but there
wasn't time. Single-handed, I pulled the boat onto the ice so it
wouldn't be crushed by the closing floes. Chris's face appeared over
the gunnel as she pulled herself back into the boat. I smiled in
encouragement, slid the boat back into the water, grabbed my oar,
and pushed us another few feet toward the beach.

We reached shore after half an hour and pulled the boat to safety.
"You're a warrior," I told her.

"Oh, gimme a break! You were worried, too, out there."

"No, Chris, a *warrior*, a soldier, a brave; you were a warrior out
there."

"There wasn't much of a choice," she responded.

I said nothing but thought, "Yes, there were lots of choices; you
could have panicked into inaction, you could have given up." We
hugged and I felt how wet she was.

"Maybe you should change your clothes."

After Chris was dry and warm, we walked toward a bluff to watch
the ice move. Fresh wolf and grizzly tracks were imprinted in the
moist sand. An arctic fox scurried to the tundra edge, eyed us, and
then slipped away. We lay in a sheltered gully amid the tundra flowers
and absorbed the warm sun. The ice that had nearly killed us
appeared as a gracefully undulating landscape of moving blue-white
splotches in a matrix of gray water.

26

The next day was July 8; we had been traveling for seven weeks. I sat on a bluff overlooking the bay and wrote in my journal:

Even though the ice is melting, the floes seem to grow more concentrated. If you break a flat plane, like a window pane, into pieces, and then move the pieces around without fitting them together like a jigsaw puzzle, then they take up more space than they did originally. Even though the ice is melting slowly and thus the pieces are becoming smaller, the inefficiency of packing accounts for the greater congestion. We could be here for a long time.

Four hundred miles separated us from the next town, Paulatuk. Five days previously, we had also been four hundred miles from Paulatuk. Even though we had traveled seventy-two miles in that time, our route had followed a convoluted coast, and now we were traveling southeast along the shore, away from our goal, because we couldn't cross Liverpool Bay.

I put my pen down and said to Chris, "Maybe we could reach Pond Inlet if we just could get going, if the trip would finally get under way."

Chris shook her head. "We launched in the middle of May; it's now early July. Jon, the trip isn't going to start; it has started. This is the trip. Can't you see that even now?" She paused. "What are you fighting against and why? Frustration doesn't make you move faster."

Chris doesn't get angry often, but she was annoyed this time and walked away across the tundra.

I watched her leave and then turned and watched the ice. We were on the same expedition, in the same boat, lovers. We hadn't seen another person since Tuk. Something rather unusual had brought the two of us—and no one else—to this ice-choked bay. Like the pin in a door hinge, we both rotated around that something, swinging in our own directions yet grasping the same pivot. Maybe if I understood the nature of that pin, I could acquire some of her equanimity.

Chris didn't share that part of me that had gone to graduate school and coveted a professorial chair. What did we have in common? Maybe to answer that question, I should ask when we were happiest together. Skiing. Okay. Outside, in the snow, skiing. Better. So was the pin simply that we liked to be outside?

It seemed to be a trivial answer to a lifelong search that had led past the chemistry lab, abandoned marriages and lovers, abandoned children. Everybody likes to be outside. I looked at the empty landscape. But clearly everybody doesn't toil to the Arctic. I was missing something obvious.

27

After four days, the wind shifted again and drove the ice north, leaving only a handful of mavericks milling near shore. The day was sunny with a gentle swell, and we broke camp. For the first time we were in a small boat on a big wet ocean, rowing to the far shore. Halfway across the bay a loud whooshing sound seemed to announce some new problem, but it was only a bearded seal rising out to breathe and stare.

We rowed through a cross-swell to the other side of Liverpool Bay, where a wolf was cruising the beach. After the wolf sauntered off, a lone caribou followed us along the shore, like a dog that didn't want to be left behind. When we turned in to make camp, a signal registered in its caribou brain—people, predators, time to run—and in a gait halfway between that of a moose and that of a horse, it clambered up a steep bank. It lost footing on the loose sand and slid back down. On the beach once again, it studied us closely and then escaped along the coastal plain at a full gallop. As we dozed off to sleep that evening, Chris said, "Listen. It's the sound of waves lapping against the beach; it's so much softer than ice grinding against ice."

28

Once upon a time, mosquitoes couldn't have cared less about people. They kept to themselves on a remote little island and seldom paddled their kayaks more than a day's journey from this island.

But there was a man who robbed and cheated and stole his neighbor's wives. Thinking that no one would find him, he paddled away to the mosquito island. But his neighbors followed him and came to the island, too. They beat him to a pulp with their clubs and left him there on the rocks.

After that, mosquitoes always attacked people, for now they had tasted human blood.

Inuit legend, in Lawrence Millman,
A Kayak Full of Ghosts

We spent most of the day in the boat, out of mosquito range, but we could watch the uneven battle on the beach. A caribou's antlers are marvelously adapted to scraping snow and ice from mosses and sedges. They are a bull's main weapon in fighting for a harem and are a deterrent to wolves and even bears. Many Asians believe that powdered antler is a powerful aphrodisiac. But the antlers are not effective for swatting mosquitoes. Caribou scratched with their paws and twisted their necks to swing the regal antlers, but still tormented, they ran along the beach to escape. A caribou can't keep running until the mosquito plague ends in late August, and whenever the caribou stops, the mosquitoes catch up. Harassed and embattled, the caribou splashed into the surf and sat in the cool water. But there is nothing to eat in the ocean, and hunger soon drove them back to the tundra. During summer, the caribou are thin and unhealthy looking despite the lush and blossoming tundra. You would lose weight, too, if every time you sat down to eat, mosquitoes covered your naked body and the only relief was to run or to jump in a frigid ocean.

For a brief period at the end of the summer, the weather is cool enough to drive the mosquitoes away, yet winter has not set in. During this time, the caribou fatten to build up the reserves they will need for their long trek south in search of winter forage.

29

On July 15 we reached the abandoned town of Stanton at the mouth of the Anderson River. Stanton consisted of one well-preserved missionary building, a smaller trading post, and several deteriorating shacks. We hadn't seen any people since Tuktoyaktuk, and except for the shack on Cape Dalhousie and trash along the beach, we had seen no sign of civilization since McKinley Bay. Therefore, the discarded newspapers, calendars, and comic books were almost welcome, and we decided to rest here for the afternoon.

Even though I had never gotten enough to eat on our full rations, we reduced rations when we realized how slowly we were moving. Chris was more tired than hungry and took a nap while I set out in search of food. First, I remembered the sculptor's advice and set a fishnet along the beach. Then I loaded my .22 rifle and wandered across the tundra to hunt ptarmigan. Mosquitoes covered my hands, bit my face, crawled into my ears. I tried to estimate how many calories I was losing per mosquito bite, how many bites per minute, how many minutes I had been traveling. After I added the calories used for walking, I began to doubt whether this hunt was a good idea. I saw no ptarmigan. Tired and dejected, I returned to camp, looked into the water, and saw a huge fish tangled in the net. I rowed out and carefully wrapped the fish in excess net so it wouldn't slip out as I hauled it aboard. I had caught a twenty-pound inconnu, a silvery, oil-rich Arctic fish, and we had a fabulous barbecue.

A ghost town invites reflection on why people moved there and then left. Stefansson spent a year near the Anderson River in 1909 without meeting people or finding any signs of recent settlement. When he finally met central Arctic Inuit in Union and Dolphin Straits to the east, he was the first white man they had ever seen. In his own words:

> When we approached the village every man, woman, and child was outdoors, waiting for us excitedly, for they could tell from afar that we were no ordinary visitors. . . .
>
> After building an igloo for their guests, the local Inuit told us they hoped we would occupy it at least until the last piece of meat in their storehouse had been eaten, and that so long as we stayed in the village no man would hunt seals or do any work until his children began to complain of hunger. It was to be a holiday, they said, for this was the first time their people had been visited by strangers from so great a distance that they knew nothing of the land from which they came.*

As a scientist, Stefansson observed but tried not to influence people's lives. However, merely by making contact, he altered their lives irrevocably. Traders followed Stefansson and exchanged steel tools and rifles for fox skins, which the Inuit had previously used as diapers. Imagine hunting with a bow and arrow and then trading a few diapers for a rifle! Missionaries followed the traders with promises of eternal salvation, but guarantees for a glorious afterlife have a price, and the missionaries made troublesome rules that brought hardship and even death to a culture in harmony with its harsh land.

Government bureaucrats brought the third wave of white European culture to the north when they built airstrips, schools, nursing stations, electric generators, and warm houses with free rent. But government services are most efficient when they are concentrated. As a result, in the 1950s the Canadian government said something like this: "We will supply you with snowmachines to travel efficiently in search of game, and furthermore we will ship food north for the hungry times when there are no seals near your villages. You no longer have to send your old folks out into the dark blizzard to freeze to death during cold winters. You can sit in a warm house, watch a video of *Poltergeist II*, and go hunting when you choose. But these riches

*Stefansson, *My Life with the Eskimo*, pp. 175–76.

will be centralized in a few large villages." As a result, many of the outpost camps and trading posts were abandoned and Stanton became a ghost town.

30

For most of our journey, the low-lying tundra slid gently into the sea, and we could pull to shore whenever and wherever we wanted. Two days after we left Stanton, we awoke to a brisk onshore breeze. We spread out our topographical map and looked at the route ahead. Our map had contour lines drawn at 100-foot intervals. The first contour line was half a mile inland, which implied that the tundra dipped gradually into the sea, as it had for most of the journey. I reasoned that we could continue eastward despite the threatening wind. If the storm intensified, we would pull to shore. Alternatively, if the wind died down, we would be that much farther along.

As we rowed around the first bend, the coastline steepened into cliffs of compressed sand and gravel. The map wasn't wrong, just misleading. If a cliff rises vertically for ninety feet and the tundra is nearly flat for the next half mile, the first contour line on the map will be in the same place as it would be if the land rose gradually for the entire distance. Waves had undercut the cliffs and the sea gurgled against the base, dislodging cobbles that plopped into the water. It was simply bad luck that the map misled us on a day when a fresh breeze intensified into a gale.

The wind stacked the sea into steep waves that broke against numerous offshore bars. We pointed the bow directly into the waves and pulled for sea room, but before we had gone far, a steep wave broke in front of us, caught the bow, and surfed us backward toward the cliffs. Oars are ineffective in foamy, air-rich water, and we struggled helplessly until the whiteness subsided and we caught some gray-green ocean. "Pull!" I shouted, and the cliff receded. We rose and fell over smaller waves, then another large one broke and stood the boat upright again. The bow turned on the wave, broached, careened. We held her steady, immersed in the foam, but lost too much ground, and the cliff loomed close again. I pulled on the oars.

"If we can make it over this shallow bar, Chris, we'll be out of the worst of the break."

"I know."

I thought about contingencies. When I shipwrecked near Cape Horn I landed on a small beach and found a gully through the bluff. There was no beach here, no gullies, just an undercut cliff and cold water. If we failed here, waves would beat us to death against the cliff—if we didn't die of hypothermia first. Chris was a few feet behind me, but I was facing the stern and couldn't see her. She seemed so far away.

"We're making good progress," I optimistically reported over the sound of wind and breaking seas.

She didn't say anything, so I tried again. "I think the storm is dying."

She replied, "I don't think so."

Then I thought about her in the ice in Liverpool Bay, pulling herself into the boat dripping wet, grabbing an oar, and pushing a floe out of the way. Chris refused to be encouraged by my lie, but she wasn't going to give up.

I stared at the map encased in plastic and propped up on the seat beside me. There was a protected bay about three miles east, past the next rock outcrop. In flat water, we could cover the distance in an hour. But if we turned eastward, parallel to the coast, we would expose our beam to the breaking waves. Instead, we rowed straight out to sea, as I had done in my kayak at Cape Guanaco before I lost strength. This time, we held our ground. Facing backward, looking at the cliffs, feeling the waves roll under the bow, I tried to judge distance. Were we gaining sea room or sliding backward? I looked at my watch: 10:35. I forced myself not to look at it again for an eternity, then stole a glance: 10:42. I tried again: 10:57. The cliffs seemed farther away. I probed Chris again: "I think we're gaining sea room, Chrissy."

Her soft voice rushed passed me, riding the wind. "I think you're right."

"Good."

I looked over my shoulder. Three steep breaking waves approached, and behind them the sea was calmer.

"Let's ride these three and then turn east for a few strokes."

"Okay."

The boat rose elegantly, rocking fore and aft, riding her double-ended hull. The wave broke, parted, rushed past; then the second one, larger than the first, carried us toward the cliff; we struggled, met the third, almost held our ground but slid off the face backward, toward the cliffs. We rowed out to sea for deeper water, then turned and rowed three strokes eastward. Three strokes closer to safety. I stared at the map, looked at the land. How much closer were we? One boat length per stroke? Three strokes? Forty-five feet? I looked at the shore, back at the map, back at the shore, attempting to bring the sheltered bay closer by powers of concentration. Then I realized that the map was smiling. The shape of the headlands and rivers outlined a sloping forehead, a Roman nose, and a smile. It was an elemental smile, not a beacon of hope or the diabolical smile of a horrible fate. It was a day of simple things: a smile, a storm, and the classic curves of a hull that parted the waves and kept us alive.

Adrenaline is like many other drugs: The first infusion is invigorating, but the sensation sours with time. If you swig a few shots of tequila, you feel a surge as the alcohol takes over, alters senses, makes you talkative and prone to giggles. But if you drink steadily throughout a long afternoon, the giggles turn dull. In the same manner, the first breaking wave and its accompanying adrenaline rush were fresh and pure. But after several hours, we were left with a dull recognition of the danger. I fought against complacency and constantly reminded myself of what I had to do: "Pull hard on this stroke, okay good, now pull hard again, fine, now bend the oar on this one, pull."

We rowed continuously from eight-thirty that morning to nine-fifteen that evening, swallowing some candy and a handful of nuts between strokes. Finally we pulled into the bay, protected by a low-lying sand spit. The wind still howled, but there were no waves, no cliffs, no death behind us. We stepped out of the boat onto the spit. The waves broke on the windward side, sending spray into the air. Water collected on Chris's face and dripped off her eyelids and nose. She slipped her arm around my wet slicker and we held each other.

Even though we were tired, we decided not to camp here because the wind would rip our tent and the spray would soak us. Stiffly, we climbed back in the boat. At first, my hands refused to close around the oars, but once they shut they locked tightly. We pointed toward a grassy bluff and started rowing again. The bay was shallow, and we watched the bottom a few feet beneath us. The tide began to ebb, robbing precious water from the bay's interior and producing a current that threatened to push us back to sea, back into the breakers that we had fought so hard to escape. We had mentally relaxed when we thought we had entered a safe harbor, but as the current carried us back toward the sea, we had to tell our muscles to row hard again. At first the muscles refused until we screamed down through the nerves to make ourselves heard. We pulled against the tide as we had pulled against waves, held ourselves steady, and then worked up current. As the tide ran out, the water became shallower, until our oars became tangled in seaweed. Within a few minutes, the water disappeared altogether and the boat settled into the tidal swamp. We rocked gently and stopped. A few gas bubbles dislodged from beneath the algae, and the air smelled of decay.

We could have sat in the boat, brewed hot tea, and huddled to stay warm. When the tide rose, we would have drifted calmly to shore. All we had to endure was a little discomfort and the ignominy of winning our battle with the Arctic gale only to burrow, muskrat-like, into the ooze. I could have told Chris I loved her, pulled a candy bar from our cherished goody bag, and then told cheery stories as we waited through the night.

But I wanted to be in my warm sleeping bag. I didn't want to wallow in the muck.

I thought we could drag the boat to a small channel cut by a tidal current and then row to shore. However, when we stepped out of the boat, we sunk to our waists in the mud. Chris lifted her foot, but the mud pulled her boot off and she had to stoop into the frigid water to retrieve it. She called out over the wind, "I can't do it, Jon; I can't do this!"

A dark anger rose from a hidden crevice inside me. I don't know where the anger originated or why it was there. It's my monster in the basement. Many times in my life, I have gone down the creaky steps with flashlight, club, and murderous intent. I have faced the monster, poised to swing, but at each encounter it feigns defeat and slips away, only to hide, wait, and slither back up the steps when I least expect it. The monster had emerged at strategic times in my life; it chased away Elizabeth and Debby and Marion. It rejoiced when the dead beached whale in the Chilean canals beckoned from the eerie blackness of a cold ocean, shrouded by fog and rain, reminding me of my aloneness.

"You can't go on?" I screamed. "You can't go on? Then lie down in the mud and die!"

Chris recoiled at my outburst. I recoiled at my outburst. I wanted to shout, "It wasn't me! I didn't say it!" But the monster was inside, coiled around my intestines, reaching up, grasping my larynx. It was angry at Chris for bringing friendship and a strong oar into the storm. The monster wanted to see me as an old man, walking alone across the windblown snow.

I couldn't talk. I couldn't apologize.

Chris looked up, frightened and hurt, and continued pushing the boat through the frigid muck. Once we had been in the water for a few minutes, we were so cold that we really did need to get to shore, change, and start the stove in the tent. The monster released his grip and slipped back in the basement. I didn't see where he went and was too tired to chase him. Chris was crying quietly as she slopped through the swamp.

Sometime after eleven we found a sandy beach. Shivering, we spent an hour setting up camp and lighting the stove. We worked together as we had before my outburst, but the closeness wasn't there.

31

The next day was calm and sunny, and we regained our unity. Chris wrote in her journal:

Today has been as positive, easy, enjoyable, and encouraging as yesterday was negative, hard, scary, and discouraging. We packed camp and moved not knowing what the water would be like out on the bay but we did know that we had to take advantage of the tide to avoid being high and dry at low tide. Rowing out was easy like sleep walking. Out at the sandspit that had offered us protection last night, we found a welcome surprise; the wind was going our way.

Finally, the winds that had been against us for so long veered and slackened. One day we sailed fifty miles past icebergs, pods of white whales, rainbows, and hills of low-grade coal that had been smoldering and smoking for thousands of years. The next day we rowed seventeen miles in a flat sea. The day after we sailed again, and despite needing a few hours to repair a broken tiller, we traveled another thirty-five miles.

That evening, after I had snuggled into my bag and fallen asleep, Chris shook me. "Jon, there is a bear outside."

Her voice was too relaxed to rouse me, and I groaned and rolled over. Chris told me later that she sat there, as though alone in the tent, listening to my snoring and the crunch of heavy footprints in the gravel a few feet away. Then she shook me hard repeating, "Jon, there's a bear right outside the tent."

This time I woke up. It was a squally night, and the midnight sun was covered by clouds. I reached for my shotgun, but I had left it in the boat. I zipped open the tent to escape, but instead looked straight into a glistening drop of moisture suspended from a bear's nostril. The drop jiggled as the bear drew in my scent. Maybe I wiggled my nose too, but certainly I smelled the muskiness that hung between me and the tundra horizon. For a moment the grizzly and I stared at each other, nose to nose, as my sister and I used to stare in a contest to see who would blink first. A blink merely shuts out the intensity for an instant, however, and I needed more time to regain my composure, so I zipped the tent door shut. It was an irrational act, as if one millimeter of nylon would protect us from a paw swipe that could break a moose's neck. Chris and I sat defenseless in the semidarkness. For a few moments we heard nothing, no guttural growl, no ripping, not even wind blowing waves against the beach. The stillness was as intense as the stare; right out there, behind that droplet of snot, the bear was making a decision. Then stone rubbed against stone as paws disturbed the gravel, and step by step the sound became fainter. Finally Chris whispered, "I think it's gone." I unzipped the tent again and dashed naked and barefoot across the beach to the boat and the gun.

The bear had retreated a hundred yards and now turned to face me, shuffling back and forth, two steps one way and then two steps back. Tigers look like they are dressed in Lycra, ready to race, but a bear looks like it is dressed in baggy pajamas, ready for a pillow fight. Yet that awkward swinging bear gait looks menacingly efficient.

With one slug in the chamber and five more in the action behind it, with the safety off and my finger on the trigger, I felt brave. I shouted, "Go away bear!" and waved my gun. It stood up, rocked back and forth on its hind legs, and sniffed the air. I hoped it would catch a whiff of gun oil and fantasized that its mother had taught it that guns meant danger. But it wasn't put off that easily. Chris poked her head out of the tent, looked at the bear, then at me, still naked, waving a gun in the air and shouting into the night. She laughed and ducked back in to bring me some clothes. We built a driftwood fire. For half an hour the bear walked a semicircular arc around our camp, gradually widening its distance. Finally it moseyed off, bored.

32

We continued on. Our senses, long deprived of electronic stimuli, became attentive to changes in the land. My journal entries speak of the journey during the following week:

July 25: *Kind of a spacy day. Started late to let the wind die. It is sort of difficult to get a fix on things; distances and mirages are a bit confusing.*

July 26: *I woke up in the middle of the night and the sun had set below the horizon for the first time in a few months. Maybe it was psychological, but I felt chilled, not a winter chill, but an end of summer chill. The flowers are fading, grasses are tinged with yellow, and the caribou calves are getting bigger.*

July 28: *Storm day. The tent compresses and expands in the wind, like a giant bellows, and the steam from our morning tea pulsates like we are sending smoke signals.*

July 29: *This is the most barren place I have ever been in. There are*

*degrees of desolate. Western range lands are desolate. The tundra
around Liverpool Bay was more desolate. But this place is so far gone
that there aren't even any mosquitoes.*

*August 1: We paddled by sea cliffs filled with murre birds. They
seem to fill the evolutionary gap between penguins and flying birds.
Adults jump off their perches on the cliffs, then soar, using their broad
feet as rudders, like a flying squirrel, until they gain enough air speed to
fly. Going the other way, taking off from the water, is desperate, with
much running on the surface and wing flapping before they become air-
borne. Yet somehow they migrate thousands of miles to the Labrador or
British Columbia–Alaska coasts for ice-free ocean in the winter.*

But a darkness had crept amongst the images. Perhaps it had
started after my outburst in the mud; perhaps it lay deeper. For the
past few months, we had been within a hand's reach of one another
for nearly twenty-four hours a day. Even though one of us would frequently walk off alone after dinner, every decision, even the tiny
ones, had been made jointly and had affected us jointly.

Chris complained about the lack of nutmeg for our morning oatmeal. Of course, nutmeg wasn't the issue; she felt that her personality
was lost in my expedition. She had followed my dream, but now it
had begun to chafe. In turn, I felt angry that Chris had never cared
whether we made it to Pond Inlet or not. I ignored the fact that she
had rowed and dragged the boat gamely alongside me and that the
Arctic, not Chris, had stopped us.

33

On August 3, thirty-six days after we left Tuktoyaktuk, we
rowed into Paulatuk. Even though we were eager to talk with
other people, when the reality was so close, we were reluctant to pull
into town and face a curious crowd.

I still nurtured the dying vestiges of my original ambition to complete the Northwest Passage. After all, it was still the beginning of August and we had a month and a half before the ocean would start to freeze again. But for the moment, we had completed an arduous passage and were here, on the soft tundra, hungry but well, and the town and dirt airstrip lay within sight. I thought back to the beginning. When Chris first agreed to accompany me on this trip, she said that she wanted to come "because she liked the North." My fisherman friend viewed the expedition as a sequence of dangerous obstacles to overcome, with beautiful passages in between, but Chris had seen it as a sequence of beautiful passages with a few dangerous obstacles in between. I felt close again.

A teenager drove his snowmachine across the dry tundra to bring a greeting from his grandparents, who had spied us from afar: "Who are you? Where have you come from? Do you need something to eat, a place to sleep? Welcome." His words were similar to those his ancestors used when they greeted Stefansson, only two generations ago.

We followed him to his rectangular government house. His parents, Andy and Millie, greeted us warmly and invited us in for coffee and homemade brownies. Children, energized by the excitement but too shy to talk, orbited the table, grabbed bits of food, and disappeared giggling. They played, fed, and, as we learned later, slept in such a random manner that it took us a week to learn which children belonged to which parents. Millie followed our eyes and told us, "Children should be free as long as they can; the land will teach its lessons soon enough." A few older people joined us at the table, but they climbed on the chairs and squatted on their haunches, perched like wrinkled birds on top of the seats. Occasionally they joined our conversation, but more frequently they chatted to each other in their native tongue. These people were born in tents and igloos and grew up as nomads. They owned no chairs when they were children. When they die, everyone will sit on chairs with their feet on the ground.

We explained that we were passing through and wished to buy food for our continuing journey eastward. Andy shook his head and explained that the town was supplied by barge only once a year. The bad ice and storms that had delayed our progress had also delayed the barge. The store carried only flour, lard, oatmeal, tea, sugar, toilet paper, disposable diapers, cigarettes, matches, and a few boxes of cake mix. "No one has much food," he said. "We have little more than you do. We are going hunting and fishing tomorrow; you are welcome to come. If we are successful, everyone will have plenty to eat."

I explained that we would probably buy some flour and oatmeal, and move eastward the next day.

Andy shook his head. "That's a bad idea. A few days ago I spoke with the Canadian Coast Guard by radio. Polar ice had blown south and was jammed in the straits between Paulatuk and Coppermine, the next village to the east. An icebreaker was trying to open a passage and start the pack moving again, but had, as yet, been unsuccessful. You'll get caught in the ice."

"Yes," I explained, "but we have to take that chance if we have any hope at all of making it to Pond Inlet."

Andy looked at me incredulously, and even the old people stopped their chatter to listen. "Pond Inlet! You're crazy. You're too crazy. You're hungry. The char will be running soon, and the caribou are starting to get fat. You stay here and come hunting. It will be cold out there in that ice. Fall storms will be here any day. And you'll never make it to Pond Inlet no matter how hard you try."

Chris looked at me expectantly. I didn't need to ask her opinion; I was alone with my ambition.

I thought, "What did the Inuit think of the early explorers who were so eager to be somewhere else that they refused to look around and hunt. And they died."

Then I recalled the tiny distance we had traveled and the long journey ahead. Traveling at this speed, we would need four summers, not one, to achieve our goal.

I asked myself, "Now why do I want to go into the ice again?" I shrugged. "We'll stay."

Millie stood up and walked to the stove to brew another pot of coffee. Andy pushed the plate of brownies toward me, and the old folks ignored me once again and resumed their conversation.

34

ven today, the primary clock in an Inuit village is the passage of seasons and the movement of game, not the hands on the wall. To us, it seemed that there was no schedule. Certainly there was never a sense of urgency; no one was ever late. But the caribou move north in the spring and south in the fall. Geese, seals, bears, and fish migrate, each animal on its own schedule. A person who is tuned to these cycles eats well; one who is not eats flour and oatmeal.

The Hornaday River Delta lies east of Paulatuk, and every August the char return upriver to spawn, although the timing varies by a few weeks from year to year. Fishing season was about to start, and people were talking about heading out to the river. However, some test nets had come up empty, so the following morning most of the people in the village slept in. We wandered around, enjoying the rest.

A crowd was gathered by our wherry. One middle-aged man, wearing a necklace of bear claws and a thigh-length Hudson's Bay parka lined with wolverine fur, ran his hands across the gunnels and commented, "This is a good sea boat; if there were any old times left, I would buy that boat for sure."

Another man responded, "But there are no old times left," and everybody laughed. As the crowd thinned, a tall, thin, wrinkled white man approached us. He was the Catholic father, seventy-one years old, and a resident of the North for forty-five. He was relaxed, slow, and gentle. Quietly, as a secret between us and not as an affront toward the people, he told us that the old times were not gone forever. He was certain that when Western civilization has squandered its fuel resources, the white men will no longer know how to survive in the hostile North and will leave as quickly as they came. Then the old times will return, and the people will survive only by recalling the old ways.

When he was a young man, he told us, there was no town of Paulatuk and his parish was scattered across the land. He had built the missionary house at the Anderson River, where we had stayed, and used it as a base because the people always migrated past to fish and hunt. But he couldn't serve a nomadic congregation if he lived in one place, so he too became a nomad. Every spring he traveled by dog team east to the hunting camps and then back westward to the main parish in Tuktoyaktuk, where he reported on his year's progress and visited with the other priests. He spent late summer in Stanton, where he caught and dried fish for his dogs. By the late 1950s, people concentrated around the DEW line base at Cape Parry. When the DEW line was built, the bases provided medical attention, communications, and occasionally jobs. Then the government built Paulatuk. The priest wasn't quite sure why the government had put it here, although the hunting and fishing were good. He suspected that the site was chosen because it was close to Cape Parry but not too close. Houses were built and offered virtually for free. Next came electricity, water delivery, and sewage pickup, and with these services came the need for money and the availability of jobs. Finally he mused, "Now they are building a TV and radio receiver. We used to receive mail twice a year and that was plenty."

I asked him how the change affected the people and whether he thought it was good or bad. He responded that change is neither good nor bad. "One can neither encourage nor fight progress; it is a migration like all the other migrations that move across the land."

Traditional Inuit family life was ruled by strict division of labor between men and women. Men hunted, built igloos, cared for the dogs, drove the sledge, and fabricated weapons. Women cooked, sewed, and trimmed the lamps that provided heat and light. As part of their sewing tasks, women tanned hides and made tents for the summer. Both sets of tasks were essential to survival. Owing to the dangers of the hunt, male mortality was higher than female mortality, and consequently there were more women than men. Therefore, successful hunters often had two wives. Alternatively, if a hunter had to take a long journey and his wife was unable to travel, he would borrow one, because a man could die on the trail without someone to repair clothing.

Missionaries tried to replace these cultural adaptations with religious dogma that arose in medieval Europe. Polygamous men were told to expel one of their wives. But how was a man to choose between two women he loved, between two women who had borne his children? Which one should he send into the cold with no meat and oil?

The missionary who stood before me was a gentle man. Had he condemned women to loneliness and starvation to appease his God? As a traveler, I would never stay long enough to learn the answer to this question, for it is buried deeply.

35

Knowing that the locals would move faster in their powerboats than we could by rowing, we set out a day before everyone else for the Hornaday. Like the Mackenzie, this river carries warmth northward, and therefore alders and willows line its banks. These were the tallest plants we had seen in six weeks, and we rowed upriver for a mile to camp in a brushy glade. The next morning, for the first time since May, we were on the land without a destination. I suddenly felt that we were on vacation.

We broke camp late, and as we floated back downriver a large bull caribou came down to the bank to inspect us. We returned to the coast at about noon and found six white wall tents set up along the beach, but no people. We called out, and Andy's sleepy face poked out the door of the tent.

"Oh, hello, hello, please come and have some coffee, sorry we are still asleep. We had no food, so we chartered a plane from Inuvik and it arrived late last night. We came out here at four o'clock this morning."

Millie set a kettle on a Coleman stove, and sleepy faces appeared from the pile of furs, foam pads, and blankets inside the tents. We sat and chatted and told them about the caribou we had seen.

"Why didn't you shoot it?"

"We are white people and are not permitted to hunt caribou."

Our hosts had trouble understanding. "We are the people here; this is our land. You are our guests, our friends. We are out of meat, you would share it with us. We would not tell the queen in London or the prime minister in Ottawa that you shot the caribou."

Another white couple walked out of one of the adjacent tents. They had been schoolteachers in Paulatuk but had moved to Inuvik. Last night they flew in with the chartered plane to spend a few days at fishing camp. Our Inuit friends decided that all the *kabloonas* (white people) should return to where we had seen the caribou and bring home some meat. I felt embarrassed because my short-barreled shotgun was intended as bear defense only and was too inaccurate to shoot caribou on the open tundra. Jim, the schoolteacher, had a .30-30 with open sights, which is designed for hunting in dense forest, but at least it was a rifle. So four of us, with one rifle, set out in search of game.

We crossed the tundra to the place where we had seen the bull. Looking down from a high bluff, we saw a small herd on an island in the middle of the river. Jim handed me the gun, claiming that I must be the best shot because anyone who had traveled so far must be a good hunter. It is difficult to stalk a caribou in open country, but we had a plan. I climbed down under the cover of a ravine, waded the river, and hid behind a driftwood log on the north end of the island. Once I was well concealed, Jim and the two women approached the island from the south, spread out, and attempted to drive the herd toward me. The caribou spooked, as expected, but then veered, fording the river at full gallop a hundred yards away from me. I took a long shot and missed, and we returned to camp empty-handed.

We were greeted by the smell of cooking meat. A caribou carcass hung on a makeshift rack. Someone saw us and shouted, "Hello, hello, did you have any luck?" and everyone laughed.

"No, I had a shot and missed."

"You missed?" More laughter. "Then you are poor hunters; now we'll all go hungry." Laughter again.

"Where did you get the meat?" I asked.

"Oh, after you left we all went back to sleep, and when Andy got up to pee, this bull was standing right outside the tent, so he shot it."

Someone produced jars of barbecue sauce that had been delivered by the plane, and we all sat down for a feast.

Andy had been born near Paulatuk and was in his midthirties. When he was a teenager, the Canadian government had taken all the children in the central Arctic away from their families and sent them to boarding school in Inuvik. They learned to speak English and to read and write, but they lost contact with their families and were ripped away from their culture. After he graduated, Andy moved to Tuktoyaktuk and worked a steady job for thirteen years. Six years ago, he quit that job and moved to this village with his family. He earned his living driving the water-supply truck and supplemented his income by hunting and trapping. When I asked what people were going to do about water while he was out here in camp, he told me that everyone was going hunting, so no one needed service.

36

The next morning Chris and I awoke early out of habit. No one stirred, so we brewed tea and made a pot of oatmeal. By ten-thirty people began to collect outside their tents. At eleven-thirty bacon and eggs were cooking, and there was a general discussion about trying to set some nets, but enthusiasm was too low to generate action. At about two-thirty the men rallied for a caribou hunt, and I followed without a weapon. We wandered across the rolling hills, chatting and laughing in groups of twos and threes. I was disappointed; I had expected to see silent men confidently following a track that was invisible to my urban eyes. I couldn't imagine that this casual stroll would be more successful than my carefully planned fiasco of the day before. However, soon the merriment was broken by the sound of a shot. One of the younger men had killed a bull midway down the flanks of a ravine. The rest of the party contemplated the animal slumped on the steep hillside.

"You should have waited until it went up or down before you shot it. It will be a lot of work to skin it and clean it there."

There was more discussion, but no one offered to help. Finally, I dropped over the bank and helped the hunter drag the caribou to a level place where we could skin it. We carried the carcass back to camp, and the hunter's grandmother cut it into portions. She handed me the front leg and some ribs: "This is yours." When I asked why, she told me that I was one of the hunters, and each hunter is given a share of the meat. I argued that I wasn't one of the hunters, because I didn't carry a gun.

"No matter, you went out with the men, you are a hunter."

I protested that I was a traveler, that I would be gone in a few days, and that the meat would spoil. She told me patiently that travelers need to eat too. The old woman handed me the meat saying, "It is our way."

I picked up my share and started toward our tent, wondering what to do with this huge quantity of meat. Then I walked through camp, announcing, "Everybody come to our tent for a feast." People smiled; we started a fire and ate it all.

After dinner, Andy thanked me for the fine feast but announced that his wife could cook a better one. Millie laid newspaper out on the tundra and carefully set out *muktuk* (raw whale blubber), bannock, and tea, with Jell-O for dessert. Shortly after midnight, we stood in a red glow and watched the sun dip below the horizon and rise again shortly thereafter.

When all the food was gone, Andy's brother Gil said it was sure good to be out on the land eating *muktuk* again, but if you are going to make a feast for *kabloonas*, it would be better to serve goose. We all marched over to a third tent, where Gil's wife laid out more newspapers and heaped plates with rich, fatty piles of stewed goose. By now it was two-thirty in the morning, time for coffee and fresh doughnuts, deep-fried in lard over a Coleman stove.

Even though it was nearly four in the morning when we returned to our tent and crawled into our bags, Chris and I couldn't fall asleep. Our stomachs were too busy digesting all the rich meat and fat, and the black, strong coffee kept us awake. I watched the sun shining through the nylon and followed its path as it swung southward, before it began its travel from east to west.

Chris snuggled against me and murmured, "Tell me a story."

I recounted a story about an Inuit boy who was orphaned and was left alone with his feeble grandmother. They had nothing to eat, and the boy was too young to hunt. He fashioned himself a crude harpoon, and one moonlit winter day, when the hunters were leaving through the semidarkness, he trudged behind. The men shouted insults, called him a baby, and told him to return to his igloo with the old woman, but he didn't listen. The hunters outpaced him, and he followed their tracks, alone, across the ice. The men killed a great white bear, a *nanuk*, and as they were skinning it and proportioning out the meat, the little boy finally caught up. Solemnly, carefully, and with absolute fairness, the men gave him his share of the meat and hide because he had been out with the hunters; he was a hunter. The next day, this time wearing a *nanuk* claw around his neck as a talisman, he followed the men again. Once more he reached the hunting grounds long after the kill had been made, and according to custom, he returned home with food for himself and his ailing grandmother. Of course, the little boy grew up to be one the greatest hunters.

Chris rolled over and drifted off to sleep while I lay in my bag daydreaming. I felt that I had been the little boy these past few days. Our friends not only had shared their meat, they had taught me about the land. There were so many gurus to teach me: the people, Chris, and the land itself. The land had taught me that you can't overpower the ice or Arctic storms. Chris was happy to pass through the land without the need for accomplishment. My friends, and their ancestors before them, believed that a stomach full of *muktuk* and goose fat is the greatest happiness of all. I must listen to these voices.

I started to doze. I wanted to listen but not copy. Maybe I could mold the lessons around my own personality. I had wanted to row to Pond Inlet. In a few days I would walk into an airplane and fly home. The ending seemed so tame, so dissatisfying. At least I had failed honorably at Cape Horn, hobbling back to Puerto Toro, haggard and lean, with a broken boat and an injured shoulder.

37

The next morning I wanted to climb back into the boat and continue on, but success was impossible and the summer was closing. In any case, we had lost the momentum. We asked Andy about the plane schedule, and he told us, "Go see Nora. She's the airline agent."

Nora was the oldest woman in camp, and her tent was twenty yards away. She was sitting outside, and when I came close she looked up. "Tea?"

Water boiled in an open kettle on the Coleman stove. I sat crosslegged on the tundra, and we chatted. Nora told me about the ghosts and about throwing babies off the cliffs during the hungry times, which I wrote of in the prologue to this book. Then she swatted mosquitoes and told me that she had already booked our plane reservation.

"Sometimes the plane stops at Sachs Harbor first, unless no one at Sachs Harbor wants to go anywhere, then it comes here. Maybe you will fly to Holman before you go to Inuvik, I'm not sure, but the pilot will know where he is going when he gets here."

We sold the boat to a man named Tony. After he handed me the cash, he ran his hands over the smooth teak gunnels and said, "Next I will buy a dog team. Then I will be able to teach my children how to travel in the old way both in summer and in winter."

Thursday morning Tony sped us to town in his powerboat. A hard rain fell as the plane taxied down the dirt strip, gravel plinking against the underside of the wings. As we shook hands good-bye, I realized that Tony was standing in the rain in a woolen shirt. I took off my raincoat and handed it to him.

He said, "No, you will need this."

I replied, "No, I can buy another one where I am going."

He thanked me and I climbed the ladder.

The flight attendant closed the door, replacing the rain, the smells, and the expanse of the Arctic with the enclosed comfort of a dry, well-padded aluminum tube. I fastened my seat belt.

With a clever strategy, we could have completed the Northwest Passage.* It would be silly to fight against myself and pretend that I wasn't attracted to goals, just as it had been futile to try and bulldog my way through the ice. Surely there was a way.

The plane took off; we banked and headed west. I found an old Inuvik newspaper on the magazine rack. Nora was the correspondent from Paulatuk, and I read her column:

---

*The Northwest Passage was completed in 1988 by kayak, the first nonmotorized traverse in a single season.

The sun came up on the 16th of January and the long winter is nearly gone again, especially for those who trap in such cold weather. It is very hard for some who go out on long traplines and come home sometimes with nothing. I always have a great feeling for those who try hard and come home with nothing. There is a lot of snow drifts between the houses again. It is not easy to go next door for a visit in the winter. The trapping has been very poor this year. Three skidoos broke down out of the settlement this year. The men had to walk their way home. Most of the men are on a dog team now. The planes come in once a month. So far everyone has not been sick with the flu yet, and we are thankful. That is all. Nora.

Part 3

DOGSLEDDING

ON

BAFFIN ISLAND

Once there was a hunter who kept losing his meat. He'd store a cache in his cave and next day it would be gone. The hunter was not too happy about this. He vowed to stab whoever was making off with his meat and then fling the lifeless body into the sea. And thus he hid himself in the back of the cave. One day passed, two days. Finally he saw a group of children who seemed to appear out of nowhere. They were gathered around his meat. Now the hunter was furious and raised his spear, hoping to kill each and every one of them. Then he realized: They were the Northern Lights Children—spirits of stillborn children who danced with their afterbirths in the sky. They told him that they had been going through a very hungry season. Which was why he hadn't seen any Northern Lights recently. Wouldn't he allow them to take his meat? If not, the sky would be empty forever more. The hunter relented. "Please take what you want," he said to them.
And several days later there were Northern Lights in the sky once more.

Inuit legend, in A *Kayak Full of Ghosts*,
Lawrence Millman

1

We returned to Southern Cross, picked huckleberries, baked homemade bread in Chris's wood cookstove, smeared it with fresh huckleberry jam, forgave each other for the hard times, and reminisced about the good. But the romance wavered. We had spent too much time in one boat an arm's length apart, on a cold, gray ocean, torn by conflicting dreams.

In a small space, such as Chris's kitchen in Southern Cross, people continually bump into one another. You can pass with a gentle touch on the hip that says, "I'll go this way, you go that way, and as long as we're this close, remember, I love you." Or you can bulldog forward and announce your temporary turf with a stare that says, "I'm going this way." We didn't argue, but when the body language changed, it was time to leave.

I cleared my messy desk, threw the homemade desktop and legs in the firewood pile, and replaced a potted plant in the corner where it had been before I arrived. Then I loaded my books and typewriter in the trunk of my car, two file boxes on the back seat, and camping and climbing gear in every remaining crevice. We hugged and kissed, and mumbled something about "seeing each other soon." I drove down the mountain.

Noey had asked to spend the school year with me, so I drove to California to pick her up. I try to ignore complex emotions when I am driving long distances alone. Even during normal times, thoughts get twisted around the dashed line in the middle of the road. But this wasn't a normal time. I needed loud music, mainlined straight into the eardrums, to overpower thought. I put on the headphones and turned up the volume.

Even music wasn't strong enough. Was I making a bold dash for freedom, an affirmation of *me*, Jon Turk, defining a unique lifestyle? Or was I just confused and acting stupid?

Fifteen hours, two quarts of coffee, a Big Mac, and a gutful of crispy fried chicken later I began to accept the second explanation. What was so confusing? It shouldn't be that difficult to figure out

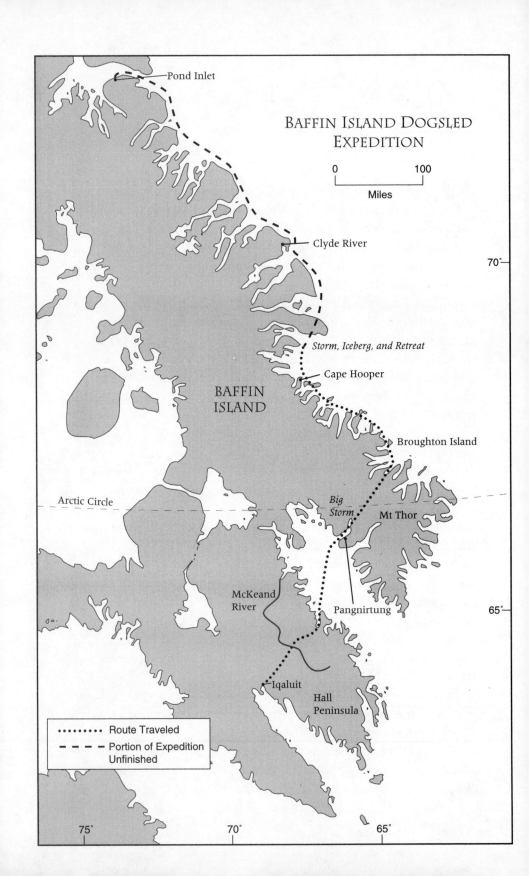

BAFFIN ISLAND DOGSLED
EXPEDITION

0   100
Miles

Pond Inlet

Clyde River

70°

Storm, Iceberg, and Retreat

Cape Hooper

BAFFIN
ISLAND

Broughton Island

Arctic Circle

*Big
Storm*

Mt Thor

McKeand
River

Pangnirtung

65°

Iqaluit

Hall
Peninsula

•••••••• Route Traveled
– – – Portion of Expedition
         Unfinished

75°   70°   65°

what made me happy. I'd been faltering for a decade. About a third of my life.

"I'm not stupid," I told myself. "I walked out of chemistry because I thought chemists' faces looked sallow and saggy, and I wanted to go skiing. I went to Cape Horn to . . . do what? Find spiritual contentment within the swirling mists?

"Swirling mists" sounded poetic enough until you reworded the phrase to "cold damp gales." Much of the time I was plagued by the hardship. So why did I go on the second expedition to the Northwest Passage?

I couldn't capture any simple image to guide and calm me.

I turned onto the freeway and kept my foot on the gas.

I met Noey near Santa Barbara and we went to a pizza parlor to discuss plans. I had sold my house in Telluride, and except for a few books and files stored in Southern Cross, everything I owned was in my car. I was thirty-seven years old and had no home and no particular destination. Noey suggested that we visit our friends Jock and Francie, who owned a sheep ranch in southern Colorado. That sounded as good as anything to me, so we drove south to Los Angeles and then swung east across the desert.

We set a wall tent by the river and went to town for supplies. I began work on another environmental science textbook. Noey was supposed to go into the fourth grade, but we ignored the school bus that passed along the main road every day. I read Hemingway aloud, and she struggled to understand *For Whom the Bell Tolls*. Bob Dylan sang from the car stereo for our poetry lessons. Jock taught her to milk cows and tend sheep. Francie attacked her with a hairbrush, and after removing the tangles led her to the garden to harvest. Jock's brother, Doug, taught her how to steal chickens. He was careful to remind her that it wasn't a good idea to steal chickens, but if you were ever down-and-out and hungry, you could slip into the henhouse at night, grab a chicken by the legs, and quickly flip it upside down. An upside-down chicken won't squawk and wake up the farmer.

I lay in my sleeping bag one morning, watching the early-fall frost sparkle on the inside of the tent, and decided it was time to initiate a social studies lesson. When Noey woke, we started a fire, cooked a pan of scrambled eggs, and planned a trip to the Yucatán Peninsula in Mexico.

Noey suggested that we invite Chris. Noey wasn't an insightful child-therapist, trying to save her daddy from a lonely old age. Chris was her friend, and Noey thought we'd all have fun together. I watched the eggs cook and put another stick on the fire. Why couldn't Chris and I maintain our identities in each other's presence? I finished breakfast and walked to the main house to borrow the phone. Fortunately, Chris was beginning to miss me, too. In Chris's words:

> After Jon moved to Colorado with Noey, I had my cabin, job, and pace of life to myself again. The emotional and physical stress of the journey left both of us wanting to retreat to our own spaces.
>
> I worked on a forest service timber crew and spent my days walking through the woods making an inventory of the timber stands. We left the truck each morning and traveled game trails to reach a stand, followed a compass bearing for a predetermined distance, and then studied habitat, size, and age of the trees.
>
> Trees in western Montana are small compared to ones that you would find in Washington and Oregon, but compared to the treeless tundra it was a wonderland of giants. An early September frost had turned the low huckleberry bushes a brilliant red and the other vegetation a wide range of yellows and golds.
>
> After a month of living life at my old pace I started to miss Jon. He called just as I was laid off for the season. A trip to the Yucatán with Jon and Noey sounded perfect after an especially cold week in the woods. I booked a flight to Denver.

We flew to Mexico, snorkeled along coral reefs, and visited ancient Mayan ruins. Chris and I forgave each other for the hard times and fell in love again. Chris asked us both to spend the winter with her in Southern Cross.

Noey went to school nearby, I worked on a book, and Chris and I skied together nearly every day. One afternoon, while we were drinking hot chocolate after a ski tour, our neighbor Carl knocked and told me that I had a phone call. There was nothing unusual in the summons; Carl had the only telephone in the neighborhood.

"Do you know who's calling?" I asked as we walked across the snow.

"Oregon State Police."

I reviewed my recent travels and tried to recall any ignored traffic violations, even parking tickets, but could remember nothing.

"Hello."

"Oregon State Police officer Jensen speaking. Do you know a twelve-year-old girl named Reeva Saria?"

"Yes, she's my daughter. I haven't seen her since she was a baby."

"We picked her up as a runaway in the Portland bus station. She says she'll stay with you but would run away again if we returned her to her mom's. Will you take her?"

I made all the necessary arrangements with social workers and judges, sent a plane ticket, and met Reeva at the nearby airport in Butte.

I recognized her mainly because she was the only unaccompanied young girl who walked off the plane. Her hair was blow-dried and teased, and she wore city clothes. I handed her a pair of boots I had brought, but she wouldn't take off her low-cut street shoes. I explained that we lived in the snow on a mountain where there were no paved roads or sidewalks. She told me that the boots looked ugly.

Chris's tiny mountain cabin was perfect for one person, crowded with two, and chaotic with four. The girls had to sleep on pads on the floor, and we had no electricity for hair blowers and curlers.

Chris and I hadn't welded together strongly enough to sustain the pressure. I talked about moving to Alaska and maybe trying another expedition. Chris wanted to stay in Southern Cross and maybe raise a family. We accepted that we could be friends and lovers for now, but not forever.

In the spring Noey flew back to California, and Reeva visited Jock and Francie's ranch. I traded my car for a pickup and moved out of Chris's cabin for the second time.

I drove across British Columbia in a trance, unable to believe that I was alone again. I slept for a few hours, drank a thermos of horrible roadhouse coffee, and took the wheel again. I remembered the glorious moments in Chile when I had overcome fear and emptiness and faced the world unhindered. Sure there were dark times, but I always overcame them. I zoomed through the taiga forest and fell into a rhythm: drive a thousand miles, sleep two hours, drink coffee, eat, drive. The customs agent at the Alaska border took one look at me and said, "Get out of the car, put both hands on the front fender, spread your legs apart, and don't say anything."

Okay, my hair was disheveled, I had a three-day growth of beard, and he thought I was a middle-aged drug addict. But he couldn't bust me for looking like shit because I had left my woman and was so afraid of myself that I couldn't sleep.

2

Throughout the fall and winter of domestic upheaval, I had quietly planned my next expedition. Chris and I had thought that our wherry was light enough to maneuver through the Arctic ice, but we were wrong. We had rowed and dragged only five hundred miles in the Beaufort Sea and had flown home with fifteen hundred miles unfinished. When you fail so spectacularly, you must modify your strategy.

The Inuit developed two unique technologies: the kayak and the dogsled. Both were adapted to an icy world, and when times were tough, both were edible. Kayaks were made of sealskin, which could be boiled into a meager soup, and dogs could be butchered. Dogs were more nourishing, but an old man told me that during hard times people generally ate their kayaks first.

Today the Inuit in Canada usually travel by motorboat in summer and snowmachine in winter. They fly in commercial airplanes. But when old men reminisce about their adventures, they always talk about dog teams. In northwest Greenland, even today, a male is not considered a "man" unless he is a hunter, and you cannot be a hunter without dogs.

Andy and Gil, our friends in Paulatuk, told me that their boyhoods in the nuns' dormitories had irrevocably robbed them of their formative years on the land. However, the Inuit in the eastern Arctic had refused to send their children to school in central villages. As a result, many never learned to speak English, and most were excellent hunters. Andy and Gil assured us that we were welcome in the central Arctic, but *kabloonas* like us were wasting our time here when we could be hunting with the real Inuit on Baffin Island.

I decided to fish all summer and make enough money to buy and train dogs during the fall and early winter. Then I planned to fly to Iqaluit on the southern coast of Baffin Island and sledge eight hundred fifty miles to Pond Inlet, our destination on the previous journey.

After the encounter at the border, I asked myself why I was planning a third expedition when the first two had both been failures; I hadn't achieved my goals and I hadn't been happy along the way. The Wrangell Mountains slid past. Mick Jagger told me that he had "no expectation to pass through here again." I stopped for gas, grabbed a burger-to-go, and slipped back behind the wheel. What was the question again?

I had walked out on my lover. I didn't have to answer questions anymore. Fuck it. Okay, I might grow up to be a weird old man. Fuck that, too. I was going to go to Baffin Island, in the winter, with a dog team. Because I wanted to.

3

After fishing season, all three children—Nathan, Reeva, and Noey—flew to Alaska. We planned to move to a remote cabin, wait for winter, and train a team. Nathan had recently turned fourteen, Reeva was thirteen, and Noey was eleven. I traded my small pickup for a large one and met the children at the airport.

I am not a natural animal trainer. I like animals and believe that they trust me, but I don't have the correct combination of persistence, discipline, and leniency to train them. I had dogs as a child that loved to romp in the woods. Some could sit and shake hands, but that was about it. Once, as an adult, I was caretaking a house for a friend while she was away on vacation. After showing me how to water the plants, she led me to the tank of tropical fish. "I've trained the fish to swim in circles to ask for their food," she said. She tapped the side of the tank with her finger, and incredibly two orange- and yellow-striped fish approached and swam in tight circles. "Fish aren't smart," she explained, "and need constant reinforcement. I would appreciate it if you would maintain their training schedule." When she returned, the soil in the cactus pot was dry as it should have been, and the rubber plant was glossy and waxy, but the fish were swimming in circles only when they felt like it, not when I asked them to. The fish fiasco haunted me, for now I was planning to train a pack of dogs and travel with them into the Arctic winter, where our lives would depend on one another.

A friend in Colorado had known Susan Butcher, a woman who ran the long-distance Iditarod race from Anchorage to Nome (and won it several times since I met her). I wrote to her, told her of my plans, and asked if she would teach me how to buy and train dogs. She wrote back that she would.

Fairbanks is linked to the civilized world by paved roads to the south and east, but the few gravel roads that reach out to north and west are long and lonely. Motorists carry extra gas and tools. The directions to Susan's house read, "Follow the road west for about 100 miles, turn right past the creek at the bottom of a long grade, and follow a rough driveway until you hear 100 howling dogs."

Susan wasn't overjoyed to see me. The bonds of allegiance to friends of friends had led her to answer my letter, but she had never expected me to arrive, smiling, with my muddy truck and entourage. I offered to help with the chores in exchange for advice. Free labor was appealing, but the children really convinced her. Susan loves living creatures. She was charmed by the girls and intrigued by Nathan, and once she learned that I knew how to handle a chain saw, she let us stay.

My first lesson was that you don't teach dogs to pull. They can't be compared to a tropical fish that learns to perform for its dinner. A sled dog wants to pull, loves to pull, lives to pull, and if it doesn't have that attitude, it's not a sled dog.

A sled dog is given freedom as a puppy, but after that, until death, it is either tied to a chain or harnessed to a sled. It never roams about, sniffs fire hydrants, or plays with suburban children. Instead sled dogs lope across the frozen landscape and sleep with their teammates in a soft snowbank under the aurora.

I spent a week with Susan and bought two dogs, Mac and Cameo, from her neighbor, who ran a sprint team. They were too heavy and slow for sprint racing but ideal for me, because I needed larger dogs to drag loads across vast distances. Cameo was a white female with a pink nose. Mac was only two years old, colored like a Siberian husky, and unusually alert and inquisitive. As we were about to drive off, Susan asked me to wait and ran to the truck with a puppy. "Here is a present for the children," she said. "His name is Ben." The girls took possession immediately. "He will learn to pull the children on skis. He's a good dog but has a congenital malfunction in his trachea, so he's short-winded. I can't use him for racing or breeding, and I would like someone to have him. There is only one condition. He comes from my best breeding stock. Dog racing is competitive and it is my livelihood. The genetic line that I have been building all these years is unique. I don't want him to fall into anyone else's hands. The kids can take him home with them to California, but you can't give him to anyone in Alaska."

I knew that it was a gift that could come back to haunt me, but I was asking the children to live in a remote cabin in Alaska with me, and having their own dog would allow them to have their own adventures, so I acquiesced.

4

Susan advised that if I wanted to run on the sea ice in the eastern Arctic, I should train on sea ice, not in the forest. Therefore, I should move to an Alaskan Inuit community along the coast, such as Kotzebue or Nome. I knew that she was right, but I wasn't prepared to be a single parent in such a desolate place. Instead, we moved to Trapper Creek, south of Denali National Park. A fellow fisherman knew of an empty log cabin three miles from the road. It was far enough from neighbors that no one would complain about a howling dog team, close to an active mushing community where I could buy dogs and seek help, and only a three-hour drive from Anchorage.

It was early September. Once the snow fell and the swamps and lakes froze, the dogs would haul our supplies to the cabin, but in the interim, I had to carry everything in on my back. I loaded a forty-pound bag of dog food on top of the family groceries, tied Mac and Cameo to leashes, and walked home. The cabin had one room downstairs and a sleeping loft above. The log work was so poor that air flowed through the cracks. But outside the north window, the sharp features of the Cassin Ridge divided the snowy face of Mount Denali.

If you can resupply frequently along the way, a large team travels faster than a small one because it has more muscle power. However, on an expedition, you have to balance team size against the amount of dog food you can haul. I read the journals of Amundsen, Peary, and Stefansson; spoke to locals; and decided on a team of eight. Friends told me to buy eleven or twelve dogs and then sell the weakest before heading to Canada.

I bought three dogs from Rick Mackey, winner of the 1983 Iditarod: Happy, Joker, and Kenai.

Happy was his winning leader, a veteran of five Iditarods. Rick told me that he was nine years old and too old to race any more but had the strength for one more trip and the experience to pull me out of a jam.

Happy's personality never reflected his name; he was always serious and often irritable. But his son, Joker, lived up to his name. Half of his face was white, and the other half was black, giving the appearance of a medieval jester: good and evil, mirth and anger, clarity and mystery. He had the strength, speed, and intelligence to be a leader, but he was enough of a rake not to be dependable up front. Joker had run in the swing position, the post behind the leader, in the 1983 Iditarod win, but he had been a little slow at the end so Rick was selling him.

Kenai was heavy enough to pull in the wheel position, closest to the sled. Wheel dogs bear the greatest impact when the sled bounces on rough terrain. They are the middle linemen of a dog team and are subject to the worst beating and the least glamour.

Every musher dreams of a mythical leader with enough strength and spark to motivate a team and the intuition to avoid danger. As a race dog, Happy was accustomed to trails, and several people warned me that he might balk on trackless ice. However, Smokey had led teams across heavily crevassed glaciers and might have the savvy I would need. Compared to the lean Iditarod dogs, Smokey was furry and short-legged, but I needed intelligence more than speed. He wasn't for sale, so I leased him for the trip.

Susan had told me that I should look for Jake, an old dog of hers. Jake was so big and strong that Susan had placed him in wheel as a pup. Years later, Susan realized that Jake was smart enough to be a leader. But by that time he was too old, so she sold him, and his new owner placed him in his old position, wheel. Like Smokey, Jake was not for sale. His new owner wanted him for breeding but was willing to lease him.

The man who owned Jake also sold me Cisco, who had been a sprint dog in his youth, then had slowed and begun to run Iditarods. The previous year he was slow even for long-distance racing so was up for sale.

Except for Mac and Cameo, all my dogs so far were old race veterans. A musher named Joe Leonard, who had also won the Iditarod, told me that I needed some youthful enthusiasm. Sure the old dogs would pull, but I needed a sparkplug to fire them up. On this advice, I bought Apple.

The town of Trapper Creek consisted of a small cafe–general store and a post office. I drove in one day for coffee, mail, and gossip. A trapper was selling out his entire team. They weren't racing dogs but would pull well, and they were cheap. I bought Snowball and Miuk.

By the middle of September, I was living beneath the Alaskan Range with twelve dogs and three children. We had a few weeks to wait before snowfall. The dogs slept or paced circles in the dirt at the outer edges of their chains. Almost every day I made a six-mile round trip to the road and back to haul a backpack load of dog food or other supplies. We held school on the front porch. After their lessons were completed, the children were required to haul water and gather firewood, but they frequently escaped to pick blueberries.

The land around the cabin had been recently glaciated, and the receding ice had left parallel rows of swamps and long, low, eskers. The eskers were covered with spruce trees and blueberry bushes. Nathan, Reeva, Noey, and I had a simple deal. They picked berries, and I made pies. We soon learned that dainty wedges were an irrelevant regression to another lifestyle. When a pie was done, I'd cut it in quarters, one for each of us. On warm afternoons, the wood cookstove was too hot inside so we lit a campfire, rolled berries and sugar in bread dough, wrapped the turnovers in tinfoil, and cooked them in the coals.

Moose frequented the alder patches, and we often saw grizzly tracks near the cabin. A family of ermines lived under the house. We shared our stream with river otters and the nearby lake with beaver. Squirrels constantly invaded the cabin to steal insulation for their winter nests.

We went for a hike every day. Travel north or south was easy because we could stay on the esker, but we had to cross the swamps to explore east or west. A mat of vegetation floated over a layer of ooze that rested on permafrost. Most of the time, I sank to my thighs in the muck, but the children were light enough to walk on top of the vegetation.

"C'mon Dad, let's go. Why are you always so slow? Tired? Be a good trooper and put that fatigue behind you."

I'd lift one leg slowly, so the suction wouldn't pull my boot off, step onto the unbroken vegetation, break through again, and advance two feet. A little smile appeared at face level.

"How come you're so short, Dad?"

I'd reach out to grab an ankle and pull one of my wood nymphs into the bog with me, but the children knew me too well and danced away. The mosquitoes swarmed, fully aware that I was defenseless. From the next ridge I heard someone say, "Hey Dad, you better hurry up or we'll eat all the blueberries."

5

I hadn't seen Chris for five months and began to miss her again. I told myself that if I wanted my freedom badly enough to move out twice, I should maintain my resolve. Then I argued that I shouldn't perpetuate a bad mistake. I reserved the right to be inconsistent, irrational, even foolish. Now I wanted her back. I took long walks, carried heavy loads up from the road, watched winter descend down the flanks of Denali. The swamps skimmed over with ice; the blueberries froze and shriveled; the first snow fell. One afternoon, after the children had finished their home-school work, I announced that it was time to go to town for showers and treats. We hiked across the hills, through the swamps, and down the ridge, then drove to town. While the kids feasted on burgers, fries, and ice cream, I called Chris, apologized for my abrupt departure from Montana, and asked whether she would like to visit us in Alaska.

She responded, "Well, maybe."

By early October, the ice thickened and a dusting of snow covered the tundra. It was time to go dogsledding. I dragged my sled to the edge of the dog lot and connected it to a tree with a quick release latch. First one, then two, then twelve sets of dog eyes focused on me. Snowball sat up and howled, and soon the others joined. At first each dog cried out as an individual, so that they sounded like a classroom full of first graders trying to make music with whistles and cymbals. But then the noise melded into a harmony that built, rose, fell, and rippled through the forest. It was the song of a pack, beautiful and fearsome. It was the call that beckoned adventurers to explore uncivilized continents and the call that drove settlers to destroy the wilderness around their new homes.

The dogs were too excited to sit and sing for long. Joker lunged for the sled with a strident yelp that was cut short by a gurgling choke as he hit the end of his chain. The impact jerked his front feet off the ground, and he pawed the air. The others followed Joker's example, adding clashing chain to the snarling, howling ruckus.

I was shocked into inaction. Susan had taught me how to harness

147

a dog, and I had practiced a few times on patient Jake, but I wasn't prepared to grab fifty pounds of lunging, tooth-snapping wolf, wrestle it to momentary submission, and harness it to my sled. Yet that is exactly what I had to do. I assured myself that I had been feeding the dogs for a month; they were my friends. They didn't want to bite me or eat me; they just wanted to pull a sled over the frozen tundra and across the mountain ranges. They were primordial travelers, and as fellow mammals we understood each other.

Nathan, Reeva, and Noey stood out of the way, watching. I waited until Jake had hit the end of his chain, and then, like a street fighter with a momentary opening, I raced in, straddled him like a horse, dug my knees behind his front legs, and slipped a harness over his nose and shoulders. My next task was to lead him to the sled. Friends had told me that an excited dog can pull a man off his feet. To prevent the ignominy of being dragged through the dog lot on my stomach, I grasped Jake by his collar and lifted him by the neck until his front legs paddled uselessly in the air. Thus I cut his pulling power in half and led him, hopping on two legs and choking, to his place in the sled traces. People who have witnessed this procedure have remarked that it is a cruel way to handle a dog. Perhaps. But it is the only way, and it doesn't change my feeling about a sled dog's life. I'd rather get choked a little on my way to a grand adventure than bask forever in the gentle softness of a city apartment.

In Alaska, teams are harnessed in tandem, with two dogs in each row. A team of four consists of two leaders and two wheel dogs. Six dogs are harnessed in three rows of two, and so on. Traditional Alaskan dogsleds are made of wood, but I had purchased a more durable sled made with a nylon bed and aluminum stanchions. My sled was about six feet long. I stood on the back of the sled runners and held onto a crossbar bolted to the stanchions. A steel brake was bolted to the back of the stanchions. If I stood on the brake, the prongs dug into the snow and slowed the team. I also carried a steel anchor to hold the team if I left my position behind the sled. If the team was tired or the load heavy, I could step off and run behind, or push if necessary.

I decided to drive four dogs on my first journey. Jake had already won my heart and trust, so I harnessed him in wheel. Then I chose the three dogs from Mackey's lot: Happy, Joker, and Kenai. They were not only experienced but were familiar with one another and therefore less likely to fight.

Kenai joined Jake in wheel. Once harnessed side by side, their excitement increased and both leapt savagely against their lines. As I raced back to harness Happy, Kenai banged into Jake, and the two started to fight. With Happy lunging in my left arm, I pulled Kenai off Jake, clipped Happy into position, and raced back to grab Joker. I knew that the best way to avoid another fight was to let them run, so I harnessed Joker as quickly as I could and jerked the quick-release latch free. We accelerated so quickly that I almost fell backward off the sled. When I regained my balance, I looked over my shoulder at the three children, standing motionless and watching as we rounded a bend in the trail and disappeared.

We raced through a small patch of timber into the large swamp north of the cabin. As the vista expanded, Joker jumped as far as he could within the constraints of his harness, did a full body roll in the air, and landed on his back. For a few seconds, the others dragged him through the snow by his neck as his feet ran through the air. Sliding along next to his father, I sensed he was shouting "Daddy, Daddy, look! I'm running, I'm running, but my feet aren't touching the ground!" Then he rolled back over and ran along with the others. But he couldn't restrain himself and jumped again. This time he landed on Happy. Father and son rolled into a ball of tangled harnesses and bodies, which quickly doubled as Jake and Kenai overran them.

When Happy, the serious leader, was tripped by his little boy on his first day on the new job, he lashed out at Joker, who was lying defenseless on his back with one front and one hind leg tangled in the traces. Eager to avoid injury of two of my most important dogs, I hastily set the steel anchor and ran forward. I broke up the fight and untangled the lines. Then, their anger gone, they all leapt forward as a team. Before I could grasp the sled, they jerked the anchor out of the frozen ground and took off, without me, toward the distant mountains.

I felt as if I had just bought a new Porsche, driven it from the dealer's lot to the insurance agency, left the emergency brake off, and was watching as it rolled down the hill toward a concrete wall before I had time to sign my collision policy. The anchor bounced wildly across the tundra until it swung wide and, luckily, hooked a small tree, jerking the team to a halt. Five minutes later, when I arrived, the dogs were waiting patiently, looking back at me as if asking, "Where have you been?"

I straightened the lines again, returned to the sled, and cleared the anchor. As I was beginning to relax and enjoy the ride, I saw that we were headed straight toward a small lake. Winter had only begun, and although the shallow swamps had frozen, I was uncertain about the deeper lake. I called "gee" and then "haw," the commands for right and left, but the dogs ignored me. I tried my foot brake, but the snow was too thin and I couldn't get adequate purchase on the frozen ground. The dogs jumped a small bank, and the sled flew through the air to land on the ice. The impact formed a wave on the surface of the ice like an earthquake wave traveling over a roadway. The wave sped toward the far shore, then reflected back. The reflected wave amplified the outgoing one, the ice broke, and I fell into the frigid water with the sled. The two wheel dogs were dragged down with the sled, but Happy and Joker were on thicker ice close to the far shore. I lost my grip on the sled and went under. When I rose and cleared my vision, the two lead dogs had dragged Kenai and Jake onto the ice. I took two quick swimming strokes and grabbed the back of a runner with one arm just as the team reached shore and started to gain speed again. I slid across the last stretch of ice on my stomach, but when we reached the shore I swung my legs around, dug my feet into the bank, and jerked the team to a halt. They stood quietly, tongues hanging out, big eyes watching me as I regained the sled and stomped the anchor solidly into a grassy hummock. Ice was already forming on my hair and mustache. I ran forward, turned the team toward home, stood on the sled, pulled the anchor, and yelled, "Yo, yo, let's go!!"

Nathan, Reeva, and Noey were waiting for me at the edge of the swamp as I returned and set the anchor. "What happened, Dad? How come you have icicles hanging off your ear?"

The children were unsure how I would react, but when I laughed, they joined me.

"I fell in. Thin ice on the lake."

Meanwhile, the four dogs in harness were jerking on their traces, ready to run again, and the eight dogs on their chains were howling and leaping, eager to join the action. I tied off the sled, chained the dogs to their posts, and ran inside to change clothes near the fire.

6

The next day I went to town again to call Chris. I told her that we had spent only five months of the last thirteen together and that maybe we should spend some time together. She should have screamed, "You *jerk*, what do you mean *maybe we should spend some time together!* Maybe you shouldn't take off and leave me every few months!" She would have been justified in slamming down the receiver and unhooking the phone for the rest of the day so I couldn't call back to plead and grovel. But she accepted my offer for a plane ticket. I met her at the airport with three unwashed children and a gift-wrapped down parka.

Chris greeted each of the children, then met me with a kiss and hug that didn't linger. We talked about friends and recent events as we drove home and walked to the cabin in the darkness. We ate supper, put the kids to bed, and were finally alone.

"Want to help me feed the dogs?"

"Sure."

We turned on our head lamps and went outside. I broke up chunks of meat with an ax. Ermines peeked out from under the cabin, their ears twitching at the familiar sound. I showed Chris how much meat, chow, and fish oil to add to each dish, and as we carried the food to the dogs, the ermines scampered out to feast on scraps that lay scattered in the snow. The dogs howled discordantly when they smelled dinner, screaming as individuals, "Feed me, forget the others, they are not my friends." When we approached, the dogs lunged against their chains, snapping their jaws, reaching for the food. Chris backed away and watched me as I fed them. Then we walked to the edge of the frozen swamp, turned off the electric glow of the head lamps, and watched Denali shimmer under a quarter moon and curtains of aurora. When the dogs finished eating, they howled in harmony.

After the dogs settled down, I introduced Chris to the team. Cameo cuddled up to her, happy to have another female in the family. Smokey sniffed for food, then accepted a scratch behind the ears. Joker pretended not to care about her affection but pressed against her briefly. Snowball didn't need to feign indifference; if she wasn't going to harness him to a sled, he didn't care about her.

When we reached the end of the dog lot, I scratched Chris behind the ears and told her that it was fine to live out here with the children and the dogs, but that I was glad she was back.

Chris looked up. "It's time for a real kiss now."

"My mustache is all icy. Shouldn't we wait until we go inside?"

"No, now, here, out in the snow."

"But the ice will melt and drip all over us."

"We'll press our top lips together and breathe out the bottom lips, so we won't melt the ice."

I held my icy mustache up with the back of a mittened hand and pulled her close.

"Remember," she mumbled. "No breathing out your nose; you have to breathe out the bottom of your mouth. Maybe this is why they rub noses up north."

We kissed, breathed, started laughing, and pulled away.

Chris ran her tongue over her top lip.

"Salty."

"I warned you."

"Let's go inside."

7

Winter advanced quickly: the lakes froze, snow fell. Over the next two and a half months I dogsledded twelve hundred miles across the swamps and forests of south-central Alaska. Often I went out on day trips, either alone or with one of the children or Chris. As the dogs calmed down and I became more skillful, I learned to drive eight dogs and, on rare occasions, ten. I bought a second, smaller sled, and soon Chris learned to drive a team so we could travel together.

I learned to handle the dogs but grew worried about my leaders. Happy had run many thousands of miles on trails, and if we came to a Y in the road he would "gee" or "haw" without breaking stride. But I needed a dog who could lead the team across trackless ice on the east coast of Baffin. One day I harnessed Happy and Joker in lead, drove the team onto a lake, and ordered them to leave the trail and head toward the far shore. Happy looked in the direction I commanded but refused. Joker pretended he hadn't heard. I walked forward, grabbed Happy's collar, and pulled him off the trail. He ran a few yards, swerved, and then looked back to inform me that we were lost. I worried about the expedition.

Although central Alaska is a great wilderness, it is warm, sheltered, and densely inhabited compared with eastern Baffin Island. Even on longer trips, we crossed a trapper's trail or cabin at least once a day. My proposed route from Iqaluit to Pond Inlet covered eight hundred fifty miles. The east coast of Baffin Island is cooled by currents flowing south from the North Pole, so I had to be prepared for fifty-below temperatures on the expedition. I would cross two mountain passes and travel the rest of the way on sea ice. There were three villages where I could resupply and rest and one DEW line station where I could seek emergency help. In between these havens I could expect windblown snow and broken pressure ridges. In a blizzard, sea ice is exposed and deadly. I was a novice musher.

None of the experienced dog handlers in the region wanted to join me. The expedition was too long and too expensive; besides, most of the mushers were training to race the Iditarod. Chris knew that this expedition would be even more arduous than the Northwest Passage trip, and I told her that I planned to strive hard for my goal this time. Some of the old bad feelings from the Northwest Passage expedition surfaced. As a result, she planned to return to Southern Cross. I prepared for another solo.

One evening, after we had fed the dogs and eaten our dinner, as we huddled around the woodstove reading by kerosene lamps, the dogs started to bark. All the grizzly bears should have been in hibernation, and we never had visitors, so I ran outside into the darkness, full of curiosity and apprehension. The dogs were staring down the empty trail from the main road, and soon a strange dog team appeared, driven by a giant in a blue parka with a wolverine ruff. His team slowed to a well-behaved trot, and the giant tied them off efficiently.

"Hi, my name is Dave. Are you Jon Turk?"

"Yes."

"I hear you're taking a dog team to Baffin Island."

"Yes."

"I'd like to go with you."

Dave was six foot seven, and he bent slightly to shake my hand. I noticed that he was wearing thin cotton gloves even though the temperature was close to zero. I knew nothing about this person, but I thought about a winter solo across one of the harshest and most desolate regions of the Arctic.

"Well, Dave, I haven't had a very good success record lately. I've failed on my last two big trips. I don't really know that much about dogs, and I don't have a dependable leader. But I have a pretty good record of coming home alive. If you're still interested, stake out your dogs and come in for tea."

We talked about the expedition, and Dave reiterated his desire to join me. Most of the mushers I knew bred race dogs, but Dave had built a stronger, slower team. They were a disjointed-looking lot of various colors, sizes, and breeds, but they were obviously accustomed to harness. I agreed to join forces.

Dave nodded and rose to leave. It was late and we invited him to spend the night.

"No," he said. "I'll be back."

We followed him outside. His team, sleeping in their harnesses, rose.

"Gee around!" he called.

The leaders pulled the team around in a tight circle on the narrow trail.

"Hup, hup!" They trotted into the night.

It's always dangerous to head into the unknown with a stranger. But it is also dangerous to go alone.

"What do you think?" I asked Chris.

"He doesn't talk much. I didn't feel any warmth from him. But his team sure knows how to behave."

We went back inside to put the kids to bed.

8

athan and Noey returned home to California, and Reeva flew back to the ranch in Colorado. No one wanted Ben. That left me in a bind; I had promised not to give Ben away or sell him in Alaska, but I had no home for him elsewhere. Even though he was too young for a long trip, he had been pulling well, so I decided to take him. Snowball developed stomach cancer, and the vet put him to sleep. Miuk fought too much, so I gave him away.

After the children left, Dave, Chris, and I made longer forays into the forest. Dave ran with his full team of eight. I had ten dogs left and drove six while Chris harnessed four to her small sled. Dave had more power and was therefore faster than we were, so he ran ahead. Generally, when someone you are traveling with reaches a trail junction first, he or she waits to make a joint decision about which way to go. Dave never waited. He went the way he wanted, and we could follow if we liked. When I tried to discuss the issue with him, he ignored me.

At camp, in the darkness of the Alaskan winter, we seldom spoke and never shared food. Dave ate his dinner; Chris and I cooked ours. One evening, Dave piled a branch loaded with spruce needles on the fire. The blaze flared up and an ember burned Chris's new down jacket. I asked him if we could have a smaller fire. He said nothing but piled another branch on the blaze, daring me with his eyes. I walked off out of the fire's glow, toward my bedded team. Cameo raised her head to ask me whether we were preparing to move on. I scratched her chin and she settled back down, covered her nose with her warm tail, and went back to sleep.

I stood in the darkness and slipped my hands inside my pants to warm my fingers. Dave was brewing tea in a small pot that held enough water for one cup. Chris was melting snow for two cups. The dance of shadow and firelight emphasized her slightly raised cheekbones, half covered by her long hair. Chris might disagree with me, but she would never boil one cup of water while I looked on. Suddenly, I wanted to return to Montana with Chris and go skiing. Then I looked around at the spruce forest that enveloped us and at the dogs that lay sleeping. I knew that I would feel empty and haunted if I sold the dogs and moved south. Over the past few years my dreams hadn't always led me to happiness. I would have to confront that contradiction.

9

We moved out of the Trapper Creek cabin in early January. I wrote in my journal:

I have an acute sense of the planet racing through space toward the other side of the sun. Until it completes its half circle, warmth is a transitory luxury and cold is the expected norm.

We planned to drive five thousand miles from Anchorage to Montreal and then fly to Baffin Island. Chris would travel with us as far as Edmonton and then fly back to Montana.

We stopped in Anchorage to buy supplies, and I staked the dogs at a friend's house. When I returned, Kenai's foot was bleeding and he was limping badly. A suburban dog had attacked, and Kenai, disadvantaged by his chain, had lost. The vet told us that the bite broke several metatarsals and that Kenai would never run again. I had originally planned to rotate Kenai, Snowball, and Jake in wheel, giving one dog a rest every third day. But now with Snowball dead and Kenai injured, I had only one wheel dog and would have to move lighter dogs into this punishing position.

I delayed our departure to bring Kenai back to Rick Mackey. A sled dog lives on a chain or in harness. If you take away the harness, you take away the dog's reason to be. As I clipped him to a chain for the last time and patted him, he lay his head down on his good paw and shut his eyes.

10

Iqaluit is the largest city in the eastern Arctic, with a population of three thousand. It supports the region's only "skyscrapers," several multistory buildings that serve as administrative centers for the eastern Arctic. Iqaluit lies at 64° north latitude, below the Arctic Circle, about the same latitude as Trapper Creek, Alaska. Therefore, we had about seven or eight hours of daylight—plenty of time for travel. But Iqaluit is much colder. We stepped out of the plane to a dull, low-angle winter sun and forty-below temperature. My body was still warm from the airplane cabin and I was building my mental strength for the journey ahead, so I didn't feel the cold. I turned to Dave.

"This doesn't seem that bad."

He responded, "Just wait."

The cold, dry, polar air brings little snow to Baffin Island in winter. Less than a foot covered the ground, not enough to soften the rocky outcrops that offset the low hills beyond town.

The door of the airplane hangar opened, and the warm moist inside air collided with the cold, forming a cloud of ice crystals. A forklift emerged from the swirling ice fog with a pallet full of dog boxes. We strung a cable between two utility poles and staked the dogs so they could stretch and relieve themselves after their cramped flight.

A friend of a friend, Kathryn Garven, met us at the airport. As we introduced ourselves, a battered green pickup roared to a stop, and a Caucasian man wearing a thin jacket jumped out.

"Where are your dogs from? Where are they going?" he demanded.

"They came from Alaska and are headed for Pond Inlet, and we're going with them," I responded.

He looked at the team closely, then, finally, at us. "My name is Brent. You're going to need some help. I run dogs here on the island, and you can count on me for support."

Brent and Kathryn decided we should stake our teams out at her place, where they wouldn't fight with Brent's dogs. When we were on the trail in Alaska, the dogs dug warm, comfortable nests into the deep snow. But wind had scoured Kathryn's backyard, leaving only a few inches of hard pack. I watched Cameo as she scratched down to the frozen tundra, lay down, then stood up again to scratch and sniff. She walked in a tight circle several times to satisfy herself that this was the best possible bed and then curled up in a tight ball with her nose pressed against her anus and covered by her tail.

After the dogs bedded down, we went inside for tea. Brent suggested that the high Arctic might be too harsh for the Alaskan dogs and that we should train for a month before setting off northward. I was humbled but not deterred; we agreed to train for a week and then head toward Pond Inlet as originally proposed.

11

Brent had to work the next day, so we arranged a training run with his partner Rene. I had forgotten the beauty of space. It is like an open roadway after a traffic jam or a quiet walk in the night after a crowded party. The dogs must have felt the release as well, for they stretched out, not in a frantic run but in a loping all-day pace.

Despite the dogs' enthusiasm, we moved so slowly that I stopped to check the sled runners. No problem—the white nylon was unmarred. Then I picked up a handful of snow, opened my mittened palm, and blew on it. The crystals rose into a puffy cloud like fairy dust that sparkled rainbows across my frozen breath.

In warmer environments, where the temperature hovers near freezing, the sharp edges of the snowflakes melt and then recrystallize. During this melt-freeze cycle, airy snowflakes consolidate into rounded crystals and the snow pack settles and becomes denser. However, in the extreme cold, a reverse process occurs. Molecules sublime directly from solid to vapor. Some of the vapor refreezes on the outer edges of the crystals, forming long airy needles and blades. Thus very cold snow has no structural integrity. You can't build a snowman at forty below. Sled runners sink through this light fluff and scrape on the rocks below. In addition, the sharp needles restrain the sled, like sandpaper. Snow is most slippery when its surface melts to form a lubricating layer of water. Cold snow is about as gritty as a paved roadway.

After about ten miles, Rene swung his team onto the sea ice. Dave's dogs followed without hesitating. My dogs balked. Happy tried to turn the team back toward shore and snapped at Joker when he tried to proceed. They tugged, fought, stopped, and looked back as if asking for directions.

I watched Rene and Dave grow smaller in the afternoon twilight, then checked the thermometer hanging on my sled handle: thirty-five below. I thought, "I should have trained more on trackless lakes or better yet on the Alaskan coast as Susan Butcher suggested." But I hadn't. The town was invisible around a low ridge to the east, ice stretched southward toward the reddish-gray horizon, and the tundra rose behind me.

I walked to the head of the team, grabbed Happy and Joker by the collars, and pulled them forward. They resisted, then acquiesced and trotted slowly on the other teams' trail.

After we returned to town, I staked the dogs out, fed them, and walked back into Kathryn's warm house. Several people had gathered to meet us. As I shed my goose-down parka, an Inuit man laid his hand gently on my shoulder. Quietly, to avoid insulting me, he remarked, "If you wear those clothes on your journey north, you will die."

I stared blankly at the short, broad-chested figure before me. A quiet smile separated his wispy beard from his scraggly Fu Man-chu mustache. His ancestors had stabbed mammoths to death with spears in the windswept corridors between Pleistocene glaciers.

"What's wrong with my clothes?" I asked.

He picked up my parka and ran the edge of his palm along the inside of the garment. In doing so, he scooped up tiny ice crystals that had collected there as my body moisture froze. We both watched the ice melt in his warm hand.

"If you hang the parka up in a warm house, it will dry overnight. But if you travel for days on the land, the frost will accumulate, enter the down, and freeze inside the feathers. Then maybe a cold storm will come and . . ." He drew a forefinger across his neck as if slicing his throat with a knife.

"What can I do about it?" I asked.

"You need a caribou anorak."

Brent had walked into the room and overheard the conversation; he nodded in agreement. In fact he had already made arrangements.

The government housing in Iqaluit has spread a monotonous mediocrity over the landscape. I followed my hosts up the street into a pale-green cubic fourplex, designed in Montreal for shipment to the North. Four older women were sitting on chairs and couches as they half-watched a program on a television set in the corner. A pile of caribou skins on the floor offset the shiny linoleum and formica counters. One woman stood to measure Dave and me with a knotted string. Like many older people on Baffin Island, she spoke only her native tongue. She wrapped the string around my chest, arms, and torso and chatted with her companions, but she wrote nothing down. Then she squeezed me and told a joke that started the women giggling. When she turned to Dave, she had to stand on a chair to reach his shoulders, and she slowly whistled, pantomiming that she was amazed at how big he was. Then she reached the string down as if to measure his penis. She whisked the string away, opened her toothless mouth as if in surprise, and broke into a wrinkled grin. The grin cascaded into hysterics, and she climbed off the chair for a moment to avoid a fall. Then she finished her measurements, and we discussed our wardrobes through an interpreter.

Aboriginal Inuit wore two layers of clothing in the winter. The inner layer was prepared with the soft hair against the body, and the outer garments were reversed, because animal fur sheds snow. Anoraks were usually made from caribou, but pants were made of more wear-resistant polar bear hide. Overboots, called *kamiks*, were sewn out of sealskin, the most waterproof material available. We decided to use our synthetic underwear, pants, and boots, but we bought caribou anoraks.

The following day, as Dave and I were outside doing chores, a boy and an Inuit man with a shaved head and no hat strolled past. The two stood aside watching us, and then the boy spoke. "My cousin, Jacopie, heard that you were going to Pang by dog team."

Pang is short for Pangnirtung, the first town along our route, and I nodded.

The boy asked, "Do you have a good map?"

"Yes, why?"

The boy continued, "Jacopie says that people less experienced than you might get lost out there. Of course you could probably find the way, but it would be difficult." Then he exchanged some words with his cousin, who nodded.

I looked at Dave, and he muttered, "Jesus Christ, another warning."

I responded, "We were going to take a compass bearing across the Hall Peninsula toward the sea ice in Cumberland Sound. Then I thought we would recognize the entrance to Pang Fiord."

The boy discussed this with his cousin and continued, "That would be a good idea except for the cliffs."

"What cliffs?" Dave asked.

"Oh, didn't you know that the east shore of Hall Peninsula is full of cliffs? There is only one good route down to the sea ice."

"And how do we find it?" I asked, alarmed.

After a lengthy exchange, the boy answered, "Maybe you should follow Jacopie's tracks. He just remembered he should visit his aunt in Pang and bring her some fish. You could follow his snowmachine tracks if they don't get covered by a storm."

"When is he leaving?"

"Oh, when will your parkas be ready?"

I wondered how he knew about our parkas and answered, "Day after tomorrow."

"Good. Jacopie needs to leave day after tomorrow, also."

I nodded to Jacopie and offered my hand. Before Europeans came, Inuit didn't shake hands, and he took mine awkwardly and limply. I reached out and put my palm on his shoulder; he nodded and turned away.

12

On February 1, the morning of our departure, the temperature was forty-six below, and a gray ice fog hung over the town. Jacopie swung by on his snowmachine pulling an Inuit sled, called a *komatik.* Jacopie had tied on extra fuel, camping gear, and a small pile of frozen fish wrapped in canvas. He was still hatless as he slowed down to wave, but he reached for his hood as he accelerated toward the edge of town.

We followed behind at our much slower pace. At the edge of town, the trail climbed slowly toward the plateau, and I stepped off the sled and jogged behind the team. My heavy breathing drew frigid air past the guard hairs of the polar bear ruff around my hood. The cold scraped against my face, frostbiting the skin on my cheeks and chin. Then, tentacles of cold reached inside, flowing up my nostrils into the usually well-guarded sinuses. As I jogged toward the plateau above town, my heavy breathing drew more cold into my lungs, where it spread like tiny pinpricks into the alveoli. But the warm blood finally held the line so that my heart, only a few centimeters from the lung membranes, remained at normal body temperature. I had been warned not to allow my lungs to be frostbitten, because the damage could cause pneumonia, so I stepped on the sled for a moment to ride and slow my breathing. The dogs looked back as if to say, "Hey, we have lungs, too." Chagrined, I stepped off and called a rest for all of us.

A maze of snowmachine tracks crisscrossed the first hill, but Jacopie had marked his track with wooden stakes and red flags. Within a few miles the tracks thinned out, and endless waves of wind-rippled snow spread out before us. I stepped back on the sled as the grade leveled and the dogs accelerated. The tunnel of my tightly drawn hood made Dave seem far away, as if I were looking at him through the wrong end of a telescope. He was stooped over to grasp the handle of his sled, so he looked almost bearlike in his fur clothing. Gradually, the ice forming on my ruff and eyelids blurred his outline. As he disappeared even farther down the telescope tube, frost froze my upper and lower lids together and rainbows danced from the crystals that clouded my vision. The sparkles were too fanciful for the bear image so I imagined him to be a shaman crossing the edge between reality and the void. An Inuit legend tells of a shaman who danced with walrus on the ocean floor during hungry times. The walrus enjoyed the shaman's dance and assured him that hunters would be successful. In my own dream images, Dave became a dancing walrus surrounded by choreographed fish in a warm, watery world.

Dave drove to the top of a long hill and called out for a short rest. Because I was behind, my dogs were forced to stop while still on the uphill grade. When the rest was over, we would start against gravity. It was a small matter, but I felt that life out here was hanging by a knotted string of small matters, so I asked if he might stop next time a few yards past the crest. He silently poured some hot tea from his thermos and drank it as if I hadn't spoken. I looked hard at Dave, and he stared back silently.

I wanted to ask, "Why do you want to be on this trip if you don't want to be my friend?" But maybe I was imagining his indifference, and I didn't want to start an argument.

He yelled, "Yup, yup!" and his team trotted down the grade. I rocked my sled to free the runners and pushed hard to get it moving, then yelled to my team to start.

13

The Hall Peninsula is a broad plateau with few prominent landmarks. Our untrained eyes saw only windswept snow, featureless undulations, and nondescript rock outcrops. The compass needle staggered and bounced, slowed not by the cold but by the proximity to the magnetic north pole. At the magnetic pole, a compass needle points straight downward, toward the earth's metallic core. Baffin Island is close enough to the magnetic pole that the needle is pulled downward until it drags against the compass rose. To obtain a reading, I placed the compass on a flat rock and tapped it until the needle hopped and skipped to a bearing. But multiple readings from the same place varied by about twenty degrees, introducing an uncomfortable margin of error. Jacopie had grown up learning the name, history, and location of every hill and depression and probably had stories to tell about most of them. He had known that without this local knowledge, a *kabloona* from the south would surely be lost.

Inuit readily joke about misfortunes, especially their own; they warn people about specific dangers that may be avoided, but they never insult a person's competence. So Jacopie hadn't said, "Look, you are new here, you will get lost and die; you shouldn't go." He simply showed us the way by inventing a trip to his aunt's. But the thin crosshatched snowmachine track was a frayed lifeline that could easily be erased by snow or wind.

At any instant we were safe; our body temperatures were normal, and except for frostbite nips, we were relatively comfortable. No yawning abysses or raging polar bears threatened us. We weren't climbing steep rock cliffs or kayaking down turbulent rivers where a single off-balance movement could lead to disaster. We were walking or jogging along a snowmachine trail and occasionally riding on the back of a sled at a sedate five miles an hour. But we were vulnerable. If a storm obliterated our trail, if our stove failed, if the tent ripped, or if some other unseen problem arose, troubles would compound quickly.

If danger lies directly ahead, adrenaline shoots through the bloodstream closing down the sphincter and enlarging the capillaries in arms and legs. But when danger is simultaneously real and nonexistent, fear takes a different form. It gently lays a hand on you, exerting a pleasant pressure, pushing you toward heightened awareness. Check camp before you leave and don't forget a tent pole; watch the sky for signs of a storm; memorize a sequence of landmarks backward to Iqaluit in the event that the trail is erased; study the ripples in the snow to plot your forward travel with respect to the prevailing winds.

14

Brent had guessed that our fast Alaskan dogs would travel forty miles to the McKeand River in a day. However, when the Arctic twilight darkened the landscape, we were still climbing toward the top of the plateau and were obviously not near a river valley. We had no idea how far we had gone, so we stopped in the shelter of a large boulder and set camp.

Once inside the tent, we lit both burners of a two-burner Coleman stove and set candles around the perimeter. The flames warmed our small space, and soon the frost melted from our faces. We removed our mittens and anoraks and sat comfortably in long underwear and light pile jackets. Then we melted snow, boiled water, and settled into a quiet cup of hot tea followed by a big bowl of rice and steamed caribou.

It was our first camp, and we both relaxed with nothing to do but eat and sleep. All the planning, training, and traveling were behind us. Dave explained that he had thought about running the Iditarod this year but had changed his mind after he met me. He felt that the Iditarod was a reenactment of an expedition, whereas this was the real thing.

I was happy to talk about plans and dreams because I felt the conversation brought us closer together. Maybe my apprehensions were wrong. Wilderness changes people, and now that we were on the land—alone, together—we could shed the shields that protected ourselves from each other. We had a long way to go.

After traveling all the next day we still hadn't reached the river. In Alaska I had traveled eighty miles in twenty-four hours, but here the cold snow, the heavy sled, and the long uphill grade reduced our progress to less than twenty miles a day. The cold deepened to fifty below. We descended into the river valley by midmorning of the third day. Dave and I treated ourselves to a cup of tea from our thermos and a frozen candy bar, and we rewarded each of the dogs with a morsel of fish. When it was time to move on again, Happy looked ahead at the uphill trail and turned the team back toward Iqaluit. I set the brake, ran forward, grabbed him by the collar, and swung him back toward our route. But he had made up his mind, and he veered around again. We repeated the tug-of-war several times. Dave was already on top of the first level bench above the river and watched my struggles.

"Kick him!" he yelled.

Happy was nine years old, had been a sled dog all his life, and had led a team to an Iditarod victory a few years previously. He wasn't merely being cantankerous. He had always known that he was more experienced than I and that he was the true leader. Now he was telling me that we were all too close to the edge out here, and it was time to go home.

"Kick him!" yelled Dave from above.

Maybe Happy was right. At this speed we barely had enough food to make it to Pangnirtung, and at these temperatures, small mistakes could quickly turn to disaster. Maybe I should go home to the warmth of a Montana winter and escape this brutal cold and the unfriendly giant who railed at me from the top of the hill. I pushed those thoughts aside.

I removed Happy from the lead, put him in wheel, and switched Joker into lead with Mac. Mac and Joker wavered, then trotted purposefully onward. For the first time since I had known him, perhaps for the first time in his life, Happy pulled halfheartedly. His line fell slack, and the others jerked him forward. He pulled for a while, then he slowed, looking back over his shoulder.

We climbed all afternoon and camped on a large lake on top of the plateau. When I unharnessed the dogs and staked them, each immediately dug a depression in the snow and curled into a ball with nose tucked under tail. But Happy stood, legs apart, staring onto the back trail, looking south. I sat in the snow next to him and wrapped my arms around his neck.

"C'mon Happy, get it together. I know you're old, but we'll be in Pang in a week. When you're done with this trip, your work days are over. You retire to stud. Rick Mackey will feed you and bring you women. All you have to do is lie around. It's an easy life."

He remained statuesque. I grabbed his outside two legs and jerked him onto the ground. Then, grasping his neck and tail, I pulled him into a ball. When I let go, he stretched out on the snow to expose as much body surface to the cold as possible.

I went into the tent, cut him a choice chunk of caribou, and boiled it with a little seal meat and a few morsels of fish. When this stew was done, I dressed again and walked back outside into the Arctic night. I put the hot dish in front of Happy's nose. His teammates smelled the delicacy, pulled at their chains, and yelped excitedly. Happy opened his eyes but didn't raise his head. A cut on his nose glistened with white frost. Yesterday he had tried to discipline Cisco, but he was too old and slow to be the boss dog, and Cisco had lashed back.

I stood in the cold and checked the thermometer: sixty below. Curtains, arrows, and spirals of aurora chased each other across the sky. The electrical pulses seemed to beat against my eardrums with an inaudible, low-frequency hum. I imagined I was inside an ice-lined cavern, surrounded by huge bass speakers playing an African drumbeat at such a low frequency that I could hear nothing but feel everything. There was no moon, but the fluorescence reflected from the white snow to illuminate the rock along the lake shore.

In his final lesson, Happy was teaching me that despite all my warm clothes, high-tech tent, and Arctic sleeping bag, my main survival weapon was the will to live.

I whispered quietly, "I knew that, Happy."

I remembered early mornings as a boy when the house was quiet with sleep and I propped myself against the heat vent in the bathroom and read adventure stories. I recalled an image from a Jack London story, "To Build a Fire." London's hero was traveling along a frozen riverbank with the temperature at sixty below. He stopped to spit, and the spit froze solid before it landed with a crackle on the snow. I held out my boot and spit. Liquid spittle landed on the toe, spread out, and then froze. London was wrong. I returned to the tent.

15

I needed to escape to a few friendly words with my companion, who sat cross-legged drinking tea, a few feet away. I said something simple, a quiet plea for understanding.

Dave shrugged. "It's just a dog; he wasn't much good anyway."

I tried to fly away, but I couldn't escape this man's words and presence. What happened to the friendship we had shared for the first two days? Why couldn't he offer me a kind word? Even though it was still early, I slipped into my bag, pulled a hat over my head, faced the tent wall, and closed my eyes. The previous winter, I had skied every day with Chris, even if it was only one run after hours at the keyboard. Most days, one or more of our friends joined us. In the evenings, people visited, shared food, bathed together in a community sauna, danced late into the night during spontaneous parties. The old Finn who had attacked me that first day never forgave me for winning the heart of "his Wanapeka." He warned Chris that I was "a lazy good-for-nothing," but between his vitriolic attacks, he shared his treasured vodka spiced with heavy doses of garlic, offered me day-old discount Danish that had become week-old Danish because no one had gone to town recently, and told me old stories of strikes and battles with the scabs in the copper mines.

I think Happy chose to die because he was getting old, this land was too harsh, and he couldn't imagine that he would ever retrace all those steps—the plane rides, the long drive—back to his home in Alaska. Now I wanted to retrace my steps back to Southern Cross. Part of me didn't care about Pond Inlet, my ambition, or its seemingly intangible rewards.

When I awoke the next morning and looked into the predawn grayness, Happy's frozen corpse lay stretched out on the lake. I tried to talk about the death during breakfast, but Dave ignored me and discussed the mechanics of the day's travels. We broke camp and roused the dogs. None of them looked at the body or sniffed. Maybe I was the only one who saw it, as in a haunting daydream.

Like a lover hoping for a hug after an angry argument, I looked at Dave, silently pleading for a soft word. But he harnessed his team methodically and didn't speak until he yelled to the dogs, "Yup, yup, let's go."

The sun rose, offering light but little heat. I harnessed Smokey and Mac in lead, started my team, ran for a few moments, then stood on the sled runners. I needed a voice to break the silence so I turned and spoke to the dot on the landscape, recognizable only because I knew what to look for. I quietly said good-bye.

Smokey took charge and followed Jacopie's snowmachine trail at a steady trot. I ran behind the sled again, across the lifeless landscape, then rode on the back runners as we picked up speed downhill. Softened by space, one death seemed insignificant. But Happy had been my friend. I consoled myself by rationalizing that Happy was an old man; perhaps he had chosen well for himself.

16

Cape Horn introduced me to wetness. I embraced space on the Northwest Passage. On the Hall Peninsula, cold became the overriding sensation. It hovered in my dreams, wrapped around me when I harnessed the dogs, trotted alongside me as I ran, and deepened as the evening fell and we made camp.

At suppertime, we warmed the tent to about fifty degrees above with our stove, but when we turned off the stove to sleep, the temperature dropped rapidly. We pulled the hoods of our sleeping bags tightly around our faces, leaving only our noses and mouths exposed to breathe. The moisture from our breath froze to the outside of the bags, and by morning the nylon was coated with ice. This layer melted during breakfast, and moisture seeped into the insulation. By the middle of the week, the bags were damp and not as warm. My body understood that it had only one defense left: motion. So I slept and my body stayed awake, shivering intermittently throughout the night to keep me alive. When I awoke, mentally restored but physically exhausted, I sat up and waved my arms violently to move blood throughout my upper body. Then I pulled on my boots to go outside and pee. Before returning to the tent, I jogged rapidly in place to pump life-maintaining blood into my legs. Breaking camp, harnessing the dogs, resting for lunch, making camp—it was all the same. When I wasn't running behind the sled, I was running in place or waving my arms to maintain blood flow and stave off the cold.

One morning, as I followed the sled across the nearly featureless plateau, a loud sound broke the silence. The dogs stopped, alert. The noise repeated—a distant *craaak* like a rifle shot, then a prolonged *zing,* changing in pitch as if a bullet approached, passed, and disappeared toward the horizon. But it wasn't a bullet. The cold had penetrated so far into the ground that the permafrost was fracturing, like the ice on a lake.

On a warm day in the tropics, your body feels like a cooperative system: Heart pumps blood to the lungs, lungs absorb oxygen for the heart. But out here I felt that each organ, each extremity, was separate, suspicious, and guarded. My intestines tried to hoard all the food until the toes called up, "Hey, if you don't send some energy this way, we won't take you to Pang and we'll all be in trouble." Then the intestines would relent and ship down a few calories, but just enough. My brain, like a politician backpedaling after drawing a nation into war, told the rest of the body that it had nothing to do with this project. Every morning it transmitted a few generalized instructions for the day, "heart—pump, legs—jog," and then drifted off on its own. As my feet headed toward Pang, my brain and I wandered across the blank landscape, drifted backward and forward through time, and lapsed into peaceful warmth. We checked in with reality occasionally to be sure that we were still on Jacopie's trail, that the dogs were all doing well, and that none of the extremities were complaining too loudly. Those are the glorious moments on an expedition, when you become detached from everything and meld into the landscape.

17

On the sixth day, we reached a small lake near the top of a broad pass. Jacopie had built an igloo on the lake and spent the night. We had traveled eighty miles in five and a half days and had a little over one hundred to go to Pangnirtung, but the remaining distance was downhill or along the level sea ice of Cumberland Sound.

The downhill trail was steep. We swung onto a river that cut through the cliffs. I rode the brake as the sled skidded on the bare ice and threatened to slam against the wheel dogs. The temperature rose to eighteen below, and I stripped off my anorak. The river ice was only a foot thick and had fractured where the stream tumbled over boulders. Cold water flowed out of the cracks onto the surface. Vapor from the liquid rose and crystallized, creating streamers of ice fog like cirrus clouds that had fallen from the sky.

I thought back to my days as a chemist. There is one unique combination of pressure and temperature, called the *triple point,* where water, ice, and vapor all coexist at equilibrium. Although I lived in a safe world where water was water and not everything together, I dreamed that if I could climb inside the triple point, the world would be magical.

I had learned my chemistry well enough to know that what I was experiencing now was not the triple point of water, but it felt like the spiritual triple point. I had climbed from under the fluorescent laboratory lights to an Arctic landscape where the world was composed of water, ice, and vapor. A pale sun shone through the suspended ice crystals and projected hazy rainbows that danced in the whiteness.

The dogs were not so enchanted. Smokey, in the lead, refused to step into the water, and the team backed up against him in a tangle. I couldn't control the sled, and it banged into Jake and Apple in wheel. Luckily the dogs were too exhausted to fight, and I ran forward and pulled them through. When we stepped off the wet ice onto dry snow, I checked their feet and tried to pick out the ice encrusted between their already shredded pads. But my fingertips were frostbitten, and I could do little for my friends.

18

We reached the sea ice on February 7, after a week on the trail. Despite some ominous clouds, good weather had held and the dangerous portion of the journey was over. The remaining trail to Pangnirtung followed the sea ice, which was heated by the ocean and therefore warmer than frozen ground. As a result, the snow that covered the ice was more slippery and less needlelike. In addition, no rocks lurked beneath the snow to cut the dogs' feet. Although my dogs had balked at travel over the sea ice on our first excursion in Iqaluit, conditions here were so moderate compared to what we had been through that they picked up speed. The final stretch of the Iditarod race in Alaska crosses the ice into Nome, and most of my dogs had run Iditarods, so perhaps they associated sea ice with the end of the trail. I couldn't tell them that Pangnirtung was only the first leg of a longer journey.

Friends in Iqaluit had told us about a small shack in an abandoned village called Kipisa, a few miles away. The shack was maintained as an outpost camp, open to all travelers. A few miles from Kipisa, Dave, in the lead, stopped to inspect a red object in the snow. It was a five-gallon plastic jug filled with diesel fuel. We knew that the outpost camp had a diesel stove, but we had left town too loaded to carry fuel.

The wood-frame shack was about fifteen feet on a side with a low ceiling and a flat roof. Bladed ice crystals hung from the ceiling. The interior was painted hospital green and contained a formica table and chairs and a small bookcase with Western novels and a few *Playboys*. The centerfold women hanging on the walls looked frigid without their clothes on. A castiron cookstove stood against one wall. Someone had installed a diesel burner in the old firebox and connected it to a reservoir mounted on the wall. We poured our precious fuel into the reservoir, opened the valve, and lit a match. The cold metal sucked the heat out of the match and extinguished the flame. We leaked some fuel into the firebox, lit a few pages of a Louis L'Amour novel, and dropped the burning paper onto the pool. It caught, and an orange flame spread around the circular burner. Within a few hours, the icy coating on the inside walls melted. The room was above freezing!

Our anoraks, like our sleeping bags, had absorbed body moisture during the week. For the past few days, they had frozen during the night, and we had thawed them over the Coleman stove in the morning until they were supple enough to wear. However, the moisture soaked into the leather, which became whitish and soggy, like an old shoe left out in the rain.

We were low on food, so we felt pressed to continue on to Pang-nirtung, but the following morning we still had three gallons of fuel left and we had no desire to harness up. Inuit hunters had butchered seals along the beach, leaving innards and blubber behind, which we thawed and fed to the dogs. For ourselves, short rations in a warm cabin were luxurious. We spent the day reading, writing letters, and napping.

As we loaded the sleds the following morning, Dave suggested that because his team was faster, he take additional weight for our final run to town. I was surprised at his generosity and thought that perhaps our successful crossing together, followed by a warm night, had kindled our friendship. I handed him the stove, fuel, and most of the remaining food. Then he proposed that I leave first and he would catch up in half an hour. We looked at the map and plotted our route. It was about the same distance either to the left or to the right of a small island, so we decided arbitrarily to travel to the left.

Even though we never talked on the trail, I always felt his presence, and now I was relieved to be alone. Numerous snowmachine trails crisscrossed where hunters had searched for *aglus* to hunt seals. When I reached the island, I stopped for a rest and a cup of tea from my thermos. I looked back, expecting to see the giant hunched over his sled stanchions. Instead, I saw only whiteness. Had we miscommunicated? I waited until I cooled off and began to shiver. Then I circled around to the right side of the island. No sign of Dave.

Pang was still two days away. I had little food and no stove, and because I needed the stove to melt snow, I had no water. I speculated that his generosity in taking the extra weight was merely a ruse to steal the stove and food. Then I felt guilty for my mental accusation. He was a strange man, but he wasn't capable of murder. And even if he were, why had he left me with the tent? No, I must be slipping into insanity even to contemplate that he had abandoned me; something terrible must have happened. I had to return to Kipisa and find him.

As I turned the team around, a thick fog spread from the southeast. The snow was so windblown that I had left no tracks. I tried to navigate on a compass bearing but reached land in an unfamiliar place in the descending darkness. I staked out the team, pitched the tent, drank the last sip of tea in my thermos, and crawled into my bag. It was too early to sleep and my mind was racing. What would I do if I didn't find him? Was it better to risk death in a desperate dash for Pang, or should I wait in the shack, slowly burning the remaining fuel, in the hope that some hunters would visit? What were my chances either way? I dozed off.

In my dreams, an eight-foot-high ornate castiron woodstove stood in the corner of the tent. I put my hands against it, but it was so cold that my fingers froze to the metal. I opened the door and saw that it was full of wood, but the wood wouldn't burn because the flue was blocked by hundreds of dampers. I opened the dampers frantically. The fire flared and warmth poured out. Then I awoke. Large platelike ice crystals covered the inside of the tent. Where was Dave? What had gone wrong?

The fog lifted the next morning, and I discovered that I was only a mile from Kipisa. As I headed back, I saw a dog team in the distance running toward the island. They were too far away to respond to a shout, so I fired a shot into the air. No response. I fired again, and again no response. My dogs caught the scent and pursued until we caught up.

"What happened, Dave?"

Dave explained that as he was preparing to leave the shack, two snowmachines roared in from the south. The local hunters had shot a seal. They relit the stove, warmed the cabin, and boiled a big pot of seal ribs. The food was good, the warmth embracing, and he remained, assured that I would return by evening. As we talked, the dogs sensed a rest and curled up in the snow.

"You don't leave your partner, Dave, even for a good meal. We are not communicating; something is unsaid."

"Nothing, Jon, nothing is ever unsaid. I just thought you'd figure out that I wasn't coming and return to camp. I didn't count on the fog."

I had spent a night in the Arctic without food or water, and if we had missed each other this morning, both of us would have been in trouble. I had never been abandoned like this, never heard of anyone being abandoned like this. One of the joys of an expedition is to travel with someone who will watch out for you, risk his or her life for you. If you protect your partner, you are protecting yourself, but partnership transcends expediency and implies an unbreakable code. On an expedition, your partner's well-being is as valuable as your own. Dave had broken the code.

I turned away, called, "Yah, yah, let's go," and the dogs trotted onward. I jogged behind the sled for a quarter mile then stepped back on the runners to calm down and catch my breath.

I reviewed the events. Dave had never before been generous, but he'd offered to carry more of the weight. Had he set me up? Had he known that people were coming? I thought, What would a character in a Jack London novel have done?

Maybe I should shoot him.

I started shaking, deep under the furs.

Bad idea.

"How could Dave have known that people were coming? Probably the whole incident was just sloppy expedition style."

No, the incident went beyond carelessness. Some psychological game was going on here, and it had started a long time ago. My self-esteem demanded that I break the relationship, but we were still out here on the sea ice with one tent and one stove, two days from town.

The cliffs guarding Pangnirtung Fiord shimmered in the distance. The temperature was twenty-five below, warm enough to soften the queasy vulnerability yet cold enough to nip the frostbite scars on my face and fingers.

I jogged for a long time, forcing fatigue to overpower thought. I didn't know what had happened, but we had crossed a barrier from aloofness to mistrust. I was on this expedition—alone. Dave was on the same expedition—alone. We had one tent, one stove. Dave's team still responded to commands better than mine did, so I was stronger with him than without. I could lean on him and use him, but I couldn't depend on him. I didn't have to like him. It was a narrow line. An unfriendly line. An unsafe line.

Time, space, and cold spun my thoughts into wispy filaments. By midafternoon I was back on the trip, but its character had changed irrevocably.

19

We spent two nights on the ice, and on the third day we were close to Pangnirtung as darkness turned color into shadow. The dogs smelled town and accelerated, so we let them run and switched on our head lamps. A well-worn snowmachine trail led through the jumbled ice in the intertidal zone and toward the village. Children appeared out of the darkness and ran along with us, yelling, "The dogsleds are coming! The dogsleds are coming!" We had no destination in town, so we stopped arbitrarily in the middle of a street. Streetlights illuminated straight roads and geometric houses. The dogs were so tired they lay down in their traces and curled up; their job was done.

A door opened and a woman stepped onto the porch. "The dogsleds! Come in for coffee!"

She had a throaty yet melodious voice. "Hello, my name is Meeka. Let me take your anoraks." I bent over, facing her, and she reached across my back to slide my anorak over my head. I smelled the caribou muskiness mixed with my own stale sweat. Then, with the faintest female touch along my arms, she slipped the heavy anorak off and I straightened up, smelling her perfume. She smiled and turned to help Dave.

We were still on the porch, and the cold night air penetrated my thin underclothes. I was hungry, tired, and ready for a rest, but I already missed the sea ice and high desolate plateau.

I removed my boots and stepped out of the thirty-below-zero night into a carpeted seventy-degree room. The hundred-degree temperature change, bright lights, and room full of people made me feel awkward. I stood, embarrassed that everyone was looking at me, embarrassed by the rank smell of my body, uncertain what to say to the half dozen people who watched silently. A middle-aged woman named Rosie asked me to sit, offered me a cup of coffee, and introduced me to two older women who didn't speak English.

On the television, women in bikinis and muscle-bound men splashed through a tropical ocean singing and waving bottles of Pepsi.

Meeka turned our anoraks inside out, shook them, and ran her fingers over the smooth white hide. Then she frowned and handed them to the two older women, who also inspected them carefully.

Meeka turned to us. "Where did you get these?"

I told her that a woman in Iqaluit had sewn them for us.

"Shame on her," she said. "These are *kabloona* anoraks, for tourists. These are not anoraks for hunters. You men are hunters, not *kabloonas*. Look at your faces," and she poked at the frostbite scars. "You could have died in these anoraks. They were not properly tanned. The hide is dead. It doesn't breathe. Feel this; sweat has collected here under the armpits. And feel how wet the leather is near your mouths. Don't these furs freeze at night?"

We explained that they did but that we held them over the stove to melt the ice in the morning.

"Shame on that woman," she repeated. "She knew that you were traveling by dog team in the middle of winter. First, the moisture from your bodies collects in the hide and makes you cold. Then it freezes and ruins the leather. Shame on that woman. You men are traveling in the old way. You should be treated as travelers were treated in the old days, not as tourists who ride on the airplane."

Then she handed an anorak to each of the older women, disappeared into the kitchen and returned with two *ulus*, traditional Inuit knives. An *ulu* has a curved blade with the handle mounted on top like a chopper. Both *ulus* were old, with walrus ivory handles and blades thinned by many sharpenings. One woman deftly cut out the discolored and soggy portions of my anorak while the other worked on Dave's. Nonchalantly, between coffee and conversation, they started chewing the hide. They chewed, spit, rubbed the spit into the leather, and worked it again with their mouths, moving slowly in a spiral from the necks toward the waists.

A man entered with a raw frozen fish and set the fish on newspaper on the carpeted floor. The older women smiled, showing their teeth, which were worn nearly to the gums from years of hide preparation. They set our anoraks aside, squatted in front of the fish, and cut off long slices with their *ulus*. Following our hosts' example, Dave and I reached for our knives, cut oursleves a slice of fish, and ate.

After dinner, our hosts arranged for us to sleep in the parish church and told us to stake the teams out in front.

20

The following morning I walked to the store to buy breakfast. I met Jacopie and thanked him for leaving a trail that guided us across the plateau. The last time we met he didn't understand English, but this time he conversed.

"Had to bring fish to my aunt."

I pressed the issue. "I think you made the trip especially to help us, and I thank you."

But he objected. "Oh, you don't need help. You are dog mushers from Alaska."

Then he touched me on the elbow. "You find can of diesel?"

"Was that yours? Yes, we found it before Kipisa. We burned the fuel to warm ourselves at the outpost camp. Did you leave it for us? Thank you."

"Oh no, I didn't leave it. I am bad traveler. Fell off my *komatik*." Jacopie laughed at himself. "Very dumb to tie things poorly on my *komatik*. Very dumb." He looked down at his shoes. "Could I have the can back?"

"Of course. I will fill it up with diesel for you."

"Oh, no! I was too dumb. You should take the can; it is yours; I lost it. But you don't need it. Dogs can't drink diesel! It fell off my *komatik*."

After breakfast I filled the can and returned it to Jacopie.

Dave and I didn't talk much about our future plans, but by default everyone assumed that we would rest and then continue toward Pond Inlet. Meeka asked the local radio station to announce that we were traveling in the old way and should be welcomed in the old way. I chose to ignore my distrust of Dave. It was all an aberration; we would rest and continue on. As we were drying out and relaxing in the warm church, visitors brought seal meat for the dogs, and caribou and fish for us.

I doctored the dogs but knew that they really needed time, not medication. Cisco ran half sideways in his harness, and one flank had rubbed raw. I treated it with salves and sewed a soft scrap of caribou hide into his harness. Baby Ben remained strong, although he wasn't eating well. I bought commercial dog food for him to provide a familiar taste, but he needed fat to combat the cold. Jake and Apple had done more than their share in wheel. Jake's feet were in bad shape, but Apple, who was younger, was better off.

Dave and I needed rest and food, so we relaxed with the pace of the town. Occasionally, hunters hitched *komatiks* to their snowmachines and drove onto the ice to hunt or fish. Teenagers raced their machines back and forth through town, and younger children did endless wheelies on the ice with their bicycles. The blue-green glow of television screens shone out of living room windows.

We visited Meeka and her friends daily. Meeka's father had worked for the Hudson's Bay Company and was the first Inuit on Baffin Island to learn how to write. Meeka had refused to leave home to go to high school in Iqaluit but learned her lessons well enough to go to college in southern Canada. After graduation, she became a spokeswoman in Ottawa for Inuit rights and then returned to her home in the North.

We also spent long hours in the church, reading and reorganizing for the ongoing journey. Older men came by and sat in the parish pews, chatting among themselves and watching us. Some were dressed in blue jeans and flannel shirts, and others wore sealskin *kamiks* and polar bear pants. Many couldn't speak English, so we served tea and smiled. After sitting patiently, as if waiting for the preacher to begin the sermon, they would rise silently to leave or walk to the corner to examine our harnesses, tents, stove, and clothing.

Many people gave us seals, and when their generosity was exhausted, we bought more. We fed the dogs as much as they could eat and, at the same time, put meat aside for the trail. We stacked frozen seal carcasses like cordwood outside the church. One morning while I was breaking one apart with an ax, an Inuit man suggested that I bring it inside to thaw and then butcher it with a knife.

"Bring it in the church?" I asked.

"Why not?" he replied.

The church was a single room with plywood pews and a white and blue linoleum floor. One wall was adorned with a picture of Jesus' tomb under a gnarled cedar. In the picture on the other side of the room, three crosses stood on a hillside above the fortified city of Jerusalem. Jesus sagged on the center cross and his head hung limply, directing his gaze toward the whiskered faces of the dead seals. Ice clinked to the floor as the carcasses melted.

This didn't seem right. I grabbed one of the seals by its hind flipper and started to drag it outside again. At the door I almost walked backward into Rosie and one of the older women who had chewed on my coat. Rosie asked what I was doing, and I explained that I had brought the seals inside as instructed but felt uncomfortable thawing them in the church. Rosie agreed, but when she translated, the older women shook her head. There was nothing in the Bible against dead frozen seals in church, and there were no Inuit taboos against it.

More women arrived to organize a rummage sale. The younger women asked us to remove the seals, but the older women overruled. They had been born in igloos and had waited through hungry times as the men hunted with their teams. One explained, "God loves dogs, and look at how lean these dogs are. In the old days people prayed and feasted in the same igloo. Surely the carcasses should remain."

I dragged the seal back to a corner under the picture of Jesus on the cross. As a guest I try to be noncontroversial, but I felt we were driving a wedge between generations. People still welcomed us, but it was time to move on.

21

The next passage led through the Weasel River Valley, across Auyuittuq Pass, and then descended to the village of Broughton Island about one hundred miles away. The pass lies within a national park and is a popular hiking destination during the summer. The trail passed up frozen rapids hemmed in by huge granite cliffs, higher and steeper than those in Yosemite Valley. I needed more power, especially in wheel position. There were two dog teams in town, and I bought a heavy Inuit dog named Asgard from one of the owners. In Norse mythology Asgard is the home of the gods, and one must cross a rainbow bridge to reach this magic place. Mount Asgard is also an imposing granite spire near Auyuittuq Pass. It was dangerous to buy a strange dog who had not bonded with the team, but I was desperate for any dog that was strong and acclimatized.

I told Meeka that we were leaving the next day, but she explained that tomorrow was Sunday and it was bad manners to leave on the Sabbath. In any case, our anoraks weren't ready yet, and she had a dinner party planned. So on Sunday, we went to Meeka's.

The old women showed us our repaired anoraks. They had cut out the damaged portions and replaced them with new fur. The new inserts were white to offset the golden brown and were arranged into diamonds that zigzagged across the garments.

One woman pointed her finger and admonished us sternly in her native language. Meeka translated: "Don't be bashful. You must tell the women in Broughton to care for your garments when you get there. Fur clothes must be mended all the time. It is the old way."

Dave responded, "I thought it was the old way to take women with us to care for our anoraks every night on the trail."

Meeka translated, and the old women laughed. "Oh yes, you are right, we should come with you, sew your clothes, and keep you warm at night. But we are too old for you, and the younger women won't do that."

Rosie wrote a letter from the women of Pangnirtung to the women of Broughton Island. She rolled it into a scroll, tied it with a ribbon, and asked us to take it, as a memory of the old days when every traveler carried the mail.

22

Several dozen people gathered Monday morning as we loaded our sleds. I hitched Apple and Asgard in wheel, then Jake and Cisco in front of them. As I returned to the stakeout line to harness

Cameo, Cisco dug a comfortable depression in the snow and went to sleep. By the time the whole team was harnessed and I said good-bye to all the well-wishers, only Apple and Asgard remained standing. Apple barked in youthful excitement, while Asgard looked back over his shoulder toward his old home, as if to ask, "What am I doing here; why am I harnessed in this funny line with strange dogs?"

I thought about the first, wildly enthusiastic training run from my cabin in Alaska only a few months before. Now we were all sobered, stronger, more methodical. As the people watched, I walked forward and lifted the two lead dogs, Joker and Smokey. The others acquiesced and trotted through town at a comfortable pace. We left the city streets and followed the snowmachine trail into the intertidal zone. Suddenly Jacopie stepped out from behind a block of ice and walked slowly toward us, his bare head conspicuous in the morning cold. He had forgotten his English again, but he smiled, offered a greeting in words that I didn't understand, and abruptly turned back toward town.

Despite their original reluctance, the dogs trotted along strongly, and we traveled eighteen miles to the head of the fiord by noon. A braided glacial river led through the valley, bounded on both sides by imposing granite walls. Thin snow on the river ice provided good traction, and my dogs maintained their pace. However, Asgard lagged, and his tug line frequently fell slack. Dave predicted that he needed a few days to become adjusted to the new team and then would pull as an Inuit sled dog should.

We climbed a gradual rise to Windy Lake. Fast-moving cirrus clouds coalesced into ominous lenticulars that rested on the peaks. The clouds told us that the wind was howling at hurricane force up there, and we saw that the storm would surely descend to the valley floor. We had experienced extreme cold on the Hall Peninsula, but no storms. I felt afraid and excited at the prospect of my first Arctic winter blizzard. The park service had built emergency shelters throughout the valley, and if we could reach the first shelter we would be safe.

A previous storm had blown all the snow off the lake, leaving smooth, black ice. But the wind had also driven sand into portions of the ice, forming elongated patches of ice with a sandpaper-like surface. When we stepped onto the clear ice, the dogs slipped and fell, their feet sliding outward like Wily Coyote in a cartoon animation. Smokey and Joker stopped, regained their footing and dignity, and headed for the closest sandy patch. The dogs had good footing on the sand, and for a few moments the sled continued to slide on the smooth ice behind. When Smokey and Joker stepped onto the bare ice again, however, the sled scraped onto the sand. As a result, the dogs lost their footing when they needed more traction to pull the sled over the rough surface. In their minds, the going was easy when they were on the sand and nearly impossible when they were on the ice. But in my mind the problem arose from changing surfaces. We would be better off maintaining a steady pace on the smooth ice and avoiding the sandy patches altogether. They didn't understand that the sled was so far behind that it was on smooth ice when they were on rough, and vice versa. Smokey, using his best dog-brain reasoning, steered an erratic course for every sandy patch, while I, using my best human-brain reasoning, tried to direct them along a sinuous route that remained on smooth ice.

Soon Smokey and Joker simply ignored me. They went their own way and looked back irritably whenever the sled scraped on the sand, as if I were trying to make their lives miserable. Finally, they stopped. The first gusts of the storm struck my face. Up-valley, clouds lowered and snow fell. In an hour we would be caught in the swirling blizzard. I ran forward and jerked the dogs into motion and then ran along beside them, holding Smokey's collar and directing him along the smooth ice. He acquiesced, but when I let go to return to my position behind the sled, he ran to the next sandy patch and stopped again.

More gusts raced across the lake, blowing wispy snow across the ice. I tried to imagine the power when the wind blew with such ferocity that it embedded sand into the ice. It would surely blow us off our feet and slide us across the lake in a tangle of harnesses and gear. The dogs sniffed the air and then turned toward the nearest shore, but previous storms had blown the snow away, and I knew we couldn't maneuver the sled through the rocks. The shelter stood out plainly as the only geometric shape in a chaotic landscape of fractured granite. Finally, I grabbed Smokey's collar and ran ahead of the team, as the new lead dog.

By the time we reached the shelter, the blizzard was building rapidly. We staked the dogs in a small gully that provided some protection. I reached into the sled and pulled out the stove and some fuel, while Dave grabbed a bag of food. I stood up, felt the wind, and ducked back down into the gully. Dave held a gauge above our heads and recorded wind speed of fifty miles per hour. The temperature was twenty-five below, producing a wind chill of ninety-six degrees below zero. The cabin, only fifty yards away, was nearly shrouded by the blowing snow.

When I stood up, the wind drove the cold past my nose and throat, deep into my lungs. My body, desperate to defend itself, closed my windpipe and I gagged, unable to breathe. I turned my face out of the wind and tried to walk backward, but stumbled and fell. Lying on the ground, I remembered stories of people who had died within sight of camp. I rose to my hands and knees, clutched the stove and fuel against my belly, and crawled awkwardly toward the shelter, breaking the wind with the top of my hooded head. Dave was beside me, also crawling. We reached the door together and brushed shoulders as we entered the shelter.

The contact was an insignificant jostle in the bedlam of raging storm, but it was a human contact, and I wanted to give Dave a big hug, jump up and down, and hoot, "We did it, Man! We're safe! We're a team! Yahoo!"

I held back. Then I thought, "No, it's stupid not to let my emotions flow. Maybe we're not connected because I'm not putting out enough positive energy. I should break the barrier between us with a bear hug." But I was afraid that he would rebuff me. Dave, oblivious to my thoughts, turned to fill the stove with fuel. If I hugged him now, he would spill gasoline all over the table. I had lost the moment.

The shelter was a small A-frame, larger than our tent but smaller than the outpost camp at Kipisa. It was built of stout timbers and well insulated, so we could heat it to above freezing with the Coleman stove. Furniture included two bunks and a small table. It was the most comfortable storm bivouac I'd ever had. We were dry, and we barely heard the wind. We had a table to sit at, books to read, enough food, and plenty of fuel for the stove.

Dave's girlfriend had given him several nude photographs of herself, and he crawled into his sleeping bag, pulled the hood over so I wouldn't peek, and looked at the pictures. When he emerged for tea, we had nothing meaningful to say to each other and talked constantly about quitting. I wrote in my journal:

> *The day-to-day experiences on the trail aren't fun. So why don't I quit? The explorers who preceded us were rewarded for their accomplishments. Martin Frobisher kissed the queen's hand, Francis Drake was knighted, and Robert Peary became an admiral. But today, old adventurers drive around in rusty cars and bivouac along the side of the road en route to the next destination.*
>
> *So, I guess I am here because I said I would do it and now others expect me to continue. Emotionally, I am ready to fold, but when the storm subsides I will be too embarrassed to return to Meeka's kitchen in Pangnirtung.*

I drew a line across the page indicating that my thought was complete. I took a nap, woke, and stared at Dave's back as he stared at those photographs.

I thought, "God, this is grim. No friendship, no laughter."

I reminded myself that I was a happy person—somewhere beyond this emotional vacuum. Then I brewed another cup of tea, dressed, and crawled out into the storm to pee and check on the dogs. They were curled tightly and, fortunately, well insulated by drifted snow. I wished I could make them more comfortable, but there was nothing I could do. I held the wind gauge up again, but moisture had collected around the indicator ball and frozen it solid at zero miles per hour.

The wind-driven snow raced under my belly, swirling around my hands and feet so that I imagined I was flying rapidly over a stationary landscape. I recalled the storms I had weathered, the shipwreck near Cape Horn. If nothing else, a good blizzard every now and then rearranges your personal dictionary, editing definitions of words like *danger, security, safety, fear.* I had been outside for only five minutes, but when I returned to the shelter I was cold, so I drank more tea and warmed my hands over the stove. Then I picked up my journal again.

> *I can't cross the Arctic in winter simply to avoid embarrassment. So I'm out here because even the storm has its own beauty, and the harsh misery cleanses and refreshes. If I turn back, what does that mean? How*

far back do I go? To Southern Cross? To Colorado? To the chemistry lab? Maybe if I turn back I will not only forfeit this trip, but I might convince myself to forfeit the lifestyle. I'm not at peace with this adventure, but I'm afraid of myself if I abandon it. I'm not ready to become a different person.

23

The wind died the following day, and we dressed to travel. My anorak was soft and supple, unlike the stiff frozen garment I was accustomed to on the journey from Iqaluit to Pangnirtung. The mastication had worked!

The sun shone and the air was still. We harnessed the teams and started across the frozen lake. I played a word-philosophy game with myself. "What does it mean to go back? Time doesn't go backward, so maybe I can't go back. Well of course I can go back. I can go back to Pangnirtung. But I can't go back to the chemistry lab. There's a wide swath between the two. Where do I fit in? Maybe right here, behind this dogsled, jogging through this valley, with one storm behind me and another, somewhere, in front."

After a short jog across the remainder of the lake, we encountered the first of several steep, frozen rapids. We unloaded the sleds and backpacked the loads to the next level bench. Even with empty sleds, the dogs had a hard time on the cascading ice. Dogs pulled one another off icy ledges, and several times all nine lost traction together and slid back down. My old veterans were remarkably tolerant. They had lost their fight long ago and were working together. But Asgard blamed each inconvenience on his neighbor. I ignored his repeated snarls, but when he nipped Apple in the Achilles tendon, I lost patience. It was bad enough that he wasn't pulling well, but if he injured one of the others, I would be at a serious loss. I slipped him out of his harness and let him go. He looked at me and the team for a moment, and then trotted back toward Pangnirtung.

The top of the falls is guarded by Thor, the largest overhanging granite wall in the world. In Norse mythology Thor is the ruler of the gods, and he throws his magic hammer to produce thunder. The imposing face is nearly a vertical mile above the valley floor, so I felt as if we were running through the earth's interior, not across its surface. The rock had absorbed the February sunshine and was now reradiating the heat, raising the temperature to a balmy fifteen below. The valley reminded me of the Utah desert, with its slot canyons and overbearing heat. I thought about Chris and about our first nights as lovers beneath the sandstone spires.

Snowball had died; Kenai had lost his foot and his lifestyle; Happy had stretched out on that frigid lake. But the hard times were over. The sun rose higher every day. We had crossed the Hall Peninsula, and now we were cresting our final pass. I thought about returning to this place in the summer, with climbing shoes and rope. Compared to the mile-high cliffs, a climber would seem no bigger than a quartz crystal in the granite. I imagined living on a vertical plane where my life depended on grace and balance. What would it feel like to be halfway up one of these walls, attached by a fingertip and a toe, with an eleven-millimeter rope and an aluminum wedge to hold me if I fell?

I was unable to make much human contact with Dave. I was alone, far from Chris. But that day I felt that I belonged here even though I couldn't explain why.

On the downhill side of the pass, the river was congested with boulders, and we had to pick our way through the talus. Wind had blown the snow off the surface and deposited it in crevices between the rocks. The sled rested on snow for a few feet, then on rock, then back on snow. Dave and I worked together to push or lift the sleds over rough spots. The sharp rocks cut the dogs' feet, and drops of blood were left on the trail. Jake injured his right rear pad and began to limp.

As we descended back toward the sea ice, we left the talus to cross a small coastal plain covered by hummocky permafrost. One lone willow, about as thick around and as high as a pencil, poked through the snow. It was the most prominent plant we had seen since we arrived on Baffin Island. Joker, in lead, stopped and lifted his leg to urinate on it. But then Apple, in wheel, surged forward to leave his scent, and the team bunched up. Cisco tried to join but was blocked by Mac, who was by now snarling his way into position. Unable to reach the stick, Cisco pissed on Mac. Mac fought back with one leg up and a stream of urine flowing, and pissed all over poor Cameo, who wasn't sure why the boys were so excited.

The pace accelerated again when we reached the sea ice, and the team ran strongly, except for Jake, who now hobbled pathetically on three feet, trying to keep up and do his share of the work. I called a rest and put my arms around Jake as I had done to Happy so long ago. "We only have twenty miles to town. Don't give up. I won't ask you to go past Broughton Island. I promise. I'll send you back to Brent's and he'll care for you till I can take you home to Alaska."

The next day we broke camp early to reach town, but by late afternoon we were still about five miles away and the dogs were tired. We were low on food and fuel, but we could all sleep on a light supper, so we established camp against a sheltered pressure ridge near shore. Three Inuit on snowmachines raced past us a few hundred yards away. They were obviously out for a short jaunt, because they weren't carrying rifles or pulling *komatiks* with camping gear and extra fuel. They disappeared around a point, then turned, reappeared, and drove into our camp. One of the young men wore a cotton baseball cap, light nylon jacket, and tennis shoes. The others wore canvas anoraks. The temperature was twenty-five below.

"What are you guys doing? You were supposed to be here a few days ago?"

I thought about my scrolled letter. Today, the two-way radio carries the news, not the dogsled.

"Oh, I guess we're slow."

"I guess! Anyway, you're only five miles out of town. Why don't you come in tonight and party?"

"The dogs are tired. They won't understand. It would be cruel to harness them back up and make them pull again."

Our visitors persisted. "It's just around the corner."

We declined.

24

The following morning we left without breakfast, had coffee and doughnuts in town, and looked for a place to stay. Two contractors were doing the interior finish work on several houses. They were behind schedule and were happy to trade work for room and board. So we settled into a large, insulated tent, similar to those used at permanent camps in Antarctica. It had a plywood floor and was heated by a diesel stove. In exchange, we worked four hours a day hanging doors and installing trim.

No aboriginal people had lived on or near Broughton Island. Fishing and seal hunting were better to the south, and caribou hunting was better northward. The Hudson's Bay Company built a trading post between these two regions to intercept families as they migrated between camps. The government followed with a police post and a nursing station and then built the rest of the town on the site.

After four days of mixed work and rest, a man named Moosa invited us on a seal hunt. The following morning, as a thin red line in the eastern sky began to overshadow the nighttime aurora, four men drove to our tent on snowmachines. Moosa had lashed a plywood box onto one *komatik*, and we huddled inside for the ride. The staccato pop of the two-stroke engines broke the silent dawn, and the oily exhaust spread a haze between us and the orange sun, which was flattened by high-latitude distortion.

In the first hour we covered about twenty miles, a good day's run by dog team. Several towering icebergs were frozen into the planar sea ice, giving relief to the landscape. We bounced along the snow-covered sea ice past scattered seal carcasses. Moosa stopped to explain that this region had already been hunted out and that we must continue farther east. I asked why previous hunters had been so wasteful and left valuable meat and sealskin behind.

He responded, "In the old days people used everything. They ate meat, fed meat and entrails to the dogs, used the blubber for food and fuel, and the skin for clothing, kayak shells, and summer tents. Today we are not so careful."

When we came to an appropriate place, each person found a fresh *aglu* and stood over it, rifle ready. Moosa told us to wait until a seal poked its nose up to breathe and then blast it in the head at point-blank range. To prevent the seal from sinking, we were then instructed to drop our rifle and harpoon the dead animal. Others would hear our shot and run to help chop a hole in the ice to drag the seal out. In the old days people made the kill with a harpoon instead of a rifle, but otherwise the strategy was the same.

A seal can hold its breath for only twenty minutes, so if all the adjacent *aglus* were guarded we should soon be successful. But *aglus* are well camouflaged in rough ice, and it is easy to miss one. I have read accounts of hunters standing over a series of *aglus* for ten to fifteen hours without success. Our friends were not that patient. After half an hour, Moosa left his post and wandered around, looking at everyone else's *aglus* but ignoring his own. Then he called us together for a parley. If the old ways didn't work, we would try a new trick. Seals retreat from the sound of a snowmachine on the ice above them. Therefore, if we drove the snowmachines in a wide circle and then spiraled inward toward a single *aglu*, we could herd a seal to one predetermined location. Moosa told me to drive his machine while he waited at the *aglu*. I drove slowly in a circle about a quarter of a mile in diameter. After three loops, I accelerated and tightened the arc. Below the ice a poor, frightened seal retreated from the encircling vibration and rose to take its last breath. At the rifle report, I abandoned the spiral and headed straight to Moosa, who was already dragging the seal onto the ice. He took his gloves off so they wouldn't get bloody and, bare-handed, slit the seal down the belly and removed the entrails. The temperature was twenty below.

"Don't your hands get cold?" I asked.

"Oh yes, then I dip them in water." And to prove his point, he immersed his hands in the open water of the enlarged *aglu*. "Water can only get so cold and then it freezes. So in winter you warm your hands by putting them in water."

I nodded, unconvinced.

Sam, one of the hunters, lit the ubiquitous two-burner Coleman stove and melted snow for tea. When tea was ready, we squatted on the bloody snow around the still-steaming seal, sliced off chunks of hot, raw liver, and devoured them. I had been chilled waiting over my *aglu* and then driving the snowmachine, and the warm food and tea were welcome. The men chatted about snowmachines and previous hunts as they passed around a bag of chocolate chip cookies to round out the meal.

25

We swung a wide arc on the way home, checking the ice to the north for future hunts. Moosa spotted a polar bear track, and we followed it over a pressure ridge to a blood spot adjacent to an *aglu*. The patient bear had waited by the breathing hole. When the seal had appeared, the bear had smashed the ice with one blow of its paw and at the same time had hooked the seal with its claws. Then it had dragged the prey to the surface and eaten it, bones and all.

Bouncing home, Sam's snowmachine suddenly pitched nearly onto its side and stopped so abruptly that the *komatik* rammed it from behind. The left ski had fractured and the metal stub dug into the ice. The careening *komatik* had then pierced the gas tank. A trickle of gas dropped onto the snow. As we gathered around, Sam rested on his machine and lit a cigarette.

Dave remarked, "Maybe you shouldn't smoke so close to the leaking gas."

But Moosa reassured us. "You white guys watch too many movies. Gasoline only blows up in the movies. You guys worry about everything. You guys worry too much."

I didn't argue, but I stepped back.

A snowmachine ski has a metal wear bar bolted on the bottom. The ski broke in front of the wear bar. Sam removed the wear bar from the broken ski and another wear bar from his good ski. Then he proposed to use the wear bars to splice the two broken parts of the ski together. However, no one had a drill to puncture new holes for the bolts. Undaunted, Sam took out his rifle, shot four holes in the ski, and bolted it together with the wear bars.

When I complimented him on his ingenuity, Sam shrugged. "In the old days, if someone broke a *komatik*, he chopped a hole in the ice, caught a fish, sliced it in half, let it freeze, and spliced the runners together with the frozen fish."

With that comment, he pulled the starter cord, slung his rifle back over his shoulder, and headed home with a thin gasoline mist spreading rainbows around the damaged tank.

26

The following day we started preparations for the continuing journey. The next village was Clyde River, about two hundred fifty miles north. The route followed the sea ice the whole way, so there were no plateaus or passes to climb.

Jake's foot needed a few months to heal, not a few days, and I had promised him a rest, so I shipped him back to Iqaluit by plane. When I returned from the airport, a ten-year-old boy was waiting by our tent.

"I hear you lost some good dogs."

"Yes, I have. The others are going to have to work all that much harder."

He smiled, swayed back and forth, and kicked some snow. "My dog would like to go with your team. Her name is Kathy."

I knelt down to be at eye level with him. "Kathy, huh. How do you know she wants to go?"

"Oh, she does. She is always on the chain and gets bored. She wants to go."

"Well, let's go take a look at her."

Kathy was a young female Inuit sled dog, a little fat from lack of exercise, but the extra weight wouldn't last long on the trail. She had never run with a team before, but the instinct had been bred into her for the ten or twenty thousand years that northern people have been using dogs.

"Okay," I responded. "Do you want to go for a sled dog ride to see how she pulls?" The boy nodded excitedly.

I showed him how to harness Kathy, and I hooked up the rest of the team for a short run around town. I placed youth with youth, harnessing Kathy next to Apple. When Apple barked and lunged in anticipation of the run, Kathy looked at him, perplexed, but when the team set off, she trotted along contentedly with a taut tug line. The boy's only request was that I return Kathy when I was done.

27

We set off the following morning, March 6. The first day out of Broughton we reached an outpost camp at Kivitoo, about thirty-five miles away. Although the cabin was similar to that in Kipisa, we had no diesel fuel to light the castiron stove, and it was frigid inside. I suggested we sleep outside in our tent, which we could heat with our Coleman stove. But Dave was depressed that we had left town and were on the trail again. He snapped that he wanted to "eat dinner sitting at a goddamn table, dammit."

We cooked on the Coleman stove, ate at the table in our furs, and held our spoons in mittened hands. I was too cold to be comfortable, and I didn't feel like talking. Dave complained that we should have brought some diesel and chastised me for returning the fuel can to Jacopie. I snapped back that he had his morals and I had mine. It was the first night of the third leg of our journey, and Clyde seemed far.

After dinner, we put our stove and food away and prepared for bed. Soon we heard a snowmachine approaching, and a few moments later a figure in skin clothing burst through the doorway. He looked around the room. "What! Are you guys crazy? Why don't you light the stove? This place is fucking cold!"

He disappeared into the night and returned with five gallons of diesel. He poured most of it into the reservoir, and then, rather than carefully priming the burners, he splashed diesel over the stove. A small stream of oil dripped onto the floor.

Muttering and shaking his head ("Jesus, you guys are too fucking crazy"), he dropped a match on the stove top. The orange, sooty flame built as it spread across the stove top. A drop of fuel caught fire as it dripped over the edge of the stove. Like a miniature napalm bomb, it burned as it fell and ignited the growing pool of diesel on the floor. Unperturbed, our visitor casually dispersed the spreading flame with his foot while he took off his mittens and held his hands over the stove.

"Don't you guys like to be warm?"

Soon after the conflagration had settled down, a second snowmachine approached. This one sputtered sickly as if one cylinder was firing regularly and the other limped along when it felt like it. An older man, also dressed in furs, walked in and looked around. He remarked, "Hi, guys, no tea yet?" and went back outside. He returned with his Coleman stove, pumped it up, and lit it, but like his snowmachine, it sputtered. He shut the stove off, went back outside, and returned with another stove. It didn't light either. He grabbed a pair of pliers out of his pocket and pulled both stoves apart, spreading generators, valves, and burners over the table. Selecting the newest components of each, he built a stove, threw the rejected parts into the corner, and started a kettle of tea.

After tea, he placed a large pot on the stove, filled it with water, and ceremoniously poured in a single packet of Lipton's chicken noodle soup. Diluted by about four times as much water as the directions called for, the tiny noodle stubs floated on the surface, agitated slightly by the convection currents rising from below.

"See this. This is what white men eat. Right?" He didn't wait for a reply but tasted a spoonful of the still-cold mixture. "Blah . . . white men don't know how to make soup!" He went back outside and returned with a sack of frozen caribou, seal, and char. He tossed meat and fish in the pot, added a few handfuls of spaghetti, and sat down to wait. In half an hour, the rich oily soup was ready and he pointed at us with a spoon. "Eat!"

Although we had already eaten, we helped ourselves, and then he filled his own bowl. Between mouthfuls he explained, "This is Inuit soup. Good soup. White men don't know how to make soup." Then he waved the Lipton's packet in the air for emphasis and repeated, "Blah!"

After dinner, he announced, "Gotta fix my snowmachine." I followed him outside. Aided by the light of my head lamp, he found a set of socket wrenches in his *komatik,* and bare-handed in the thirty-below night, he unbolted the cylinder head to expose the pistons. "Son of a bitch, burnt a hole in the piston. Can't fix the son of a bitch. Burnt it out driving too fast, like a kid." And he smiled at his own foolishness. "Guess I'll have to drive it home the way it is."

"Why don't you spend the night here and go on in the morning?" I asked.

"No sleeping bag," he responded.

"And if the machine dies on the way home?"

He rummaged through his *komatik,* found a saw, and held it up like the torch on the Statue of Liberty. "Build igloo."

Then he bolted the head back on, pulled the tired engine into half-life, called his friend to get going, and sputtered off into the darkness.

28

Traveling light and on the level, we covered the one hundred miles to Cape Hooper in three days. A conspicuous white radar dome marked a DEW line site. We drove up the hill to say hello and possibly beg a meal and a warm place to sleep.

Each DEW line base was a vital link in the strategic defense of North America. If one were removed, enemy bombers or missiles could fly to the heartland undetected. Therefore, I expected to see guards outside in the frigid Arctic night, protecting the radar dome. But the place was empty and silent. We stood on the crest of the hill and looked over the ice below. Nothing moved, and the nearest people were a hundred miles away. Dave remarked that a couple of commandos with snowmachines could sneak in and blow up the whole place. Several metal buildings stood next to the dome. We staked out the dogs and then tried the closest door, but it was locked. Circling the compound, we finally found one that was open and entered into a warm hallway.

A sign on the door to our left said "Top Secret. Radar Room. Authorized Personnel Only." We turned right and walked down the narrow hallway. In the distance we heard a television set. Unsure of the reception we would receive, we stepped into the doorway but didn't enter the room. We were still dressed in our caribou anoraks, and Dave was so tall he had to stoop. Four men were sitting on couches and chairs, watching the screen. The room had been planned and decorated by a Pentagon bureaucrat with instructions to make the place look homey. A few motel-art prints adorned the walls. The couch and chairs had matching maroon upholstery, and plastic flowers rested in maroon vases that vaguely matched the furniture. But the men in the room were interested only in the television program. Even though we were facing them, they didn't see us. I mused that we had emerged out of the night and were invisible. But I also felt ridiculous standing there, so I broke the silence. "Hi, guys."

No response. The television faced away from us so we couldn't see the action, but we could hear the sound of gunfire. I tried again. "Hi, guys."

Someone looked up. "Hey look, Sasquatch!"

They all turned back to the TV while we remained in the doorway. Dave finally walked to the center of the room.

"Could we have a cup of coffee or something?"

The spell broke, and the men welcomed us for the night. The food was good, and the buildings were so warm that I enjoyed a cold beer. But the men at the DEW line talked endlessly about the horrible boredom of the north and about their eventual return to home, wives, trees, and green grass. Their depression activated our own.

When we settled into our warm bunks, Dave retreated to those pictures of his girlfriend. I dreamed of skiing and wondered if Chris had found a new boyfriend.

29

We left the next morning and plotted a course across the sea ice. The cook had fed the dogs warm meat scraps. Refreshed and strengthened, they trotted purposefully. Once again, we were two tiny smeared-out dots on a broad white landscape.

Out on the ice again, I fought against the monotony and the cold, and tried to grasp the contentment that I had felt among the granite spires of Auyuittuq. One moment my mind skipped across the wind ridges and drifted with the dogs' wagging tails. Then, inexplicably, there was only labor and hardship in the landscape.

Clearly I had defined my lifestyle so I could live outdoors. But outdoors didn't have to mean Baffin Island in the winter. It could mean skiing untracked powder through spruce forests, followed by wine and lovemaking amid down comforters. Was I chasing the wrong dream?

I jogged, rode the sled, and jogged again. If I looked down at my boots, the snow ripples sped by so rapidly that I felt as if I were on a spirit journey with an Inuit shaman. But when I looked into the distance, time and motion, like the sea, had frozen. We were running on a treadmill to nowhere. I looked east toward a fog that formed where fractured ice had exposed the ocean to the frigid air. Then I turned my gaze west and watched cirrus clouds race over the rock cliffs. Soon darker clouds advanced, and light snow fell, swirling around our feet like dry-ice clouds in a high school play. I held my mittened hand across my hood to keep the wind from eddying into my face. Dave stopped, and I pulled up to talk.

Dave's face was half hidden in the furry shadow created by his hood. Frost sparkled on the outside guard hairs. Even inside, his eye-brows were frosty, and the frostbite scars on his cheeks stood out clearly. Despite the emotional struggle between us, we had passed through hard times together. He was strong. I was strong. We were under control.

A large iceberg had frozen into the ice a few miles to the north, and we decided to bivouac on its lee side. The dogs trotted strongly, and the wind didn't intensify. The berg, which had seemed minuscule at a distance, was as large as a house and provided a comfortable windbreak. We staked the dogs in a soft snowbank that had collected behind the berg and dug our tent into more soft snow a few yards away.

We had four days' worth of food, but could easily stretch it to five, and we calculated that we could travel to Clyde River in three or four days of good weather. If the storm lasted one day, we were fine. If it continued for longer, we would have to reduce our rations. If condi-tions seriously deteriorated, we could retreat to the DEW line base and then back to Broughton Island.

The storm continued all afternoon and evening, and when I awoke the next morning, the back pressure of the wind was vibrating the tent. Storm days in a mountain tent are always boring and uncomfortable. Moisture rises from the teapot, freezes on the inside of the tent, melts, and drips onto your body and clothing. Tentmates crowd toward the drier center of the tent, collide, spread apart, and creep back toward the center. After a month and a half together, even good friends have told and listened to too many stories. You can only discuss the trip logistics for so long, and then there is nothing to say. So you roll over to take a nap, but you bump against your partner, move away, doze off, and wake again when a drip of water lands directly in your ear. Partners can overcome these inconveniences with friendship and a sense of humor, but with underlying tension and no giggles, storm days drag on.

I read, tried to talk to Dave, tried to ignore him, then incurred his anger when I asked to see the nude pictures of his girlfriend. Chastised, I went outside, walked ten yards north to the outer edge of the iceberg, turned, and tried to pet the dogs, but they barely rose from their sleep. I walked back to the tent, thought about going inside, but continued five more yards to the southern edge of the berg. I ventured out into the storm and circumnavigated the iceberg. I was cold by the time I finished the journey and returned, reluctantly, to the tent.

I brewed another pot of tea, and we talked. We decided that if the wind died by the following morning, we would head north; if the storm lasted another day, we would retreat back to Broughton.

The next morning was warm and sunny, a perfect day for travel. We rejoiced at our luck and reaffirmed our plans to head toward Clyde. Dave always harnessed his team faster than I did. When he finished, he looked at me thoughtfully and then called, "Gee around!"

His dogs turned back toward the DEW line and Broughton Island, southward toward home. I called out, but he ignored me. Then I stared incredulously at his receding figure.

What happened? We had come so far. I thought about the abandonment back at Kipisa and wondered again why he left me at that time. Then I returned to the present. Apparently his discontent with the monotony, the cold, and me had passed a threshold. Had he been planning this retreat all yesterday afternoon, even as we agreed to continue? Or had he reacted impulsively, after he harnessed his team and looked at the empty sea ice between us and Clyde River?

I would never know, and it didn't matter. I thought about nothing as I watched Dave, the giant, grow smaller against the planar whiteness.

I finished harnessing and sat down on my sled. He had the stove; I had the tent. I had to follow him. But I didn't move and the dogs curled up.

The sun cast an orange glow on the east side of the iceberg, offsetting the gray-blue shadows. The storm had blown fresh snow into crescent-shaped drifts around our shelter. I reaffirmed a memory from Cape Horn: "Jon, look around, breathe deeply, you will never be here again."

Dave receded until I imagined him to be a dark spot without life, personality, or motion. I didn't want to be close, yet I knew we would share the same tent for another few days. I fantasized that he would vaporize into the space that had been our companion and our scenery for so long. Finally, I stood up. Maybe he wouldn't stop at the DEW line. Would he abandon me altogether? I didn't know anything anymore.

I sat back down on the sled and began planning the next expedition. Then I stopped myself. Planning the next expedition! How ridiculous! I claimed that success was important to me, but I had failed three times in a row. For the past six weeks I spent half my time wishing I were anywhere but on an expedition. Truly, I would drive myself crazy this way.

I stood up, rallied the dogs, called "gee around," and followed Dave's trail. I started to feel better as soon as I began jogging behind the team. Motion soothed me. Maybe I should think about that. When I left Chris, what did I do? I drove. When Debby and I split up, I bought a sailboat. Motion.

Suppose I was just born to be a wanderer. It was a beautiful day. I was alone. If I was genetically programmed to wander, maybe I could learn to accept myself. I took a deep breath of cold air. My lungs had learned to accept the harsh intrusion. Now I had to train my mind to embrace the journey. The day we had gone seal hunting, Moosa had called me Qitdlaq, the name of a legendary Inuit explorer. People laughed when I had asked about Qitdlaq, but between the jokes I learned that he led a small party from Ellesmere Island to Greenland. Along the way, he had been consumed, driven insane, and eventually killed by his wanderlust.

Against all reason, I decided to follow Qitdlaq's footsteps to Greenland. Without the madness and the death.

Part 4

To
Greenland
by Kayak

Know, my friends, that the idle and indulgent life which I led after my return soon made me forget the suffering I had endured in the Land of the Cannibals and in the Cavern of the Dead. I remembered only the pleasures of adventure and the considerable gains which my travels had earned me, and once again longed to sail new seas and explore new lands.

Tales from the Thousand and One Nights
Author unknown, translated by N. J. Dawood

1

I drove back to Southern Cross and staked the dogs out in front of Chris's cabin. We shared spring skiing and a trip to the desert, and the magic of our romance returned. Chris had a job with a mineral exploration company in Alaska, and I planned to work on a fishing boat again, so we drove north together. During the long drive, Chris told me that she wanted a more stable life: a home and children. I wasn't prepared for this commitment, so when we reached Anchorage we went out to dinner, made love, and broke our relationship for the third time.

I loaded the dogs in the truck and reviewed our conversation as I drove out of town. "I want to wander. You want a family. We don't think we can do both at the same time. I love you, you love me. See ya later, Bye."

Sometimes I understood the reasoning, but sometimes it didn't make sense.

I drove into Talkeetna and walked into a friend's house. I sat down, poured myself some coffee, broke off a chunk of cinnamon roll, and caught up on the news. I was among friends; everything was going to be okay. I sold my dogs and flew to Bristol Bay to fish.

After fishing season, Nathan, Noey, and Reeva flew north, and we all moved to Seldovia, a small town on the Alaskan coast south of Anchorage. Seldovia is cut off from the road system by several glaciers, so it is a virtual island. I bought a small speedboat and started a new textbook. The children and I explored the bay and hiked into the hills.

One day we decided to motor to Homer, a large town across the bay. My fuel pump failed, so we rowed into the harbor. The dealer told me that the new part would arrive in a week. We went to a restaurant, and the children chattered away. I didn't want to spend the money to fly to Seldovia and back by bush plane, I didn't want to row home, and I didn't want to hang out in Homer for a week. I wanted to forget this stupid hassle and go see Chris. We had fought,

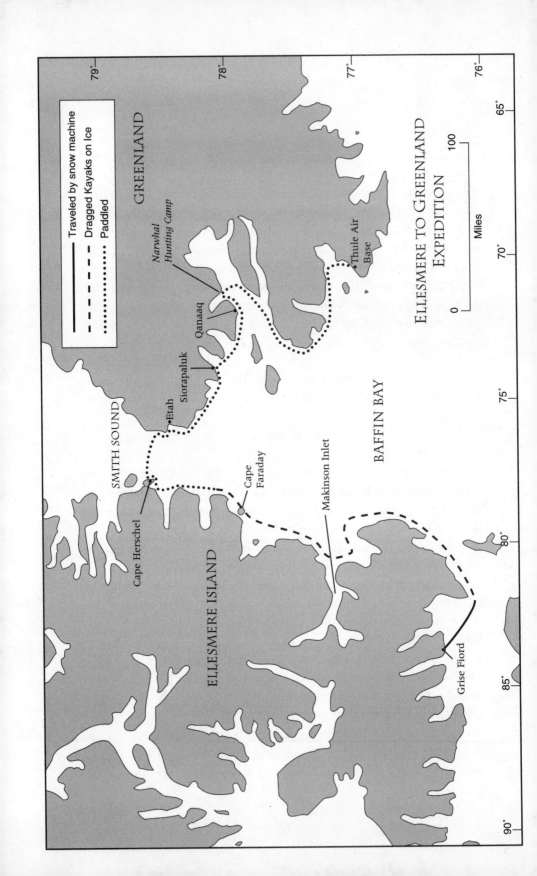

ELLESMERE TO GREENLAND
EXPEDITION

GREENLAND

*Narwhal
Hunting Camp*

Qanaaq

Siorapaluk

Etah

SMITH SOUND

Cape Herschel

ELLESMERE ISLAND

Cape
Faraday

Makinson Inlet

BAFFIN BAY

Grise Fiord

Thule Air
Base

Traveled by snow machine
Dragged Kayaks on Ice
Paddled

Miles
0   100

separated, loved, fought, and separated. Now I wanted to be with her again.

I decided to fly the children back to Seldovia on their own, fly into the interior by myself, find Chris, and ask her to marry me. Then I could return to Homer, install the new fuel pump, and run the boat back to Seldovia.

Chris was working at an isolated camp south of Galena. I could fly from Homer to Galena commercially but would have to hitchhike a ride to the camp. I evaluated my fellow passengers as we boarded the jet in Anchorage. The man with a chain saw as a carry-on looked like a trapper. I guessed that the man with cardboard boxes as luggage was born in Galena and was returning home. Women with children probably wouldn't be much help. But what about that clean-shaven man in spotless blue jeans and a white polo shirt? Midway through the flight I walked down the aisle and tapped him on the shoulder.

"Excuse me, do you work for Anaconda Minerals?"

He looked at me guardedly. "Yes, I'm camp manager, why?"

"I'm Chris Seashore's boyfriend, and I was wondering if I could hitch a ride out to camp with you."

"I didn't know Chris Seashore had a boyfriend."

"She doesn't either, but I'm it."

The man shrugged. "Sure, if there's room in the bush plane, you can come."

After the jet landed in Galena, we boarded a one-engine Cessna and flew south to a rough dirt strip. My benefactor pointed to a substantial plywood building and told me that someone over there would know where to find Chris.

I climbed the steps and entered a spacious room filled with maps, cores, and computers. Three people were hunched over keyboards or drafting tables, and two others were lounging on office chairs. A man told me that Chris was working at a remote site several miles from camp, and I could wait and make myself comfortable. Then one of the loungers announced casually, "I'll take you out there."

I had no idea what type of vehicle he drove, but the journey was becoming almost as much fun as the quest. We walked to a shiny jet ranger helicopter. He motioned me to the front passenger seat, and I climbed in. I fastened my seat belt and placed my headset and walkie-talkie over my ears. The pilot revved up the engine, lifted us a few feet off the ground, tested the chopper's response to the controls, and took off. His voice sounded far away through the headset.

"There'll be a few guys in camp who won't be too happy to see you."

I pushed the talk button. "That's their problem."

We crossed a few ridges and a swamp. He veered wide to avoid scaring a moose, then rose over a high hill.

"I'll put you down right here. Chris is working on a seismic line due north. When you step out of the ship, be sure to latch the door and exit forward. And, oh yeah, make lots of noise. All those gals working on the seismic line carry guns. No one is expecting you. It'd be a pisser if someone thought you were a bear and shot you."

"Thanks for the ride and the warning."

I stepped out, exited forward, and ducked to avoid the wind blast when he took off again. A faint trail led to the seismic line, which was a linear slash across the landscape. I saw no one, and for lack of a better direction, turned east. When I crested a low hill, I saw Chris crouched over some instruments.

I ignored the pilot's warning and walked down quietly. Chris finally looked up when I was a few feet away.

"Jon!"

She stood up and we hugged.

I whispered, "I'm tired of all this bullshit, Chrissy. Let's just get married. We'll work things out somehow."

She pressed against me, and I felt her head nod slowly against my chest. "Okay."

2

That fall, Nathan and Noey flew to California, and Chris, Reeva, and I drove south toward Montana. It was the fourth time I had driven the five-thousand-mile route between Montana and Alaska. The first time I had been alone, haunted and hassled; the second journey was with Dave and seventeen dogs, headed—unprepared—toward a dangerous expedition; the third journey was with Chris, discussing and preparing for our imminent separation. This time we were a family planning a future together.

My fishing season had been successful, and Chris had saved her summer wages, so together we had enough money for the down payment on a house. We talked about building a modern, energy-efficient structure, but Chris argued that we would probably start the project and run off on a series of expeditions, condemning ourselves to a life among piles of insulation and sheetrock. Reeva looked forward to buying any house and moving in, as long as she could paint her room pink.

The taiga flowed past. I suggested that we return to ski the high peaks of the Yukon some spring or summer. Chris seemed to glow, thinking of carving turns through the high cirques.

I had married Elizabeth in the fall of 1967, seventeen years before. Seventeen years in a whirlwind of wives and lovers, interspersed with time alone. Yet in one moment, sitting in the restaurant in Homer, contemplating the logistics of a broken fuel pump, I had decided to marry Chris. Now I felt truly committed.

Chris was sleeping in the seat beside me. Reeva was reading a book about horses. Gravel plinked against the underside of the truck. I chuckled to myself at all the confusions.

We drove to southwestern Montana and bought a two-bedroom house in the woods. I met a climber in Missoula named Gray Thompson, and he taught me expedition strategy. Gray knew how to rest and wait when conditions were unfavorable, and how to push hard when necessary. In the summer of 1987, we traveled to Auyuittuq Park on Baffin Island, backpacked heavy loads to the top of the pass, and then in thirty hours of continuous climbing completed the first ascent of a route on a granite wall on Mount Freya. As I lounged in the sunshine after our climb, I reminisced about the mixed frustration and elation I had felt in this same valley during the dogsled trip. Then I remembered my resolve as I sat behind the iceberg north of Cape Hooper and watched Dave's figure recede. I had unfinished business in the Arctic.

3

When Dave and I were seal hunting near Broughton Island, Moosa asked, "How come you guys travel so far from home? Are you like Qitdlaq?"

The others laughed but wouldn't explain the joke.

I asked friends in Broughton and then continued my inquiries in Iqaluit on my way home. Everyone knew portions of the Qitdlaq story, and I gradually pieced the chronicle together from fragments. Much later I researched it in libraries, but that was after I had camped in Qitdlaq's camps and stored my kayaks on the stone pillars he and his people had built.*

Qitdlaq was born in about 1800 near Cumberland Sound, on the southeast coast of Baffin Island. He became a powerful shaman, an *angakkuq*, who was feared and obeyed by his people. Sometime between 1830 and 1835, while hunting caribou, Qitdlaq crushed a companion's skull with a rock. There is no known motive for the crime. None of the other hunters discussed the murder after they returned to camp, but another *angakkuq* saw it in a dream and ordered several sled dogs to attack Qitdlaq.

Qitdlaq escaped and migrated north with a small group of loyal followers. They settled briefly near Pond Inlet, but fought with a local tribe, lost the battle, and fled again, this time south, down the west coast of Baffin Island.

By 1853 Qitdlaq had moved north of Baffin to Devon Island, where he met British naval commander Edward Inglefield. The two leaders met in the ship's chart room, and Qitdlaq asked about land even farther north. Inglefield spread out a map of Ellesmere Island

---

*Although written accounts are similar, no two are identical. For consistency, I have relied mainly on a single source. My only deviation from this source is to call the hero Qitdlaq, not Qillaq, to agree with other chronicles and with numerous oral accounts I heard in Greenland. My source is *Qitdlarssuaq: The Story of a Polar Migration*, by Guy Mary-Rousseliere, trans. Alan Cooke (Winnipeg, Man.: Wuerz Publishing, 1991).

and western Greenland and explained that Ellesmere was uninhabited but Inuit lived along the Greenland coast. Qitdlaq saw that if he followed the east coast of Ellesmere far enough north, he could cross easily to Greenland.

Qitdlaq's group remained on Devon Island for five years. Generally, the people were prosperous, although Qitdlaq's enemies sent evil spirits to harass them. On one occasion, as the small band traveled across the ice, Qitdlaq saw a long-haired giant on the shore. He cried out, "You, Giant, you are nothing but baleen." Qitdlaq's magic was stronger than that of his enemies, and the giant disappeared. When the Inuit investigated, they found only a whale's jawbone with some baleen attached.

Hounded by invisible *angakkuqs* and restless at heart, Qitdlaq took frequent spirit journeys to the North and returned to tell his people of rich hunting, green grasses, and friendly hunters. Finally, the entire band of forty men, women, and children set out for Greenland, directed only by Qitdlaq's visions and a five-year-old memory of a map in Inglefield's chart room. They probably left in the early spring of 1859, when the sun was returning but the ice was still firm.

They carried all their belongings on ten *komatiks*: furs for winter, tents for summer, and kayaks for hunting in open water. The largest *komatik* was pulled by twenty dogs, an admirable feat of dog handling. The tribe stopped for the summer when the ice broke up in July. Some of the hunters explored inland to hunt caribou while others harpooned seals, narwhals, and walrus from their kayaks. They built stone igloos* and insulated them with sod for a winter camp. During the long dark time, they lived by the light and heat of their blubber lamps. During the full moon, hunters waited patiently by *aglus* to harpoon seals. They set out again in the spring.

Qitdlaq's group reached Smith Sound the following year and gazed across the channel toward Greenland. A warm-water upwelling maintains a permanent open water oasis, called a *polynya*, in Smith Sound. The travelers swung their dog teams north to good ice and crossed to

---

*An igloo is any domed winter home. Permanent igloos were built of stone and moss and covered with hides. Temporary structures on ice were constructed of hardened snow. House-building technology and terminology varied across the Arctic.

the new land. They found abundant caribou on the shore and hunted walrus, narwhals, and beluga whales in the sound. Millions of birds swarmed the cliffs, and the hunters caught them in nets and gathered eggs. They also found many stone houses, but all were vacant.

The following spring Qitdlaq led his band south until they met people. At that time, the polar Inuit of northwest Greenland were perhaps the most isolated inhabitants on earth. They were separated from central Greenland by perennially bad ice in Melville Bay and from Baffin Island by the arduous passage that Qitdlaq and his party had just completed. Before these polar Inuit were "discovered" by John Ross in 1818, they had made no contact with any other people for two hundred to three hundred years.

The polar Inuit had lost three important technologies that were familiar throughout the rest of the Inuit world: the bow, the kayak, and the *kakivak* (pronged fish harpoon). Without the bow they were unable to hunt caribou. Not only is caribou an important source of meat, but its fur has the highest insulation-to-weight ratio of any hide. Therefore, the northwest Greenlanders didn't have warm, durable winter clothes. Without the kayak they couldn't hunt sea mammals in summer and often entered winter with empty larders. Arctic char run in many rivers and the lakes abound in fish, but without *kakivaks*, the polar Inuit couldn't catch them.

These people retained the words for the lost technologies and retained the concepts in their legends. Therefore, anthropologists are uncertain why or how they forgot techniques so vital to survival. One theory is that wood was so scarce in northwest Greenland that the tools were lost when the resource became depleted. But *kakivaks* can be made of bone, bows are fashioned from caribou antler in other parts of the Arctic, and numerous shipwrecks supplied ample wood by the mid-1800s. According to a second theory, the sudden death of one or two key toolmakers in such a small population could lead to loss of the technique throughout the whole tribe. Several anthropologists have suggested that the kayak may have been lost after several icy or windy years proved it impractical. Perhaps no one built a kayak for a generation, and then, suddenly, no one remembered how.

Although this explanation might suffice for the loss of the kayak, I find it hard to believe that of a population of one hundred, no one could fashion a bow from memory, even if the best bowmakers had died.

Inuit life is ruled by complex religious taboos that vary from region to region. I wondered whether taboos caused the loss of hunting technologies. I wrote of my theory to Dr. Peter Schledermann, an expert from the Arctic Institute of North America. He responded, "I think most of these people were pragmatic enough to drop a taboo or two if it came to a point of starvation." Schledermann concluded, "The loss of these technologies remains a puzzle . . . probably the interaction of a number of circumstances was at play."

Without efficient hunting tools, the polar Inuit were impoverished. In winter and spring they hunted seal through *aglus*. Occasionally a narwhal, beluga, or walrus swam close enough to the floe edge to be harpooned without a boat. In summer millions of small birds called dovekies migrate to northwest Greenland. They swarm in huge flocks and fly seemingly endless circles around their nests on rocky outcrops. The Inuit hid in crevices in the cliffs and scooped the birds out of the air with long-handled nets. A good hunter could catch five hundred in a day, although even five hundred dovekies don't provide nearly as much food as a caribou or a narwhal. The Inuit also gathered eggs from dovekies, ducks, and seagulls.

Owing to limited technology and the harshness of the land, famine was common among the polar Inuit. In 1855 Arctic explorer Elisha Kane estimated that the total population in northwest Greenland was one hundred forty. In 1861, a few years before Qitdlaq arrived, the population had declined to one hundred.

Qitdlaq and his followers taught the Greenlanders more efficient hunting techniques. The population increased and the migrants may have saved the polar Inuit from extinction. (By 1988, the population had increased to six hundred fifty.)

Qitdlaq became great friends with a fellow angakkuq named Avatannguaq until the two argued and Qitdlaq moved his band to an adjacent fiord. Tragically, Avatannguaq chased the newcomers with evil spells. The next winter, three large falcons attacked Qitdlaq. As they approached, he saw that their claws were stained with human blood. Because falcons never appeared during the dark season, Qitdlaq knew that they were spirits sent by his enemy. He lay down on the ice and turned himself into a seal. When the falcons flew away, Qitdlaq turned himself back into a man and escaped to camp.

Qitdlaq had been on the run for most of his life. He had traveled far and found peace in the new land, but he could not absorb Avatannguaq's attacks passively. Reluctantly, Qitdlaq decided to kill his rival, even though the act would lead to exile from Greenland. As he sharpened his knife at the next spring rendezvous, he cried out, "I am sharpening it in the usual way, but this knife will strike the husband of a wife who has no other family. No! I cannot do such a thing!" He argued with himself, then sealed his fate by committing murder once again.

Soon afterward, Qitdlaq decided to escape back to Baffin Island. A few people elected to stay in their new home, but most of the migrants crossed Smith Sound again. Later that spring, Qitdlaq became sick and died. The party continued south.

4

Qitdlaq was a murderer, a shaman, a leader, and an outcast, but I thought of him mainly as a compulsive wanderer. That day on the ice, watching Dave's fur-clad figure retreat into the whiteness, I realized that if I shared Qitdlaq's wanderlust, perhaps I should share the same ice, the same coastline, and, yes, some of the same hardships.

I could have reached a different conclusion. Even though I still couldn't undertstand why, Dave and I had retreated, ignominiously, from the dogsled expedition on a beautiful winter day when the wind was still, the sun shone, and we had enough food to reach the next settlement. But the failure had started much earlier. I began the expedition without adequate preparation: I wasn't a good dog handler; my dogs were trained for the forest, not the sea ice; I traveled with a partner whom I didn't like or trust. The Cape Horn and Northwest Passage expeditions also had suffered from poor strategy and execution. A rational person would rethink a lifestyle that had foundered so dramatically and so repeatedly.

But logic conflicted with my dreams. Maybe I was more content on my expeditions than I admitted to myself. Surely I was wily enough to succeed and strong enough to stop whining, even to myself. Could I simply cut through all the bullshit, as I had when I decided to marry Chris? Could it be that easy? And that rewarding?

I decided to follow Qitdlaq across the ice.

Qitdlaq committed his first murder near Pangnirtung and wandered for a few decades before he reached Greenland. I couldn't travel that far in one season and had learned from past mistakes that it is too frustrating to set an unachievable goal. Therefore, I planned to fly to Grise Fiord on the southern coast of Ellesmere Island and follow Qitdlaq's migration along the east coast of Ellesmere and across Smith Sound to Greenland. Greenland is uninhabited in the vicinity of Smith Sound, so I needed to swing south toward civilization. It is about three hundred seventy-five miles between Grise Fiord and Siorapaluk, the first Greenland village. The nearest airport is one hundred seventy-five miles farther, at the U.S. Air Force base in Thule.

All my previous journeys had taken me through remote lands, but the routes had intersected villages and military posts. There were no settlements along the east coast of Ellesmere. The crux of this expedition was that the most difficult passage, the twenty-three-mile crossing to Greenland, was situated late in the journey. If Smith Sound were ice-choked and impassable, I probably wouldn't have enough food to return to Grise Fiord. Failure wasn't an option.

I reasoned that I had accumulated enough Arctic experience to plan and execute an expedition competently. I hoped that I had learned to cope emotionally. Of course, doubts hovered. I recalled a phrase from Stefansson:

> I fancy there are few men so sure of a theory that they are free from a bit of nervousness when they come to stake their lives on its holding good.*

But I was too excited to change my mind.

Chris said that she'd like to join me. I was half surprised and half expecting that she would come. In Chris's words:

*Stefansson, My Life with the Eskimo, p. 164.

*When Jon decided to row the Northwest Passage in 1982, he was sur-
prised that I wanted to join him. Six years after our first expedition, I
longed for magical, high-latitude lighting, the vastness of the Arctic
landscape, and the self-imposed time warp created by a long journey.
Jon accepted me as an equal partner now and trusted my skill and judgment. In addition I understood Jon a little better.*

On an average year, the ice doesn't break up in Grise Fiord until
mid-August. If we waited till then, we wouldn't have enough time to
complete the journey before winter. So we planned to leave early and
drag the boats over the ice. A similar strategy had failed on the
Northwest Passage trip, but this time we had two factors in our favor.
First, several *polynyas* lie along the east coast of Ellesmere. The
polynyas guaranteed that we would have ice-free regions to relieve the
drudgery of dragging. Second, during the 1980s, light, durable plastic
sea kayaks had become popular. We thought that these boats would
slide over the ice more easily than the cumbersome wherry.

We bought two seventeen-foot-long plastic sea kayaks, about the
length of the folding kayak I took on the Cape Horn trip. Although
the length was the same, a plastic boat is more streamlined and faster.
In addition, the hard plastic is incredibly resistant to abrasion,
whereas the flexible rubberized skin of a folding kayak will tear on
sharp rocks or wear through if dragged long distances on the ice.
Folding kayaks are open in the middle, almost like canoes, and covered with a large cloth spray deck. In contrast, plastic kayaks contain
watertight compartments fore and aft and a small central cockpit. A
neoprene spray skirt fits around your torso and wraps over the cockpit
to provide a watertight seal. If you capsize, you can roll back over
with a quick sweep of your paddle. If I had been in a plastic kayak
during my disaster at Cape Horn, I wouldn't have flopped out of the
cockpit like a rag doll. Our plastic kayaks had rudders controlled by
foot pedals to maintain a straight course in waves or currents.

We flew to Grise Fiord on June 22, one day after the solstice. The
plane landed on the dirt strip with a clatter of gravel. A few pickup
trucks gathered to collect cargo. Most of the other passengers were met
by relatives on three-wheeled all-terrain vehicles. The motorcycle-
sized engines popped and clattered on the runway and carried their
passengers off with a receding roar.

Small towns in New England nestle into the foliage as if they grew there along with the rocks and trees, but there was no foliage to bond Grise Fiord to the landscape. Several dozen brightly colored square houses and a few large metal buildings rose incongruously from the gravel beach and the scattered tundra flowers. We landed late in the afternoon, as the sun finished its flight from east to west and veered north to scribe a flattened circle above the village. Grise Fiord lies at about 77° north latitude. Thus our starting point was four hundred miles farther north than any point on the Northwest Passage trip. We wouldn't see sunset until we returned home. We hitched a ride to town and carried our kayaks down to the beach. I walked out on the white, frozen bay, kicked at the surface, and exposed solid ice hidden beneath a few inches of slushy snow. Light distorted through the translucent crystal as if it were passing through both lenses of a telescope at once, so the ice looked simultaneously wafer thin and thicker than the earth. When I jumped on it, it felt like solid ground.

Chris spoke softly, almost as if to herself. "Let's paddle to Greenland."

A local hunter assured us that a *polynya* existed to the east and that the floe edge, the boundary between ice and water, was only twenty-five miles away. He pointed to a rocky bluff rendered indistinct by a mirage and announced, "There—water."

We loaded the boats with enough food, fuel, and clothing to last eight weeks. Most of our bulk and weight were carbohydrates: rice, bulgur wheat, and couscous, but we also packed nuts, soup mixes, sugar, and milk. We stuffed in extra warm clothes, a stove and fuel, a few books, and a tent. The waterproof compartments weren't roomy enough to hold everything, so we crammed gear into the cockpits until we could hardly squeeze into the remaining space. Then we loaded more camping gear in waterproof bags, which we lashed on the back deck. I protected my rifle in a waterproof case and lashed it on the front deck where I could reach it quickly if a polar bear attacked.

An older man named Pijimini joined us over coffee in the RCMP office. I outlined our route on the large wall map. Pijimini nodded and walked to the wall hesitatingly, like a schoolboy trying to remember his assignment. He drew a precise line with his finger outward from the bluff beyond Grise Fiord and said, "Ice to here." Then he swept his palm across thousands of square miles of the Arctic Ocean. "Here—ice maybe, water maybe."

He asked to see our kayaks, and we walked to the shore. He carefully inspected the boats, hit the plastic with his fist, sat in the cockpit, and stretched our neoprene spray skirts. Then he led us to a traditional Inuit kayak. The outer skin had been removed, leaving only a skeleton of carefully shaped stems and ribs, tied together with waxed string. Pijimini had carved a flat-bladed paddle from a single board. The paddle was heavier than our paddles but well balanced. Between the handle and the blade, he had cut a delicate curve that looked like an upside-down wave. Pijimini ran his finger along the curve.

"Know what for?" he asked.

"Yes, water from the paddle blade drips off the point and doesn't run onto your hand and up your sleeve."

Pijimini beamed and pointed at me. "Understand him." Then he pointed back and forth at himself and me, saying, "Same, same, kayak-men." He ignored Chris, who stood by silently.

Pijimini assured us we would encounter polar bears, but he shrugged when we asked how dangerous they were.

"Sometimes, maybe yes, sometimes, maybe no."

However, he warned us about walrus. Walrus stalk kayakers, rip their boats apart, and then suck the person's intestines out. They don't eat the rest. I smiled as if Pijimini had told a joke, but he stared unwaveringly to convince me with his gaze.

The RCMP officer admonished, "There is no word for lying in the Inuit language. If he warned you about walrus, believe him."

5

Pijimini insisted on driving us to the open water by snowmachine. After an hour's ride, we reached the floe edge, lifted the kayaks off the *komatik*, and set them on the ice. I thanked Pijimini. He looked across the water and said simply, "Long way to Greenland."

He pulled the cord on his snowmachine, sat on the seat while it idled, and offered one last piece of advice: "You kayak man, you know. Windy, windy—no paddling—stay in tent, drink tea." Then he smiled and drove away.

The sound of his machine drifted off. Southward, across the ice, half a dozen glaciers fell from Devon Island into the frozen sea. Northward, toward Greenland, the gray-green ocean lapped against the ice. We pulled on our spray skirts, lowered into the cockpits, and slid, like alligators, into the water.

The boat felt overloaded and top-heavy. I took a few strokes and stopped. Chris pulled alongside. After all the preparations, the driving, the flights, and the visiting in Grise Fiord, we were alone. Twenty yards of the journey were behind us, with five hundred fifty miles to go.

I had forgotten the feeling of traveling across the Arctic. Normal descriptions of beauty don't work, because the landscape is monotonous, not beautiful; it isn't a picture, but a sensation. In the forest, a person retains scale. You are bigger than a mushroom and smaller than a tree. But in the Arctic you may feel bigger than a glacier yet smaller than a seagull flying overhead. Once you lose scale, you lose the concept of strength or weakness. At one moment I felt that the empty space could crush me. A moment later I took a spirit journey to Smith Sound. The ice was clear. Chris and I were strong, a team now. We wouldn't need the rescue that might be impossible. I followed Qitdlaq as he descended through an *aglu*, and we danced with the walrus at the bottom of the sea.

"You okay, Chrissy?"

"I think so. I'm nervous."

"Take a moment and feel the boat."

A person balances a kayak with thighs and knees rather than with shoulders and paddle, and thus a kayak becomes an extension of the body, more like a ski than a rowboat. I pressed my thighs against the underside of the deck and gently rocked the kayak to feel the balance point and edge. Then I held my paddle in the air, reached behind, and pressed it against the back of my neck to stretch.

Chris followed a similar routine and nodded. "Let's paddle across this bay and make camp early. It's too much to take in all at once."

I had wanted to push further the first day, but I was also glad to stop. The final planning of the expedition was hectic and confusing: arranging gear and escaping from publishers and their irritating last-minute details. Now I had to shift my mental attitude, become calm and alert, pick pleasure and danger out of a long, slow-moving day.

We crossed the bay in an hour, but ice had collected in the intertidal zone to form a six-foot-high cliff, called an *ice foot*. We paddled to within a few feet of the beach but couldn't land. The tide was low, so we paddled for an additional few hours until the rising tide lifted us over the ice. We pitched the tent, went for a walk, and cooked dinner. Pijimini had given us some caribou and seal, and we made a rich, fatty stew.

We crawled into our sleeping bags at ten o'clock in the evening, our normal bedtime. I looked up at the tent ceiling and stared at seal-blubber stains from the dogsled trip. We heard shots as Inuit from Grise Fiord hunted ducks and seal. Living in a land with continuous sunlight for three and a half months and continuous darkness for an equal amount of time, they had little regard for clocks or schedules. But during our Northwest Passage trip we had functioned most efficiently on a conventional nine-to-five work schedule. Chris cuddled against me, and I thought about the tremendous difference between her warmth and the aloofness that had separated Dave and me. It wasn't just the body contact, but the feeling that we would work together. The sharp crack of the seal hunter's rifle and the dull thud of a shotgun were the last sounds of humans as we drifted off to sleep.

6

The next day, an onshore wind stacked ice against the beach and threw a cold spray into the air. I argued that if we battled through the bad ice and paddled around the point, we would be protected and could paddle ten or twenty miles for the day. Chris didn't want to take chances so early in the trip and suggested that we wait until conditions improved. I reflected on my shipwreck in Chile and on all of our arguments on the Northwest Passage trip. Chris and I could pull against each other or work together, but the land would define this expedition. I had struggled—and failed—on the past three expeditions. Maybe this time we would move faster by waiting.

We went for a walk and talked about all the unfinished business we had left back home in the Montana forest. We should have painted the deck, finished the instructor's manual for my most recent book, recharged the battery on the old pickup. But we hadn't done any of those things. Now none of that mattered. A flock of black and white diving ducks, called *guillemots*, took off with a winged whir.

The wind dropped by early afternoon, so we broke camp and launched. After a few hours, the wind intensified and veered until it blew directly offshore. We decided to pull in, but the tide was low again and the ice foot blocked us. The wind picked up, and I thought that in an emergency I could stand in the cockpit, grab the top of the ice foot, and pull myself over. But even if I succeeded, I couldn't lift the loaded boats. Consequently, we elected to stay close to the shore, using the ice as a wind shield, and to continue until either the tide rose again or we found an opening. For the next half hour the wind slowly increased, and our worry level rose with it.

In most environments, wind shakes the vegetation or forms ripples on the water, so you can watch it approach. But here the cold air dropped invisibly off the bare mountainside. Rocks don't sway, and we were so close to shore that the water surface gave no indication of air movement. One moment, the wind freshened against my face, and a few seconds later it hit with a blast, jerking one end of my paddle over my head and forcing the other end into the water, under the kayak. The boat sideslipped and ran over the down-dipped blade. Caught between the wind and the paddle shaft, the kayak tipped dangerously, burying the leeward edge. I steadied the boat with a snap of my hips, freed the paddle, and then held the blade low to brace against the water. I glanced across and saw that Chris had also survived the unexpected onslaught, but the storm washed both of us out to sea. The wind lifted the tops off the waves and blew the water horizontally across the surface. Water rolled over the deck and buried us to our armpits.

As I drifted out to sea, I thought my luck might have run out, and I imagined floating alone in a stormy ocean with only a lingering memory of a second boat drifting out of sight. Fear closed off any sense of tragedy. I viewed the image abstractly because I didn't seem to be involved.

When we were a quarter mile from shore, the wind subsided enough so that I could lift my paddle without being blown over. I turned the boat toward shore and paddled a few feet before another gust drove me backward again. Then the wind slacked off again and I battled forward. Chris had been close by but now fell behind. I was afraid to turn my head because the motion might alter my balance, so I screamed into the wind, "Chris, where are you?"

I heard a faint reply. "Jon, I'm losing ground! I'm being blown out to sea!"

I turned my boat around and yelled, "I'll get a line on you!" Another gust caught me broadside and swept me out of control. Bracing into the waves to avoid capsizing, I washed past her. I couldn't take one hand off my paddle to throw her a line, and anyway, she couldn't catch it and tie it to her bow.

We were only a few yards apart, but the water in the air softened her face and made her seem ghostlike and untouchable. A wisp of hair was plastered against one cheek and sheets of water streaked off her forehead and chin. Even though I was moving and she was nearly stationary, it seemed like she was falling past me. In my imagination, I reached out and touched her parka but couldn't grasp it. Then the wind swirled me ninety degrees and I lost sight of her.

By the time I regained control and swung my bow back into the wind, I was fifty yards farther out to sea. I watched Chris's back and arms as she strained for shore. We both made progress. I pulled close to her again.

"I think the tide is coming up, and I see a break in the ice cliff inside that bay! Can you make it?"

"Maybe!"

The wind howled in the space between us. We were both paddling hard, but I didn't know whether we were moving forward or sliding backward.

"*Maybe* isn't good enough!"

"Okay!"

I forged ahead and again lost sight of her. The windblown spray felt like hailstones against my face. My muscles were near failure, but I felt I would make it. Then I thought about Chris, behind me. Had she lost the will and was she, right now, blowing out to sea? Should I look? I could swing back to try and help her again, but we would both tip over if I tried to tie a line on her bow. Should I turn back to cheer her on and assure myself that I wasn't abandoning her? No, I had to save myself. But she was my wife; I loved her. However, I had the ELT (emergency locator transmitter) and could direct rescue from shore. No, maybe we'd be safer if we rafted off to sea together and transmitted our position precisely from the middle of Baffin Bay. I should turn back and share her fate, whatever it might be. No, this was all foolishness; she persevered through the storm on the Northwest Passage and she'd be right behind me.

A stream had melted a crevasse in the ice just large enough for a kayak. I reached it, jumped out, pulled my boat in, and turned toward the sea. Chris was only a few yards away, and I shouted and waved my arms. A gust pushed her back; then it slacked off and she advanced. Another gust hit. I ran into the water, grabbed her bow, and yanked her onto the shore. She sat in her boat for a moment and didn't move; then I helped her out.

We crouched in still air behind a rock. Chris and I had been lovers for eight years, married for four. We had been through all those painful separations and joyous reconciliations. Now she was close, not drifting behind me in a chaotic sea.

We feared that the wind would rip our tent apart, so we collected rocks to build a wind break. I worked with the same frantic energy that had propelled me to shore but then realized that we didn't need to hurry. Even though I was wet from my lunge into the sea to grab Chris's boat, I wasn't hypothermic.

"Look here, Chris!" I shouted into the wind. "When I lift a rock I don't disturb a single worm, ant, beetle, snake, or lizard. There is nothing out here, not even bugs. We're alone." She came over and brushed against me as she bent down. The faraway feeling in the kayaks receded into memory.

Several curious piles of rocks were scattered about the small coastal plain. I lifted a rock off one pile, but Chris touched my arm and motioned me to replace it. The pile was too orderly to be natural.

We stepped back, looked, and realized that it was an ancient fox trap. We explored further and found numerous tent rings, stone igloos, fox traps, and food caches. We had stopped in one of Qitdlaq's camps.

I tried to forget the screaming wind, the nearly lifeless land-scape bounded by glaciers on land and ice at sea, and instead imag-ined a small tribe, isolated from the rest of the world. I saw hunters going out every day, teenagers falling in love, young mothers with little babies. Thinking about the long journey ahead, I felt heart-ened to realize how much strength is genetically engineered into all of us.

7

The wind continued all night but calmed by the following morning. Although the storm made us wary, we climbed back in the boats and headed north. After a few hours of paddling, we reached the end of the *polynya*. Ice extended outward from shore, toward the horizon. I pretended I didn't see it and paddled steadily until my bow crunched into the solid barrier.

Chris drifted alongside. "Well, Pijimini said, 'Maybe ice, maybe water.' This looks like maybe ice to me."

I nodded. "Now we get to test the theory. Will these boats slide better than the wherry did?"

Apprehensively, we wiggled out of the cockpits and stepped onto the ice. I tied a long nylon strap through the bow loop and dragged the kayak onto the ice. Then I slipped the strap around my waist and headed north. The kayak slid along reasonably well but slower than paddling speed. I was frustrated because the ice impeded our progress; Chris was relieved because the ice was safe. She wrote in her journal:

The gale winds on the second day out really shook my confidence. Although I am an experienced river kayaker, I am a novice when it comes to the ocean. This was really the crash course in ocean kayaking and the second day's lesson was about enough to make me want to drop the class. Therefore, it was a relief to pull our boats up on the ice and walk along safely. This was a good way for me to start to feel comfortable in this environment and to trust myself.

Although sea ice is nearly flat, it has subtle dips and ridges. The high points were covered with consolidated snow, while the low points were submerged under a few inches to a few feet of water. We wore hip boots and purposefully waded through the pools because the boats floated or nearly floated and thus pulled easily.

The water on the ice was light blue, with a faint hint of turquoise, like a pristine lagoon in a tropical ocean. When I lifted my gaze, I saw mostly dark blue sky with a thin line of blue ice beneath. Chris appeared to be walking across the sky toward a void at the end of the earth. When I lowered my gaze, the sky disappeared. With no horizon—no beginning or end—Chris seemed to be a single living organism on the surface of an infinite frozen plane. A breeze lifted mist off the water and swirled it into a fluffy whiteness around her boots. The cloud-colored mist created an image of Chris walking across an icy Inuit heaven.

A lone gull soared in air currents rising off the warm beach. More gulls perched on distant cliffs, sitting on nests to incubate their eggs. Two guillemots swam in an open lead and sporadically dipped their bills to feed. A seal basked on the ice in the distance. We dragged the boats to the edge of a lead and stopped for a rest and snack. I looked into the water and saw a few tiny zooplankton swimming by convulsive contractions.

One had to wonder how any large animals lived in this environment. Over ninety-nine percent of the ocean was covered with ice, and the land was mostly barren. The previous evening, Chris and I played a game in which I closed my eyes and walked randomly. On average, my foot touched no vegetation for seven out of every eight steps. By measuring the area of each plant and the area of my shoe, I estimated that about one percent of the land surface was covered with vegetation. Yet it was undeniable that the phytoplankton in the leads and the vegetation on land supported the animals around us. Guillemots and seals were abundant, and we saw musk ox and caribou tracks on some of the beaches.

The Arctic not only supports relatively few organisms; it also supports relatively few species. Ecologists found 26 species of birds in twenty-five hundred square kilometers in the Arctic, 135 species in an equivalent area in temperate regions, and 600 species in a tropical rain forest. One obvious explanation is that fewer species evolved in the Arctic because it is so harsh. However, humans evolved in the tropics, and therefore we define harshness in relation to our own genetic background. To a polar bear, the Amazon is harsh. Another argument is that so few species live in the Arctic because it is a young ecosystem, only recently released from the Pleistocene glaciers, and speciation hasn't had time to occur. No one knows the answer. The result is that if the beauty of the rain forest is the sound of a fully orchestrated symphony, the beauty of the Arctic is like a lone oboe.

8

Early in the afternoon of the fourth day we approached a lush, vegetated plain that stood out sharply against the rocky coast. Chris suggested that we camp early, while predictably I voted to continue. I argued that we carried food for fifty-five days and had five hundred fifty miles to travel, so we needed to average ten miles a day. So far, we had covered twenty-four miles in four days and were behind schedule. I emphasized that on this journey, ambition and drive were not the only motivating factors. We couldn't resupply or retreat between Grise Fiord and Siorapaluk. We could turn back now, or even next week, but eventually we would reach a halfway point where retreat would be just as difficult as success.

"Let's push on a bit further and camp around that point."

Chris shook her head. "Look at the topographic lines on the map; land falls steeply into the sea around that point. It might be an inhospitable rocky beach. I understand the logistics, Jon, but we're in the Arctic. When you're traveling across the desert, you camp at the water holes; when you're in the Arctic, you relax and build strength when you can, then push hard when you have to."

My arithmetic was irrefutable, but so was Chris's logic. We needed to wait at times and to push hard at others. We couldn't afford a disaster. We clashed over such issues on the Northwest Passage expedition, but we had learned to trust each other.

I nodded. "Okay."

We set camp and went for a walk. A few hundred yards across the meadow we found the ruins of eight stone igloos. Each one was dome-shaped, with a six-foot tunnel entrance, like a turtle with an outstretched neck. The interiors were about ten feet in diameter. Two whale pelvic bones arched over the largest one to support the now nonexistent caribou hide roof.

Probably Qitdlaq's party had built the igloos. Chris was right. This was an oasis, and travelers stopped here. I had tried to adopt Inuit technology; now I had to adopt their attitude.

I imagined paddling out in a wood and sealskin kayak carrying a stick with a piece of sharpened narwhal tusk tied to the end. I felt the excitement and fear as I approached a whale, the frenzy of the injured giant, the comradeship of my friends as they swarmed in for the kill, and the feast afterward. Finally, I saw myself lying in the stone house throughout the long winter night, looking up at the whalebone roof in the flickering light of a blubber lamp.

9

Two days later a steady rain melded blues and whites into a universal gray. Chris and I pulled our boats along without speaking, lost in our hooded raincoats. I watched my feet move monotonously and forgot to look at the ice ahead until I almost reached a lead. Most leads form when the ice cracks, not when it melts, so the ice remains thick right to the edge. However, the lead in front of me formed where a river melted a ribbon of ice. As a result, the floe edge was dangerously thin. I took a step back, but the ice fractured and I bobbed into the buoyant saltwater. I breast-stroked through the water and slithered onto the good ice. Chris ran up and unpacked dry clothes while I stripped down in the icy rain. Then I dressed and we continued on.

The sun came the following day. I spread my wet clothes across the boat and walked back into the heavenly world of whites and ice blues. A nearby glacier had spit numerous icebergs into the ocean, and they had frozen into the sea ice. I watched the bergs line up and fall out of line as telephone poles appear to change position when you drive by in a car. But the bergs were ghostlike and reminded me more of drifting clouds than of telephone poles. Then one appeared to move in the opposite direction from its neighbors, and much faster.

I thought, "Have I lost my sense of scale? Is the berg much closer than I imagine? Or is it something else, like . . . a polar bear!"

I called out, "Chris, there's a bear out there! No two! No three!"

I unfastened the buckles on my rifle scabbard, but the bears were a few hundred yards away, so I left the gun sheathed and pulled the binoculars out instead. The largest bear rose on its hind legs and let its front paws dangle on its chest, like a rag doll with floppy, sewn-through armpits. After staring and smelling, it dropped onto all fours, shuffled behind a berg, reappeared on the other side, and stood up again to watch us.

I knew that I should feel frightened, but the scene before me was playful and friendly. Through the binoculars, the bears looked like mimes pretending to stare curiously, then ducking with fear and reemerging self-assured. I handed the binoculars to Chris and watched the bears slowly shuffle off until their whiteness merged with the larger whiteness of the landscape.

On July 2 we came to a region where the ice was fractured into a maze of alternating pans and open water leads. Many of the pans were hundreds of yards to half a mile across, while others were house- or room-sized. In some places the pans were jammed tightly together, and we could step or jump from one to another and then pull the boats across.

Frequently, I'd look at a gap and reason, "An Olympic broad jumper could easily make the leap. I could probably do it in shorts and running shoes. Maybe I could even do it in cumbersome clothes and hip boots, but it's real miserable to fall in."

Then we would bridge the gap with a kayak, and one person would walk across the kayak deck while the other balanced the tippy boat. If the lead was wider than a kayak length, we paddled across. Sometimes we paddled a few hundred yards along a lead before it dead-ended or hooked out toward sea. In order to travel efficiently, we needed to climb in and out of the kayaks quickly. Chris thought that we were wasting too much time removing our boots, slipping into the cockpit, arranging the rudder pedals, and attaching the spray skirt—just to cross a twenty-five-yard lead. Experimentally, she sat in the cockpit with her body folded into a V, her legs dangling over the deck, and her spray skirt unattached.

She swung her boat around to face me. "It's goofy paddling, but it works. Try it."

I sat down as directed and pushed off into the water, but I felt off balance with my butt below my feet and my legs splayed out across the deck. I crossed the lead tentatively, pulled broadside to the ice, and stabilized the boat with my paddle. Then I tried to throw my weight over my feet to stand up on the ice again, but the boat floated back into the middle of the lead and I almost fell in.

Chris laughed, and I snapped, "You try it."

She surveyed the situation, yelled "ramming speed!" and paddled directly toward a small depression in the ice. Even though the ice was five to six feet thick, it rose only half a foot above the water, and in places the edge had melted to form a gently sloping ramp. Chris hit the ice with enough force that her boat slid halfway out of the water. Then she casually stood up, straddling her kayak.

"Why are you trying to do it the hard way?" she asked.

It was a hot day, and Chris wore red- and blue-striped long underwear with a green tank top and a brimmed hat. I laughed and told her she looked silly.

She ignored my comment, knelt at the edge of the lead, grabbed my bow, warned "hold on," and pulled me out of the water.

After that success, we became creative in developing techniques for moving in the collage of ice and water. In places where the ice was thin, we practiced the "duck walk," waddling along with the kayak between our legs. If the ice fractured, we fell into the kayak cockpit rather than the ocean. If a narrow isthmus of ice separated two open leads, we paddled onto the ice at "ramming speed," remained in the boats, and pushed across the bridge with our hands, like paraplegic beggars in New Delhi on their low-lying carts.

As the day progressed, we invented amusing solutions to each obstacle and cheered one another when one of us discovered some new, clever trick, even if it didn't advance our journey very much. Flocks of guillemots circled, using their small red feet as air rudders to bank sharply above our heads. In places, small pans had been forced over one another, forming layers like bedded sandstone in the Utah desert. Along the shore, a tidewater glacier formed an ice cliff reminiscent of a canyon wall. Black streaks of sediment cut across the ice like basalt dikes in the lower Grand Canyon of the Colorado.

We found a sandy beach, pulled to shore early, and hiked up a hill to a sheltered notch in the rocks. Birds had nested here, and lush grasses grew in the guano-fertilized soil. We saw open water to the north. The trip had started with apprehension followed by a close call with the storm. But we had just spent the day playing on a half-frozen ocean, and with an ice-free sea ahead, we would start to move faster.

10

The next day thin clouds diffused the sunlight into a soft gray, highlighted by orange streaks, and we launched into a calm sea. Paddling is rhythmic, relaxed, quiet, and fast compared to dragging, and our boats created soft ripples that advanced until they met the reflections of scattered icebergs. We fantasized that open water would last all the way to Greenland.

By afternoon a white gossamered line cut across the horizon. As we approached, it grew into another few thousand cubic miles of solid ice. The ice was bonded firmly to the land and then sloped northeastward. We had studied satellite images before the trip and knew that in previous years the floe edge extended about twenty miles out to sea, ran parallel to the coast, and curved back toward land near Smith Sound, where we planned to cross to Greenland. If we left the land behind, paddled along the floe edge, and camped on the ice, we would reach our destination a week sooner than if we continued dragging near shore.

The idea was tempting but dangerous. In 1986 two West German adventurers had attempted the same journey to Greenland. They encountered ice at this latitude and followed the floe edge rather than the shore. They traveled comfortably for several days, but one evening, as they slept, a west wind broke a large chunk off the floe edge and blew it out to sea. When they awoke, they were camped on a floating ice pan, out of sight of land. Fearing for their lives, they activated their ELT. The signal was detected by a commercial airplane and relayed to the Strategic Air Command rescue center in Fort Collins, Colorado. The SAC commander ran a computer search of flight plans and coast guard files and learned that no airplanes or ships were in the area. Rescues are expensive in the north, so the officer assumed that the signal was anomalous and that no one was in danger. Over the next few days the transmission persisted, drifting slowly south.

Meanwhile, the storm intensified in Baffin Bay, and waves crashed over the edges of the pan. The two men moved their belongings to the center, but the ice split in two and they scurried to a new center, surrounded by less ice. They repeated this process several times until their pan was so small that waves washed completely over it. A large wave carried their kayaks out to sea. Another blew their tent off the ice, and they huddled together in their rain gear, holding the precious ELT.

The officer in Fort Collins reasoned that if an airplane had crashed in the sea it would have sunk, and the signal was moving too slowly to be a ship. After a few days he became increasingly troubled by its persistence and called the RCMP in Grise Fiord. Someone there said, "Oh, yes, that's probably those Germans!"

The nearest land-based helicopter didn't have enough fuel to reach the stranded adventurers, but luckily a research ship with a helicopter was nearby and saved the men.

Chris and I were working hard and were perpetually hungry, but with the exception of one storm, life had been peaceful. Often we felt as if we were in an abandoned amusement park complete with clean white walkways, angular bergs, fractured glaciers, and mechanical bears. The park was unblemished by human detritus; there were no oil drums, Styrofoam coffee cups, or discarded snowmachine parts. Yet the relaxing isolation was also a constant reminder of our vulnerability. We couldn't afford to take chances, so we pulled the kayaks onto the ice, slipped into our harnesses, and resumed dragging northward.

I played number games in my head. We were walking on a chunk of ice approximately two hundred miles long, twenty miles wide, and six feet thick—about 700 billion cubic feet of ice. A nuclear power plant would have to operate continuously for two hundred years to melt that much ice. The sun felt warm on my back. Step by step we continued northward. Molecule by molecule, the ice melted.

11

On July 4, our eleventh day out, I wrote:

This is the second day of dragging after that glorious day of paddling. I really do yearn for open water, but it was sunny and calm and in the afternoon we took our first bath of the journey in a warm tundra pool. The swimming was fine but the rowdy Fourth of July picnic crowd was a bit much. Chris cooked a holiday pot of rice with some dilute instant soup for flavor. So what else is new?

Life lapsed into a familiar expedition routine: wake up, eat, break camp, drag the kayak along the ice, make camp, eat, sleep. All those back-home images became vague, and I stopped thinking about that dead battery or the unpainted porch. I daydreamed the hours away, half in a trance:

Huh, wonder where my mind was just then; 11:15, I guess I spaced out for a while. . . . Oh boy, we get some nuts in fifteen minutes. Maybe we'll reach that point by then.

Light sure is shimmery across the ice today.

That looks like an aglu up there. It's melting out a large pool for easy dragging, but I better go left a bit to avoid falling in.

Boy, if I spaced out this much in second grade my teacher would call my parents and they'd all sit around and get real serious and tell me to pay attention so I would grow up and go to a good college.

Yahoo, school's over and I'm riding down the driveway on my bike.

Look, Ma, No hands!

Crash, Freak out!

No, Ma, really, if you were still alive, would you understand what I'm doing and why I'm doing it?

Maybe if I meditate real hard you'll come to me, like my friends visited me in my kayak in Chile.

Oh that's ridiculous, I can't summon my dead mother when I want to.

It would have been a better ending if you could have seen me now. You saw me dropping out of chemistry and going through my first divorce. Cut adrift. But you didn't see where I was headed.

Sorry, Mom, I know you were worried about me when you died. I couldn't reassure you because I didn't see where I was headed either. I was wandering with nothing but a vague feeling to follow.

Five more minutes until break time and some nuts. Boy am I hungry.

First, I had to shed all those expectations of me that weren't me. It should have been easy, but it took so long. Then I kept digging down, reaching for my strongest feelings. Trusting my intuition. I was often confused because intuition is so ghostly. Sometimes I grabbed hold of the wrong emotion. Then I had to let go, reach again, and hold on. Now I know that I belong out here. It's so simple.

Don't think we'll make it to that point; it isn't getting closer.

Oh, look, Chris found smooth ice and is ahead of me. How'd that happen?

Two days later we approached Makinson Inlet, a major break in the Ellesmere coastline. We had traveled one hundred forty miles in thirteen days, for an eleven-mile-per-day average. We were a little ahead of schedule, but one storm day and we'd be back down to our required ten-mile-per-day average.

We hadn't planned enough fat in our diet, and it was hard work dragging the boats. I woke up hungry every morning. Breakfast took the edge off, but not by much, and midmorning we parceled out a few nuts. I chewed mine slowly to help digest them completely. Lunches were small, and by afternoon the hunger migrated from my stomach to my muscles, where my body was slowly eating itself for the energy to continue.

Seagulls constantly flew overhead and nested on cliffs along the shore. Eggs were a traditional staple for the Inuit, and we decided to collect some for ourselves. Most of the rock was clearly unclimbable without a rope, but one afternoon we saw a fifty-foot pinnacle split by a sinuous crack. Twenty gulls nested on top. I hiked up a talus slope into the shadow of the higher cliff and reached the base of the pinnacle. Bits of damp moss clung to small edges. I tentatively tested what should have been an adequate foothold, but my oversized hip boots twisted and slipped. With a pair of climbing shoes that mold to the feet, the climb would be easy, but with the hip boots, I was taking a chance. I opened my hand and slid the flat palm into the crack in the rock and then closed my fist tightly. My knuckles jammed against the rock, providing a secure hand hold. Then I bent one foot sideways and slid it into a wide opening. The rubber held, so I stepped up, holding my body into the rock with my hand. I reached my other hand above, felt the inside of the crack, and found comfortably sharp holds. I jammed the second foot into the crack and stood on it, and the ground receded. Unsure of my feet, I relied on positive hand jams and scraped my knuckles raw and bloody against the rock. The gulls wheeled, screamed, and dive-bombed. Images of difficult climbs drifted through my mind, and I settled into a practiced calmness. Fifty feet is too far to fall, but the rock became less steep and the holds were large enough to trust even with awkward boots. The gulls became even more agitated as I stepped onto the summit. Every nook in the rock contained a nest and every nest contained from one to three eggs. I collected a dozen eggs, leaving one in each nest, and climbed back down to level ground.

Seagull eggs are considerably larger than chicken eggs, and all that afternoon I dreamed about giant omelettes. However, we didn't have a frying pan or oil, so we boiled them. The first one cracked open perfectly and had a delicious rich, almost orange, yolk. But the second contained a chick embryo curled neatly inside. Chris wanted to discard it, but I was too hungry to throw food away. I took a bite. The remaining eggy part was hard and bland. The embryo was a bit crunchy and incipient feathers stuck between my teeth, but it wasn't that bad, considering. We made a deal. Chris ate all the eggs and I ate all the embryos. There were more embryos than eggs, so I think I got the better side of the bargain.

We were perpetually tired, and boiled seagull embryos with couscous is a little grim, even if you are hungry. However, our hardships were minor compared with those of the explorers who traveled before us.

After Qitdlaq's death, the migrants continued south and wintered at Cape Faraday north of Makinson Inlet. The hunting was poor, so the following spring they decided to rest for a year. They left their kayaks on the coast and walked inland to hunt caribou and musk ox. The small band crossed into a broad valley and looked down on lush tundra but no animals. They turned north along the glacier-free west coast of Ellesmere, but they killed only one musk ox that summer. Starving, they ate their dogs and retreated toward the east coast. As winter approached they came to a large lake filled with fish. The fish sustained them for several months but provided no blubber, so they had no oil for heat and light. Catches diminished during the dark times and hunger deepened. Several people died. Families quarreled, and the group separated into several small camps.

One day, two hunters, Maktaq and Minik, visited their neighbor Qumangapik and his family. The visitors seemed surprisingly well fed, and Qumangapik suspected that his old friends were hoarding food. When he journeyed around the lake to investigate, he discovered that Maktaq and Minik had been eating their neighbors. Qumangapik rallied the survivors, attacked the two cannibals, and drove them away; one man was killed and one wounded in the battle. Twenty people had left Greenland, and now only five remained: one healthy and one wounded hunter, two women, and a child.

They wrapped their remaining possessions in a bearskin and dragged it behind them as they fled back toward the sea ice. They built an igloo, and Qumangapik went out to hunt seals but returned home empty-handed. Then a blizzard held him inside for two days. The tiny group waited in the darkness, occasionally chewing bits of the bearskin. When the storm broke, Qumangapik set out again. Several hours later the people in the dark igloo heard footsteps in the snow. Afraid that Maktaq and Minik had followed, they huddled together and finally cried out, "Who is it?"

Qumangapik cried back, "It is me, I've done it. I've killed a seal."

They sliced off some blubber and, for the first time that winter, lit the lamps that brought heat and light into the igloo. Then they ate.

Hunting improved, and the next spring they returned to their kayaks at Cape Faraday. They rested for a year, regaining strength. The trail south to Baffin was long, so the following spring the five survivors trekked northward again and recrossed Smith Sound, back to Greenland.

12

Makinson Inlet was fifteen miles wide at its mouth and was frozen solid. We could comfortably drag the boats across it in two days and weren't concerned about camping on the ice because the floe edge was twenty miles away. Even the worst possible storm wouldn't break that much ice apart.

Numerous seals basked on the ice, appearing as black dots scattered across the whiteness. Ever alert for predators, a seal sleeps for periods of ten seconds to four minutes, then lifts its head and surveys the horizon. If it sees a person approaching on foot, it immediately flips into its hole and disappears. Inuit claim that a seal even recognizes the black nose of an otherwise camouflaged polar bear.

That evening we pitched camp in the middle of the inlet, and the following morning lenticular clouds and a rising breeze presaged a storm. Pijimini had warned us to stay in the tent and drink tea on a windy day, but he had assumed that our camp would be secure. Our stakes didn't penetrate the ice, and we feared that a strong wind would roll our tent across the inlet like a tumbleweed. I imagined trying to escape from the tent with our sleeping bags, stove, cooking pans, and sacks of food flying about as if we and our possessions were all riding in a large drier in the laundromat. With no safe alternative, we broke camp and dragged the boats toward the far shore, where we knew we would find shelter. Within a few hours, the temperature dropped to freezing, and gale winds blew water into a fine spume that froze on our clothes and boats. I tightened my hood closely around my face.

Biologists report that polar bears are attracted to food sources a few hundred miles away. No one knows whether they can smell from that far away or whether they follow other signs such as bird migrations. But bears from a wide radius concentrate around a bonanza such as a beached whale or an unusual concentration of seals. Some such phenomenon must have been occurring, because we saw six bears that day. They paraded through the storm at regular intervals: first a mother with two cubs, then a lone male, then another female with one cub. At first we were spooked at such a concentration and constantly looked over our shoulders for one that might be stalking us. However, they were all moving purposefully eastward.

Chris's left boot cracked and then her right failed a few miles later. We were continuously walking through pools of water, so her feet were soon cold and wet. I sympathized but was secretly happy that my feet were so much larger than hers that I couldn't be chivalrous and offer to trade boots. However, our boots must have been designed for a specific number of steps because an hour afterward an icy wetness picked its way through the fibers of my wool socks. The water seeped in when I lifted my foot and squished out when I stepped down.

Chris was ahead, so I dropped my harness, ran forward, and jumped into a large puddle with both feet. Water sprayed up and froze to the ice already on her rain gear. She smiled but wasn't really amused.

When we had left land the previous day, the opposite side of Makinson Inlet appeared as a fuzzy brown outline speckled with white. Now, a day and a half later, the shoreline remained indistinct, and our goal seemed to be no closer than it was twenty-four hours ago. I stared into the storm for some indication of progress. Had I seen that gully a few hours ago? When had the large blurry white spot resolved into two distinct snow fields?

No matter how many storms I live through, I will never get used to the way the wind wraps me up and isolates me. Chris was beside me. Given the conditions, we were safe enough, but she seemed far away. Beyond the hood of my raincoat, everything seemed vague. I felt shadowlike, and I wondered how I would react if I drifted off without my body into the freezing wind.

When you climb a mountain, the way back is always downhill. Here all directions were the same, and every mile forward separated us by one mile from Grise Fiord. If we had to retreat, we wouldn't expect the same storms that we had encountered on the outgoing journey, but we would expect others. What would it feel like to know that there was no retreat, no village of Grise Fiord, no airplanes to fly us back to Montana? For the early European explorers, civilization was immeasurably farther away than it was for us, but a soft world did exist out there somewhere.

The Inuit had no options; this was their home. I imagined that such vulnerability would drive people together. The Inuit shared their last morsels of food during famine and exchanged wives during springtime. If hungry times returned, one neighbor was your lover and her husband was your hunting partner who had saved your life last summer from that wounded walrus. Perhaps their child was really yours, although you might not be sure. Under those conditions, your sense of family and even your individuality would become secondary to the group. Yet before I romanticized the cohesiveness, I remembered that the loneliness and hardship reduced two men in Qitdlaq's tribe to cannibalism.

Lost in thought, I stared down at my feet, navigating by the feel of the wind against my left cheek. Then I looked up and saw individual rocks on the far shore. They bridged me back to the planet and drove away the floating isolation. I forced myself to look down again, and the next time I raised my eyes, I saw splotches of blue, purple, and yellow. Slowly, then rapidly, they became tundra flowers. We were only a hundred yards from shore and camp.

Most places provide effective shelter for a camp. In temperate regions you can hide in a dense thicket, and in the mountains you can usually dig into a snowbank or climb into a glacial crevasse. But we landed along a featureless beach. The recent glaciers had filled the gullies with debris and bulldozed excess rock into the sea. A few scattered boulders remained, but the wind swirled off the ice and eddied against the hillsides so that even the largest boulders provided only occasional shelter. Even though we were tired, we laboriously built a rock wall to protect our frayed tent and weakened poles.

The storm died down that evening. The next morning we slept late and Chris rested her blistered and bleeding feet while I explored the beach. After a short hike, I decided to climb a small rocky outcrop. My egg-collecting experience had reminded me how good it felt to move on steep rock, and I felt a perverse pleasure in climbing in hip boots. A few feet from the summit, I looked upward to plan my last few moves and saw a large white animal perched above my head. "That's funny," I thought, "I didn't know that mountain goats lived here." I looked up again to stare into the curious eyes of a polar bear.

I felt like Jack and the Beanstalk climbing up to the giant's lair in the sky. The bear's paw was as big around as my head, its claws as long as my fingers. The Inuit say that a bear always rises on its hind legs before attacking a person and then swings with its left paw, starting from its heart and sweeping toward its less vulnerable side. The bear starts its swing horizontally, so a hunter can plant a spear shaft in the snow in front of the bear and then duck under the left armpit. If the hunter is quick enough, the bear will miss its swing and drop on all fours. But as the bear falls forward, it will impale itself on the spear, and if the timing and spear placement are accurate, the point will pierce the bear's heart.

If Inuit hunters could maintain that level of control, I could stay calm. I stepped down, out of paw-swipe range, and stabilized myself with one foot jammed into a crack and the other on a sharp edge. The bear inched forward until its front paws were hanging over the rock. It then peered down with its long neck stretched out, tapering to the small black nose, like the detonator on the tip of a missile. We stared at one another for a few moments and then the bear turned and disappeared. I waited to see if it would circle to my side of the rock, but it didn't. After watching the empty beach for a few minutes, I climbed down and ran back to see if Chris was safe in the tent.

13

The next day we bandaged Chris's feet and continued toward Cape Faraday. Qitdlaq's party had wintered at the cape on both the outgoing and the return journeys, and the survivors had retreated to Faraday after the terrible times in Makinson Inlet. The ice was fractured into a maze of leads and pans, as if the rocky cape had pushed into the frozen ocean like a giant icebreaker. We laboriously dragged, jumped leads, and goofy-paddled through the obstacles until we were a few hundred yards from shore. Then we stopped to look for a suitable camp.

Chris touched my arm. "Jon, there's a red spot in the rocks, to the left of the low beach; it looks like a piece of cloth."

I followed her gaze. "No, I think it's just some flowers."

We goofy-paddled a few sinuous turns, and when the lead closed out, we paddled onto the ice and stood up again.

Chris reached for the binoculars, focused on the shoreline, and handed me the glasses. "It's a person."

I scanned the shore until the red spot came into view. A man in a red parka sat on a rock, looking out to sea. After a few moments he took out a pair of binoculars and stared back at me. I waved. He didn't wave back but walked to the beach and sat down patiently on a rock. No one spoke as we paddled the last narrow lead and crunched quietly onto the sandy beach.

The stranger, a tall blond Scandinavian, remained silent but walked down to greet us. Chris and I climbed out of the cockpits and stood awkwardly in our wet boots. In the old days, two strangers approached warily, watching for hidden weapons. Perhaps our suspicious instincts remained, or maybe we were just shy. When we were so close that we had to break the silence, I said, "Hi." The man still didn't speak but reached out and shook my hand. Once he had touched me and made sure I was real, he introduced himself as Peter Schledermann, an archaeologist digging in the ruins of Qitdlaq's camp. He explained that he had finished work and had come to sit among the rocks. Surrounded by space and silence, he had daydreamed into Qitdlaq's world and then toward Qitdlaq's spirit world.

Looking across the ice, he saw two figures distorted slightly by mirage. For a few moments he concentrated, separating reality from imagination. Then he watched us through the binoculars, and even though he saw the plastic boats and other twentieth-century paraphernalia, he daydreamed again of the small band of stone age migrants.

We explained our journey, and Peter helped drag our kayaks onto the beach. He insisted that we hoist the boats onto the old stone pillars constructed to keep sealskin kayaks off the wet ground and away from the dogs. The last kayaks had been removed from those racks between 1860 and 1865.

Satisfied that our boats were safe from the sled dogs that no longer existed, Peter invited us to his camp for dinner. He introduced us to his colleague, Karen McCullough, an athletic blond woman, weathered by years of working in the Arctic sun. They invited us into their spacious wall tent for cocktails and a predinner snack. As we talked, I mentally stalked the plate of nuts in the center of the table, wondering how big a handful I could take without appearing impolite. I carefully weighed social refinement against the abundant calories in front of me and reached for another handful. Chris was playing the same game, and we soon emptied the dish.

In the North, after travelers are welcomed and fed, people always ask about conditions on the land. These questions are not conversation fillers but matters of utmost importance. People assume that you have been observing carefully and will report accurately.

Peter told us that bears had been harassing his camp. Three days before, a bear leaned against their sleeping tent, and the day before a bear poked its nose into their mess tent. These incidents had spooked Peter and Karen and they were abandoning their dig. Peter concluded, "A helicopter is coming to pick us up day after tomorrow. Lucky you made it here so quickly or you would have missed us."

We asked about the ice, and Peter told us that the pilot of a research helicopter reported open water to the north. Our dragging ordeal was nearly over.

Peter remarked that the nuts had disappeared quickly and suggested that we cook dinner. We had potatoes, canned meat, vegetables, and wine. After our meal, we climbed onto a bluff above camp and looked at the hazy outline of Cape Combermere, where we had camped eight days ago.

Peter mused, "In the old days people traveled to see a relative, follow a shaman, or just to be out on the land. Trips like yours were a way of life."

"You know," I responded, "sometimes when we are out there on the land, I feel as if we are brave individuals on a major expedition. But, you're right, maybe Chris and I are just off on a wander and it's no big deal."

I thought about it for a while, then continued. "Actually, I'm happiest when I forget our destination and feel that I am going for a walk or a paddle with Chris. I guess I've learned from her over the years."

Peter replied, "With that attitude, you'll probably make it to Greenland."

The ocean was a splotchy pattern of ice, water on ice, and open leads. I was amazed that we had been able to travel over it. Seals rested on the dry snow adjacent to their *aglus*. They napped and then raised their heads periodically to watch for predators.

Chris had wanted to go on the Northwest Passage trip because she "liked the northern lighting." I watched the landscape change from dark blues, browns, and whites to softer shades of the same colors as the sun swung north to complete another circle above the horizon.

14

At breakfast the following day, Peter and Karen showed us a sealskin mitt they had unearthed at the site. They were excited about it and explained how the stitching pattern linked it to Qitdlaq's band. Chris and I asked if we could help dig for more artifacts, but Peter and Karen were restoring the site in preparation for departure. Instead we helped pat tundra turf over the disturbed ground. When the job was complete, the four of us packed a delicious lunch and hiked to the hilltop above camp.

We wandered around in the sunshine, nibbled on chocolate, and ate fresh oranges. From our vantage point, we saw leads reaching out toward open water. Our dragging days were over! In the distance, across Baffin Bay, a thin line formed the far shore of Greenland. We hiked back to camp, and Chris and I bathed in a freshwater pool. The surrounding rock had absorbed the continuous sunlight and the water was surprisingly warm.

As we prepared to leave the following morning, Peter and Karen came down to our camp with two large bags of food. They also told us about a geology research camp at Cape Herschel fifty miles further along the coast.

During the past twenty-four days, we had dragged the boats two hundred thirty miles and paddled twenty-five. But that part of the ordeal was over. Although our journey was only about half complete, we were restocked, we were entering the last and largest *polynya*, and there were more people ahead to assist us.

We weren't accustomed to conversation, so when I went to bed that night all the words of the past few days sped by until one sentence repeated itself clearly: "Trips like yours were a way of life."

Peter saw me as a person who was wandering for the love of the journey, and I liked that image better than that of a man obsessed with expedition success. I wondered, again, why it had taken so long to learn such a simple lesson. Chris had been one of my teachers. I reached my hand out of my bag and wrapped it around Chris's shoulder. She grunted in her sleep and wiggled toward me until her back pressed against my stomach. Then we both dozed off.

15

The following day we paddled eastward through a lead toward open water. The air was still, and the ice reflected so sharply in the mirror-smooth water that I felt as if I had been turned upside down. Small ice pans, towering bergs, columnar ice, rounded ice, and sharp ice all appeared in a perfect double image of reality and reflection. A helicopter passed overhead, and the *thump thump* of its rotors disturbed the reverie. It landed at the camp, became quiet for a few moments, and then took off again. This time it dipped low above our heads and we waved to Peter and Karen, who were smiling from inside the bubble and traveling too fast to be connected to the land.

After a few hours, broken ice from the floe edge choked off our lead. We dragged the boats over a pan and goofy-paddled to the next. I pulled my kayak onto the ice again, helped Chris with hers, then outlined a route for the next hundred yards. The pans were small and tippy, and we jumped several leads onto tenuous landings. We both concentrated on the immediate terrain. When I finally looked up at the broader landscape, I saw a polar bear a few hundred yards away, running straight at me.

I told myself, "I've had encounters with bears before, but this is the real thing! Stay calm, shoot straight, and keep shooting even if you can smell the bear's breath."

I started to unclasp the waterproof rifle case tied on the front deck of my kayak. The quick-release latches had worked so rapidly in the living room back home, but they seemed cumbersome and slow as the bear grew larger. Its torpedo-like head stuck straight out from between its shoulders, leaving only a small target on its chest. I probably had only one shot and it had better be good. I unfastened the second buckle and grasped the smooth comforting curves of the wooden stock. As I started to slide the gun out of the case, I heard a scream in my right ear.

"Go away bear!"

Chris streaked past me, running straight at the bear, yelling and waving her arms. The bear rocked back onto its hind paws, made a sharp right turn and ran away, across the broken ice, agilely jumping leads and ice ridges. I remained motionless, kneeling by the side of the kayak, with the half-sheathed gun in one hand and Chris in front of me.

I slipped the gun back in the case and reclasped the buckles. Chris turned and walked over to me.

"That was cute," I said. "And if you hadn't scared the bear, you were right in my line of fire."

She answered that the bear wasn't charging. Clearly it was running toward us, but in previous encounters bears had stood and studied us before acting. Chris thought that the bear was running toward some other destination and, like us, was concentrating on the jumbled ice. Therefore, it didn't see us even though it was running right at us. Her countercharge was merely her way of announcing our existence and telling the bear to run in some other direction.

"And if your theory were wrong?" I asked. "You were in my line of fire."

"I wasn't wrong."

We continued the last hundred yards through broken ice to the floe edge. Open water stretched out before us. We had reached the Smith Sound *polynya*, and although it had been ice-free for a few centuries, I felt as if it had just melted last night to celebrate the summer that had finally overtaken the Arctic.

Chris settled into her kayak and pulled her spray skirt tight, like a real kayaker, not a goofy-paddler. She smiled, pushed into the water, and said, "Let's paddle to Greenland."

Seals, so wary on the ice, swam close by and eyed us curiously. Several walrus grunted like pigs off our starboard side. I recalled Pijimini's warning and veered to give them space, but if one attacked, swiftly and invisibly from under the water, there would be nothing I could do.

16

The weather remained warm and sunny for the next four days. We paddled in long underwear, with our waterproof jackets tied to the deck. The air blowing through the thin material provided a welcome relief from the clammy sweat inside our storm parkas. On a vacation outing, people travel slowly in good weather to enjoy the sunshine, but here we were pushing hard to reach the Smith Sound crossing while the high pressure held. We paddled every day until we were tired, then forced ourselves to go another few miles. I espoused this strategy at the beginning of the journey, but we moved slowly at that time, saving our strength. Now we were near the crux and it was time to push hard and use our reserves.

When we arrived at the neck of Smith Sound, Greenland appeared as a hazy blue line about twenty-seven miles to the east. The crossing would wait for tomorrow or the next day. Instead we turned west, into the fiord, to find the geology camp. We came to shore near a beached speedboat and walked up the hill. The research station consisted of two permanent metal buildings and a roomy tent, all tied securely to concrete anchors. It was midday and the camp was deserted, so we climbed to a rocky knoll and surveyed our crossing.

To the south, Baffin Bay is four hundred miles wide, but Greenland trends westward and Ellesmere leans to the east, so the two squeeze together to form a narrow neck. As I explained previously, Smith sound is a *polynya* and is ice-free even during the bitter-cold Arctic winter. However, thick ice forms in Kane Basin to the north, and north of that the polar seas are ice-bound throughout the year.

We had planned to continue a few miles farther north along the Ellesmere coast to Cape Sabine, which is four miles closer to Greenland. In addition, a current flows southward through Smith Sound, and if we started at Cape Sabine we would start up-current. If we paddled due east, the combination of paddling and drift would take us comfortably to a safe landfall. If we started where we were now, at Cape Herschel, we would be forced to tack against the current to reach Greenland. Unfortunately, thick ice had jammed against Cape Sabine, forcing us to consider the longer and more vulnerable route.

A twenty-seven-mile crossing is large or small, depending on your perspective. A modern adventurer, Ed Gillette, paddled a sea kayak nearly three thousand miles across the Pacific from California to Hawaii. Compared with his accomplishment, our paddle was casual. However, we were in the Arctic, not the South Pacific, and many early explorers had died in Smith Sound and Kane Basin.

Of all the misadventures in this region, Tyson's drift was the most sobering for me. In 1871 Charles Hall planned to sail north until he was stopped by the ice and then to continue to the North Pole by dog team. Hall set sail on board the *Polaris* with a mixed American and

German crew. They landed briefly on the south coast of Baffin Island to pick up two Inuit couples, Joe and Hanna, and Hans and his wife, Mary. Joe and Hans were hired as hunters and dog handlers, and the women were expected to cook and maintain skin clothing. The Inuit couples, who expected to be away for a year or more, brought their five children.

Hall had been successful on previous expeditions when he traveled alone, but he was a poor leader. Within a week after leaving port, the two expedition scientists refused to obey Hall's orders. The ship's captain stole food and liquor from the storeroom. The German crew threatened to quit when the ship stopped in Greenland for water and other supplies.

Despite these problems, Hall doggedly sailed through the ice and passed north of Smith Sound, farther north than any ship had ever reached. He dropped anchor for the winter on September 10, and a month later he continued northward by sledge with his Inuit companions. They returned after two weeks, confident that they could reach the Pole in the spring. But this dream was never realized because Hall suddenly took sick and died.

At the time Hall's death was a mystery, but his symptoms implied that he had died of arsenic poisoning. Hall's body was exhumed in 1968, and an autopsy revealed lethal arsenic concentrations. Today, most historians agree that Hall was poisoned by a dissentient crew.

During the long winter after Hall's death, discipline and morale disintegrated. In June, one of the officers, George Tyson, and a companion made a half-hearted attempt at the Pole but returned, unsuccessful. Finally, in August, after ten months in icy captivity, the *Polaris* broke free and headed southward.

Three days later the drunken captain ran the ship into the pack, where it remained trapped for two months. They drifted slowly south, arriving in Smith Sound in early October. A gale broke the pack loose, freeing the ship again. But moving ice can be more dangerous than consolidated ice, and the wind-driven pans ground into the ship. The *Polaris* listed, and the engineer called to the bridge that the hull had cracked. The captain, fearing that the ship was sinking, ordered the crew to throw food, clothing, rifles, and ammunition onto the ice, where they could be salvaged for a winter camp. Tyson realized that most of the supplies had landed on small, tippy pans and were quickly swept under the hull and lost. He gathered a small party, jumped onto the moving ice, and ferried food and fuel toward a larger floe a short distance away. While they were working, the ship wrenched free and disappeared into the storm.

Three Americans, four Germans, four adult Inuit, and their five children were left stranded on an ice floe with nineteen hundred pounds of food. Of the sixteen people, only the two Inuit men, Joe and Hans, were competent hunters. Tyson was dressed in tattered sealskin pants, two light wool shirts, a cotton jacket, and a fur hat. He had no parka or sleeping bag.

The next day the castaways saw the ship floating upright about ten miles to the north. Tyson learned much later that the engineer had panicked and the hull had never cracked. The order to abandon ship was unnecessary. The lookouts on the ship never saw the dark mass of humanity on the ice and proceeded back toward civilization without them.

Tyson observed that their floe drifted due south toward the center of Baffin Bay. With only 120 pounds of food per person and little hope for landfall or rescue, he ordered immediate rationing. But the Germans argued that they were drifting southeastward toward Green- land. Tyson was the senior officer, but the Germans all carried pistols, and they commandeered the food.

They ate most of their rations in the first month and then huddled in igloos throughout the long, dark winter, kept alive by the Inuit hunters. The dark times passed and spring returned, but no one saw land. Several times the floe broke apart and they retreated to the largest fragment. On the night of April 20, a huge wave rolled over their shrinking ice pan, washing most of their possessions into the sea. When the storm passed, they had no food, no water, and no fuel to melt the salt-encrusted ice. Two days later Hans shot a polar bear, and four days after that he killed three seals. The party drank the blood, ate the raw meat, and regained strength. But with warmer weather coming and their continued southward drift, they didn't have much time before the ice would melt. Finally, on April 30, Tyson stepped out of his igloo and saw a steamship only five hundred yards away. He awoke the others, waved bits of cloth, and fired into the air. At first neither the rescuers nor the rescued could believe what they heard. The castaways learned that they had floated two thousand miles to the Labrador coast. The ship's crew learned that the castaways had spent seven months on an ice floe without a single death.

17

Chris and I spent a lazy afternoon on the knoll. A few ice pans broke loose from the congestion near Cape Sabine and drifted through the channel. I estimated they were a mile or two in diameter, about as large as Tyson's original floe. The ice barely seemed to move, but I knew that speed and distance were deceptive. I fixed the position of one pan, napped in the afternoon sunlight, then awoke and noted that the pan had moved appreciably. We would have to paddle northeastward to maintain a course due east. If we were swept south of Cape Alexander, we would be in trouble.

Chris spotted four people walking across the tundra. The scientist in charge, Wes Blake, was shirtless, unshaven, and jolly. I immediately thought of him as a fanciful Santa Claus, enjoying a lazy summer here at the North Pole before the busy Christmas season. We retired to the mess tent, and he explained his research over tea and a predinner snack.

Eighteen thousand years ago, much of the Northern Hemisphere was covered with a massive ice sheet. A continental glacier is heavy enough to depress a continent into the soft plastic asthenosphere, which is a portion of the earth's mantle. When the ice melts, the continent buoys back up, just as a ship rises when its cargo is offloaded. But a continent rises slowly because the asthenosphere is a plastic solid, not a liquid. Thus when the pressure is relieved, the asthenosphere oozes back over a few thousand years.

Wes took us outside and pointed to a series of terraces between our camp and the sea. Each terrace was once a beach at sea level. Wes traced the history of the glacial retreat by studying the ages and heights of the terraces. According to his chronology, Ellesmere started rising nine thousand years ago and is still rising today.

Wes also manned the weather station at Cape Herschel. When we asked him about conditions for our crossing, he replied that while we were welcome at his camp, he would advise us to leave tomorrow. The good weather that we were enjoying might not hold, and if the ice jam to the north broke up, the crossing would become dangerous or impossible.

At breakfast the following morning, one of the field assistants mentioned that the crossing must be like a marathon. When I asked him why he made that analogy, he answered that Chris and I appeared to be building our carbohydrate levels for the event, just as marathon runners "carbo-loaded." I guessed that he was referring to the quantity of toast I was consuming, so I smiled and responded, "Please pass the butter."

Wes gave us additional food, including a small sack of candy bars, a can of nuts, and a tin of Christmas fruit cake. Everyone walked down to the shore to wave good-bye. As we paddled away, I imagined the geologists slowly rising on the rebounding island.

18

Greenland was so distant that it was difficult to correlate visual landmarks with the map, but we identified a dark bluff split by a snowy gully. Although the bluff rose nearly one thousand feet, when I closed one eye and sighted along my outstretched arm, it only measured one finger width. I calculated that if we moved steadily, we could complete the crossing in twelve hours. It was now nine o'clock in the morning.

I put my hand out; Chris grasped it, and I said, "Let's paddle to Greenland."

We had been working hard for the past few days, and my elbow tendons were slightly inflamed. We should have taken a rest day, but we couldn't ignore Wes's warnings about the weather and the ice. I thought carefully about bending from the waist and using my back and stomach muscles rather than pulling with my arms. A breeze built small waves from the northeast. They weren't big enough to be a major concern, but they did hinder our progress.

To calm my own fears, allay Chris's, and pass time, I made up a story. In it, shamans from the north took a spirit journey south and joined with witch doctors from the rain forest. Together they journeyed into the past, to a time when people spoke with animals. The narwhals and hippopotamuses frolicked together with their human friends in a nameless primordial ocean.

By eleven in the morning we encountered large ice pans. The first was welcome because we paddled onto it, stretched, and took a short break. We split the first of Wes's candy bars. During the next hour, the pans became denser and more troublesome. We detoured north whenever possible to compensate for our drift, but the ice was drifting from the north, and sometimes it was more expedient to take the shorter route around the south edge of the pans. The serpentine course increased our distance, and I added another hour or two to our estimated paddling time.

At one o'clock in the afternoon, we encountered a large pan with no obvious route around it. Apparently, the ice jam at Cape Sabine had broken apart and the main pack was moving south. I thought, "Hmm, we could ride this one all the way to Labrador," but I didn't joke about it with Chris. We pulled onto the ice and started dragging. The hummocky, slushy surface impeded progress. I stopped for a moment, looked across to Greenland, and held my arm out with one finger extended. To my dismay, the rocky cliff with the smooth white gully was still one finger width high. I turned around, almost afraid to look, but was relieved to see that the Ellesmere shore had receded. Regardless, the slow dragging would add another hour or two to the crossing. To counteract my fear, I added all the factors in our favor. The slight breeze had calmed and nothing in the forecast or the sky presaged a storm. The dragging was slow, but the walking relieved my sore tendons. I replaced fear with determination. We were going to make it; there were no other options.

We spent three hours dragging across the pan and another hour and a half working our way through leads and broken ice on its eastern edge. From there we saw color and structure on the Greenland shore, and the cliff was several fingers wide. I told Chris that for me the ice was a barrier. Even if a storm came up, we wouldn't be blown back to Ellesmere.

She responded with a giggly affirmative laugh, and she held out her hand as I had done at the start of the crossing. I grasped it, and she said, "Let's paddle to Greenland."

After another hour we encountered a dense concentration of broken ice that was too thick to paddle through and too broken to walk over. Logically, the small bergs should have dispersed throughout the ocean as a drop of ink disperses in a glass of water. But the currents had rounded them up and kept them in a tight herd. I grasped the stern of Chris's boat and pushed. The bow parted two small chunks of ice and she moved forward a few feet, but I drifted back a foot. Then she grasped my bow and pulled me forward while she slid back. We were trapped, drifting inexorably southward, toward open water and disaster. We stopped, snacked on some of Wes's food, swallowed some Advil, and beat futilely into the ice again. Sitting in a kayak, with your eyes just above the water, you can only see a short distance ahead; we had to plan by guesswork.

Chris suggested that since the ice was moving from north to south, we abandon our course toward the dark cliff and swing south. The course change would add distance and reduce our safety margin, but it might break us clear of the ice. We followed her plan, and after a scary half an hour emerged from the ice into a comforting gray-green ocean, broken by only a few scattered pans.

Thousands of dovekies swam in the calm sea. At our approach, the closest birds climbed onto a nearby floe. They carried themselves like penguins, and their black and white markings were remarkably similar to those of their Southern Hemisphere counterparts, but they were much smaller. They strutted back and forth nervously, as if muttering to themselves, "Oh, if I were as big as a penguin, I wouldn't have to worry so much." The collective worry reached a threshold and all the birds took off simultaneously, dispelling the penguin image. But they were too curious simply to escape, and they circled over us several times, flying so low that we clearly heard the whoosh of their wing beats. Chris named them "canary penguins."

We drifted south of the black cliff, and the Greenland shore began to recede to the east, but we had passed through the strongest part of the current and we started moving faster. The sun completed its westward passage across the sky and swung north, announcing the onset of Arctic evening. The colors softened, and the temperature dropped a few degrees. My elbow started to ache again. We needed one more determined drive, so we had another snack and more Advil.

Finally, at midnight, after fifteen hours of continuous paddling and dragging, we reached the edge of an ice pan at the entrance to a small bay. A high hill loomed above us and an arctic hare grazed on the tundra sedges. We dragged the boats across the pan, slipped back into the cockpits, and gazed across the last hundred yards of calm water. Chris pushed her boat off the ice without fastening her spray skirt. Then she looked backward over her shoulder and suggested, "Let's paddle to Greenland."

19

We were too tired to be ecstatic when we reached the beach. Neither of us kissed the soil or danced and whooped. Chris walked off by herself, and to give her space, I walked along the beach in the other direction.

Greenland is covered by a giant ice sheet, which is up to 1.7 miles thick and covers seven hundred thousand square miles. This ice sheet is second in size only to the ice that covers Antarctica. The ice depresses the center of Greenland below sea level. If someone could magically remove the ice cap, seawater would pour in, creating a huge atoll-like structure, with a thin rim of rock circling an inland sea. Then, over the next few thousand years, the land would rise, shedding its ocean like a whale rising to the surface. I expected to camp under a wall of towering ice, but the coastline was remarkably green and warm. The glacier was further inland, hidden behind a row of hills. Although a suburban homeowner would consider the plant cover dismal, abundant grasses and sedges provided a welcome relief from the barren rock of Ellesmere. A mosquito landed on the back of my hand, picked its way through the hairs, and poked its proboscis into my skin. I blew on it and it flew away. It was the first mosquito I had seen since Montana.

I turned and walked back toward camp. Chris had also turned, and she looked like the last person on earth, walking toward me. We stopped at the boats and hugged, then pitched the tent and prepared our bedding. We were still tingling with residual adrenaline and dehydrated after fifteen hours of hard work, so we brewed a cup of tea in the evening light. I sipped silently, watching the ice flow through the straits. Clearly, the congestion was worsening; if we had left six hours later, we might have been in trouble.

Chris asked quietly, "Were you afraid, today?"

I looked into her face. We weren't young anymore. Chris had spent many days in the sun and wind, and her eyes were lined with wrinkles.

"Yes, I was afraid."

"Especially when we were caught in the dense fractured ice? Like in Liverpool Bay?"

"Yes, I was afraid then."

"Good, just checking."

We finished our tea, crawled into our sleeping bags, and pressed together, like two caterpillars cuddling from within their cocoons.

20

We rested for a day and explored the beach. Our campsite was littered with empty rifle cartridges, plastic bags, and scattered food packaging. This trash assured us that we would soon meet the northernmost inhabitants of the earth, but it was sad to leave the pristine coast of Ellesmere.

The following day we packed camp and started paddling south. We felt invulnerable, as if the expedition were over, but we still had two hundred twenty-five miles of a five-hundred-fifty-mile journey ahead of us.

Our next point of interest was an abandoned village called Etah. We paddled into the fiord, with a tongue of the Greenland ice sheet in the background. After a short exploration, we found the ruins of several stone igloos.

Inuit lived here until 1955 and then moved southward to government-built houses with central heating. I was born in 1945, so if I were a polar Inuit, I would remember living in a stone igloo on a grassy knoll beneath a continental glacier. As a baby, I would have ridden on a dogsled during spring trips to visit relatives in Siorapaluk or Qanaaq. As a youth, I would have played on the beaches, imitating the men who hunted narwhals and walrus from their kayaks.

Etah was the most northern point of human habitation for explorers heading toward the North Pole in the late 1800s and early 1900s. Robert Peary, known as Commander Peary, was perhaps the most famous of these men. Peary was one of my boyhood idols because my father told me that he was the first person to reach the North Pole and that he had traveled by dog team. Once, on a Boy Scout hike, the troop leader told us of the time that Peary had frozen his feet. When his companions asked him why he had continued in the bitter cold, he responded, "There's no time to pamper sick men on the trail. Besides, a few toes aren't too much to give to achieve the Pole."

Most of the boys thought that the troop leader was a jerk for urging us onward with a stupid story that probably wasn't true anyway, but I thought about it for a long time afterward.

For Peary, expeditions were a vehicle to fame, money, and social status. When he was twenty-four, he wrote: "I would like to acquire a name which could be an open sesame to circles of culture and refinement."

Fifteen years later, in 1895, he wrote to his wife: "The winter has been a nightmare to me . . . the cold, damp, frost-lined room has made me think of the tomb."

Why did he persist? In his own words, "unless I win *here*, all these things [fame and fortune] fall through. Success is what will give them existence."*

The North Pole is an astronomical observation projected onto shifting ice. If you plant a flag there today, the Pole will be somewhere else tomorrow. The Inuit could never understand why white men endured so much suffering to attain the Pole. They reasoned that it must have economic significance, and since iron was the most valuable commodity they knew of, they called it "the Nail." But in Europe and North America, people waited for news of their favorite explorers as closely as modern sports fans follow the pregame, game, and postgame commentaries.

Peary joined the Navy as a civil engineer and was sent to Nicaragua to survey a proposed canal between the Atlantic and the Pacific. After his return, he obtained leave from the Navy, and with money borrowed from his mother, he organized an expedition to cross the Greenland ice sheet. Over the following twenty-three years, he launched six expeditions and spent nearly fourteen years in the North. The first three journeys focused on exploration of the Greenland ice sheet. His final three expeditions were directed relentlessly toward the North Pole.

Although Peary succeeded in his life's ambition to gain fame and recognition, paradoxically five of his expeditions failed and the final one remains in question. How could he have fooled so many people? Perhaps one answer is that despite repeated failure, he was a great explorer. Peary lived with the Inuit and traveled thousands of miles across the ice by dog team. He dressed like the natives, hunted for his dinner, stoically froze his toes when the going was rough, and explored new lands.

In the end it doesn't matter whether Peary made it to the Pole or not; it was, after all, just the Nail. What mattered was that he communicated his passion to the world. And the world believed that he reached the Pole.

*All three quotations are from Pierre Berton, *The Arctic Grail* (New York: Viking-Penguin, 1988), pp. 513, 518, 558.

In his final voyage, in 1908, Peary sailed from New York, landed at Etah on August 12, and took on board sixty-nine Inuit, 246 dogs, seventy tons of whale meat, and the blubber of fifty walruses. Captain Robert Bartlett wrote, "I shall never forget the frightful noise, the choking stench, and the terrible confusion that reigned aboard." The officers celebrated the departure with canned peaches, but "the odor about us was so powerful that the peaches simply felt wet and cold on one's tongue, having no fruit flavor whatsoever."* They sailed to the northeast tip of Ellesmere and froze the ship in for the winter. Then, on the last day of February 1909, they set out across the ice for the Pole.

Advance crews cut a trail through the pressure ridges with pick-axes. Supply crews ferried whale meat and walrus blubber northward to feed the dogs. Peary hobbled behind on his toeless feet, saving his strength for the final push. The expedition averaged ten miles per day for the first month and reached latitude 87° 47' north on April 1. (The Pole is 90° north.) They were about one hundred fifty miles from the Pole, but they were low on supplies and the ice was beginning to open under the returning sun.

Captain Bartlett was the only other man in the group who knew how to navigate. Peary, who was the military commander of the expedition, ordered Captain Bartlett to return to the ship. Then Peary ordered him south and continued on with four Inuit and his servant, Matthew Henson. According to Peary's report, they suddenly encountered smooth ice, increased their speed to thirty miles a day, and reached the Pole in five days. No one could affirm or contradict his celestial readings. Henson later wrote that they traveled slowly, hacking passages through jagged pressure ridges.

On Peary's return, critics argued that he had falsified his attainment of the Pole, but after considerable debate the U.S. Congress accepted his claim and promoted him to the rank of rear admiral. Peary never returned to the North. Some modern historians believe that Peary reached the Pole, while others contend that he didn't.

Chris and I sat on the grassy hill in Etah and ate lunch. We could afford to be lazy now because Peter and Wes had replenished our

*Ibid., p. 572.

food, we had made the dangerous crossing, and Siorapaluk was less than one hundred miles away. I lay back and shut my eyes.

Chris asked, "Where do you think we should go next, Jon?"

I sat up. "What do you mean? Siorapaluk."

"No, Dummy, on the next expedition. You always seem to have the next trip in mind."

"Well, I don't know, Chrissy. I guess I've been focused on this journey. Just then, I was thinking about Peary."

Peary spent fourteen years among a people who never understood his definition of success. He lived with an Inuit woman and had a child with her. Did they ever sit on a hill and talk about their passions? Could his lover, the mother of his child, ever understand his passion for fame? Did they ever dream together about children, flowers, solitude, snow, dog teams, or kayaks? I don't know, but I do know that the fame he craved, and achieved, was linked with an unwavering passion for his goal. And his message made a powerful impression on a civilization. Forty-five years after Peary arrived triumphantly in New York, I hiked through a hot day in my Boy Scout uniform, thinking not about the glorious sunshine, but about my determination not to be a wimp, even if the scout leader had to slice off my frozen toes.

Now that I sat on a hillside where Peary had sat, in the middle of my own expedition, all those stories and boyhood dreams aligned themselves into a chronicle. I had failed repeatedly, like Peary. Finally, I would succeed, like Peary. But how could he have walked away from the North to become a desk officer and socialite? Apparently he didn't sit on the ice one day and realize that wandering made him happy. Maybe, for him, adventure was nothing more than a vehicle to success. But I couldn't completely believe that. I didn't understand the man.

I wasn't talkative, so Chris stood up and walked away. She found a bear skull and started to sneak up on me, snapping the bear's whitened jaws. I feigned fear and curled up in the fetal position. She lost interest in the game and wandered off.

She wondered where we were going next. I wasn't sure: Siberia, the South Pacific, central Asia? We had plenty of time to talk about future plans. I shut my eyes and took a deep afternoon nap.

21

After three more days of paddling, Chris and I climbed a hill and looked across a fiord at green, blue, and red rectangles. We elected to camp one more night before entering Siorapaluk, our first village in Greenland. The glacier at the head of the fiord rent apart with a thundering crack that reverberated between the canyon walls. A few hours later, an iceberg several acres in size floated into view, surrounded by a few square miles of small ice chunks. The gentle swell of Baffin Bay rubbed the ice together, producing a low-frequency rumble, similar to the sound of a distant freeway. I wondered why the grinding ice was soothing while the sound of passing trucks is irritating. Was it a difference of frequency or of perception?

The next morning we paddled across the fiord through the lingering ice. Someone on the beach saw us when we were a few hundred yards away. The figure stared, waved, disappeared into a house, and reemerged in triplicate. Two of the three ran into adjacent houses and each reemerged with more people who gathered their friends, producing a rapidly branching chain reaction. As we approached, we heard babbling voices but no other sounds. There were no cars, trucks, bulldozers, lawn mowers, chain saws, or speedboats, just sixty people talking on the beach.

When Chris and I were a few feet from shore, a boy ran into the water, grasped Chris's kayak, and pulled it to land. Three boys sprang out of the crowd and grasped mine. Then we were surrounded by so many people that it was hard to climb out of the cockpits. Everyone was talking, and although we cannot speak their language, we heard one word excitedly rippling through the crowd: "*kayaks, kayaks, kayaks*," pronounced with emphasis on the *y* and the second *k*. Dozens of hands were extended in greeting, and we had to shake each hand before it was withdrawn. Finally, a voice welcomed us in English.

"Where have you come from?"

The man had a leaner, more Oriental face than the others, but I barely noticed the difference in the excitement.

We told him, "Grise Fiord," and the crowd understood. People nodded.

"How many days has it taken you?"

I responded, "Thirty-three; we are very slow." He translated to the crowd.

Another man stepped forward, grasped Chris's hand, smiled warmly, and pronounced in heavily accented English, "Kayak Woman!" Then he said something in their native tongue, and the English-speaking man translated: "No, that is fast by kayak."

The translator invited us into his house for tea, dried narwhal, and biscuits. He was a Japanese expatriate named Ihuo who had come to northwest Greenland on an expedition and stayed. For the past fifteen years he had lived as a hunter in the north. I asked him if he ever thought about returning home to Tokyo. He answered that he had been lonely for the first two or three years but now he had a family and there was no home in Japan to return to. He earned a living hunting, fishing, and trapping, and he hadn't worried about clocks or appointments for a decade and a half. He didn't think he could hold a job in an industrial society. Then Ihuo quizzed us about the animals we had seen and the ice conditions to the north. When we were finished, he showed us a comfortable camp that was close to town but offered some privacy. Several dog teams were staked out on the hillside. The dogs rose from their summer languish, eyed us curiously, barked, and wagged their tails.

A polite five minutes after we pitched our tent, the man who had called Chris "Kayak Woman" walked across the tundra and squatted on a soft patch of moss near our tent.

"Henson," he said, and he put out his hand. The name didn't register, although it should have. His cheekbones were softer than those of most Inuit, his nose and lips larger, and his skin darker.

"Jon."

"Chris."

"Today," and he pointed toward the north, "two kayak. Kayak Man," and he put his arm around me; "Kayak Woman," and he laughed.

Then he beckoned for us to follow him. He showed us a kayak perched on two fifty-five-gallon oil drums. I thought about the stone pillars at Cape Faraday and realized that even though the materials had changed, the concept had not. The drums kept the boat off the damp earth and away from the many sled-dog pups that roamed the village.

The kayak was constructed of a wood frame lashed together and covered by a canvas skin. It was much smaller than our boats, with a sleek bow and a nearly right-angled chine between deck and hull.

He motioned for me to lift the kayak and then beckoned for us to follow him to the beach. The kayak weighed about thirty-five pounds and was a joy to carry after dragging our heavily laden plastic craft. When we reached the water, he requested, in sign language, a ride in Chris's boat. Chris nodded. We dragged the boat down to the water, and she handed him her paddle. He slipped into the cockpit, and we showed him how to operate the rudder. He paddled out to sea with a fast, definite stroke.

Several people, including Ihuo, walked to the beach to watch. Henson returned and spoke to Ihuo, who translated: "Your boats are very slow. It must be hard work to travel far. The kayak woman is strong."

Then he eschewed the translation and spoke directly to Chris. "Kayak Woman, come!" He led her to his boat and pointed toward the water.

Ihuo warned Chris to step only on the wooden frame or she would punch a hole in the canvas. She eased in carefully, grasped Henson's paddle, and headed for deep water. No one spoke, then everyone in the crowd started talking at once. Ihuo told me that in Inuit tradition, women accompanied men on hunting journeys, but not on the hunt itself. Since kayaks were used primarily for hunting and not for long journeys, women never kayaked. In olden times, a hunter would destroy a kayak if a woman touched it, because the contact would bring bad luck or death to the hunter.

I looked around, expecting tension on people's faces, but saw only friendship. Henson stood apart, proud to be the man who had broken the taboo and placed honor on an honored guest.

In Chris's words:

I was honored when Henson called me the kayak woman and asked me to try his kayak. In the olden days, taboos prevented women from even touching a hunting tool. I studied his face carefully to make sure that he wasn't joking and noticed that a small crowd had appeared on the beach. From their faces I sensed that the offer was an honor, not a joke. Almost solemnly I took off my boots and climbed in. The paddle was a six-foot-long, three-inch-wide board about half an inch thick. It was straight except for small drip notches carved at either end. The boat was crafted of wooden slats, willow, and painted canvas. This seemingly low-tech and flimsy kayak rocked precipitously as I shifted my hips. I felt twenty sets of eyes watching me intently; I didn't want to flip over and risk years of bad hunting for the village. After a deep breath to relax I found the balance point. Now it felt like I was in a sports car com-pared to the lumbering old station wagon of my larger, heavily loaded boat. Dipping the ends of the board paddle, I moved quickly around the bay. Henson's kayak was a fast, sleek, hunting machine. Except for the tiny splash sounds I heard as I dipped the paddle, I was almost silent as I moved through the sea. I imagined myself quietly chasing prey but reluctantly returned to the beach.

When Chris returned, an old man in polar bear pants, worn seal-skin *kamiks*, thick glasses, and a hearing aid helped her out of the boat with a broad smile and a silent nod. Ihuo told me that the old man was Henson's father-in-law. He was eighty-nine and was once a great hunter who had traveled with Peary.

The crowd dissipated, and Henson invited us to his house. Like the homes in the Canadian Arctic, it was modeled after a suburban tract house, including even leathery rubber plants from the Amazon Rain Forest. Henson's wife busily prepared food and coffee, children passed through, and sled-dog puppies scampered underfoot. The old man entered and hunkered comfortably on his haunches. Henson brought out a large scrapbook and opened it to show us a newspaper clipping from the *Boston Globe*. Before I read the headline, he jabbed his finger at his image within a group portrait.

"Me, Henson," he announced proudly. Then he poked every per-son in the group portrait, and with each poke he reaffirmed, "Hen-son, Henson, Henson."

I got it! How had I been so stupid?

Matthew Henson was born in 1866, the son of black sharecroppers in a small town in Maryland. His parents died when he was young, and at thirteen he took a job as a ship's cabin boy. In 1888 Peary hired Henson for his survey to Nicaragua. The two shared mutual respect. Peary commented that his assistant had "intelligence, faithfulness, and better-than-average pluck and endurance." In turn, Henson wrote that "it was with the instinct of my race that I recognized in him [Peary] the qualities that made me willing to engage myself in his service."*

Henson accompanied Peary on five of his six Arctic expeditions. He learned the Inuit language (whereas Peary did not) and served as interpreter. On the first attempt at the Pole, Henson went ahead to break trail and chop passages through the pressure ridges with a pickax, while Peary rested. Then Peary and Henson made the final dash together.

But Henson was black, so he received half the pay of white men. Before their last polar attempt, Peary reminded his servant that "you have been in my service long enough to show me respect in small things. . . . I have a right to expect you will say sir to me always. . . . You will pay attention when I am talking to you and show that you hear directions I give by saying yes sir, or all right sir."*

On their final race to the Pole, Henson again broke trail while Peary rode on the sled. Consequently, Henson reached the Pole first (if either of them reached the Pole). Peary was so furious that he refused to speak to Henson for the entire journey home, and he never said good-bye when they parted in New York. The National Geographic Society presented a medal to Peary for reaching the Pole and another to Robert Bartlett for his second-place record in reaching 87° north latitude. Henson and the Inuit guides were ignored.

After their return, Peary became rich. Henson could not find a job. After three years, Henson wrote to Peary that he needed work as "a chauffeur or messenger or some other position that I could fill." A year later, Peary used his influence to have his old companion hired as a messenger in the Federal Customs House in New York, where Henson remained until his retirement.

Henson had an Inuit wife who bore a son, Anaukaq. Anaukaq's son, Talilanguaq, was our host. In 1987 he flew to Boston for a

*S. Allen Counter, *North Pole Legacy: Black, White, and Eskimo* (Amherst: University of Massachusetts Press, 1991), p. 52.

reunion that brought together the Inuit and the American sides of both the Peary and Henson families.

Talilanguaq served us coffee, bread, butter, and Danish cheese. The bread tasted almost ceremonial; it was the taste of civilization. When we finished, the children cleared a place on the kitchen floor, spread newspaper over the linoleum, and went outside to fetch a large red plastic tub. Inside was a *kiviaq*, a dish I had heard about but never seen or tasted.

The recipe for *kiviaq* calls for one seal and 250 to 500 dovekies. As I explained earlier, dovekies are caught with long-handled nets as they fly over their nests in rocky crags. To prepare *kiviaq*, the hunter must kill each bird without breaking its skin. This task is accomplished by pressing a thumb into its breast and displacing its heart. The beak, feet, feathers, and innards are left intact. The other essential ingredient is a fresh sealskin that retains half of the epidermal blubber. The dovekies are stuffed tightly into the sealskin, which is then sewed up so that it looks like a living seal. This package is buried in a shallow grave that is cooled from below by the permafrost and heated from above by the sun. Over a period of weeks to a few months, the seal fat decomposes and drips slowly through the fermenting dovekies. When the two mix and turn green, the *kiviaq* is ready.

Talilanguaq's father-in-law had shown little interest in the bread and cheese, but he moved from his corner when the *kiviaq* was brought in. He sliced the stitching that held the seal together, lifted a dovekie, and offered it to me. Small droplets of rancid fat dripped through his fingers and glistened on the ends of his knuckles.

I try to accept other people's customs, and I have a pretty strong stomach, but I was afraid I might vomit over the precious festival meal if I got any closer. I didn't even dare to open my mouth to say no, so I smiled and shook my head.

Talilanguaq understood and motioned to his wife to bring us more bread and butter. Then he sat down with his father-in-law and other guests to eat. The raw, fermented dovekies were so soft that the diners sucked feathers, meat, and innards off the bones with a contented smacking sound. Soon a pile of bones, beaks, and feet accumulated on the floor. When everyone was satiated, Talilanguaq stored the remaining *kiviaq* outside and wiped the linoleum clean with paper towels.

The following morning, Ihuo stopped by to ask us if we would like to witness a narwhal hunt. In Greenland, narwhals and seal are still harpooned from a kayak. The harpoon is attached to a sealskin float to support and locate a wounded animal. The Inuit use a rifle for the final kill only after the prey is secured. The system reduces the probability that an animal will be wounded and escape to die elsewhere. In contrast, in Canada Inuit shoot marine mammals from speedboats with high-powered rifles. They retrieve only forty percent of the narwhals that they kill. Ihuo explained that the narwhals had concentrated about fifty miles to the east and that we should hurry because the season was progressing.

We went to the store to buy food, but the annual supply ship hadn't arrived and the shelves were nearly empty. We bought a few boxes of ship's biscuits, called hardtack, and packed to go. I thought that I was familiar with hardtack because I had eaten pilot crackers when I worked on fishing boats in Alaska, but Alaskan pilot crackers have been civilized and are soft and flaky, like a fat saltine without the salt. The Greenland hardtack was so dense that I had to soften a corner in my mouth before I bit through. Chris beat her rations into pieces between two rocks to save strain on her jaws.

Hardtack contains carbohydrates but few essential vitamins; *kiviaq* is a complete meal. Hundreds of explorers died or were maimed by scurvy because they tried to survive on hardtack and salt meat and refused to adapt to native foods.

22

We paddled to Qanaaq, the largest village in northwest Greenland, in two uneventful days. Again, a crowd gathered to welcome us. An older man made the shape of a tent with his hands, we nodded, and he escorted us to a level terrace large enough for our tent.

Talilanguaq had taught us a few words of the local dialect, so we held up our water bottles and asked, "*Inuk?*" The man nodded and led us to an outside municipal water faucet. I filled the bottle and asked, "Tea?" He followed us back to the tent, and we lit the stove and shared a cup of tea.

An iceberg in the bay rolled over with a splash and a crackle of fracturing ice. But today, for the first time on our journey, the noise of the sea and its ice was overwhelmed by the town generator and by trucks unloading a ship at the beach. From the first trash at our landfall in Greenland, to the quiet of Siorapaluk, to these noises, we were entering civilization.

We rested in Qanaaq for several days. Chris and I wanted to witness a narwhal hunt, and people told us about a group that was camped two days' paddle east of town.

When we reached the hunting camp, the four men and two women welcomed us and offered us first tea, then coffee. A narwhal, dead for about a week, lay stretched out on the tundra. It was seventeen feet long, the length of my kayak. A mature male weighs about one and one-half tons, twice as much as a moose but considerably lighter than an elephant. The hunters had split it open, cleaned out the innards, and removed some of the meat. A few flies buzzed about the carcass.

Our hosts motioned with their knives for us to eat, so we squatted on the tundra and cut off chunks of the dark, oily, sun-dried flesh. One man tapped me on the elbow with the flat of his knife blade. He then cut off a cube of raw blubber and indicated that I should do the same and eat the fat with the meat.

After the meal, we walked down to the beach, and the men inspected our boats, spray skirts, and paddles. Then each took a turn paddling. Chris tried to convince the women to try, but they giggled and refused. I looked at the local kayaks, and one of the hunters handed me his harpoon. The wooden shaft was about four feet long. He had lashed a piece of hollowed narwhal tusk to the tip of the shaft with seal sinew. Then he had tied a sharpened steel tip to the ivory. The harpoon had no barb, but when the weapon penetrated an animal, the lashed ivory and spear point slipped out of their mounts and twisted at right angles to the shaft. This double right-angle twist secured the harpoon until the hunter killed the animal and cut the weapon free. Hunters threw the harpoon with the aid of an *atlatl*, a hinged lever developed by Clovis hunters around 10,000 B.C. A seal-skin rope tied to the harpoon was attached to a sealskin float.

The harpoon in my hand was almost identical to those used before European explorers arrived in the North. The main difference was that while modern tips are composed of tempered steel, in olden days they were made of chips from an iron meteorite that had landed on the Greenland ice sheet a few hundred miles to the south. Other men used combinations of modern materials. One hunter replaced the ivory segment with a cutoff screwdriver, which is cheaper and stronger. Another used yellow polypropylene line instead of the sealskin rope, and a third proudly showed me an old piece of five-millimeter perlon rope garnered from some expedition.

People napped, did small chores, drank tea or coffee, and ate. No one was formally assigned lookout duty, but someone always scanned the water for signs of narwhals. I sat with an older man on the bluff. He said, "Narwhal," and moved his hand in a wavy swimming motion. Then he pointed to the head of the fiord. He mimed putting food into his mouth, pronounced the word *cod*, and ran his hand straight down. So the narwhals were deep-diving for cod at the head of the fiord. He grasped my hand and pulled my sleeve back, exposing my watch. It was 11:00 A.M. He pointed his finger at 12:00, repeated the word *narwhal*, and pointed to the water directly below us.

At 12:09 the lookout cried out excitedly, and all the hunters ran for their boats. I picked up my binoculars and focused on three pale brown speckled spots moving through the water. That was all—no tusks, no majestic dorsal fin, no arcing tail silhouetted against the noonday sun.

Viking explorers thought that a swimming narwhal looked like a drowned human corpse and thus named it the *corpse-whale* (*nar + hvalr*). But then the image changed. A Norse sailor killed a narwhal and took the ten-foot-long spiraled ivory tusk home to Scandinavia. A merchant bought it, carried it south, and sold it to a noble, who recognized it instantly as a unicorn horn. Medieval manuscripts claimed that the unicorn's horn was a powerful medicine. As a conse-quence, narwhal tusks sold for twenty times their weight in gold.

Four hunters paddled their kayaks to intersect the narwhals' pre-dicted course. But the animals dove, and the men returned to shore empty-handed. Soon a single narwhal swam by, and this time only one man took up the pursuit. He approached cautiously until he was a few yards from his prey. Then he carefully set his paddle on the deck and picked up his harpoon.

I felt two opposing romantic images. First, I thought, "Here in 1988, in the age of the laser-guided missile, there is a lone hunter in a thirty-five-pound boat made of sticks tied together with string, covered with cloth no more durable than a pair of blue jeans. This man holds a long stick with a sawed-off screwdriver attached to it, with a steel point tied to the end of the screwdriver. With this device, powered by a levered throwing arm that was invented before the bow and arrow, he intends to kill a whale." I wanted to be out there with him, back to the primeval, the noble savage.

But I also saw the narwhals romping through the waves, free and alive between glaciers, mountains, ocean, and sky. It was the unicorn of the sea. My daughter Reeva had a picture of a unicorn on her wall. It stood defiantly on its hind legs in a sea of flowers that evoked images of picnics and love. Chris's wedding ring is a silver narwhal that swims endlessly around her finger. I didn't want to see all those beautiful images reduced to a frenzied thrashing in a blood-red sea. I thought, "We are not living one hundred years ago, we are living now and must preserve the wild creatures that remain."

The man raised his harpoon as the boat glided silently. His arm shook with anticipation, then steadied with the calm control of a practiced hunter. But before he threw, the whale sounded and escaped.

23

The narwhals didn't return, and two days later the hunters loaded their kayaks into their motorboats and sped back to town. Left alone, we decided to head toward Thule Air Base and home. We had one long crossing of Inglefield Bay and then coastal travel to the base. In the middle of the bay, we saw three narwhals. We paddled slowly toward them, eyes focused on the moistened patches of skin. They swam in a scalloped motion, alternately swooping a few feet below the surface and then rising to breathe. Sheets of water ran off their skins, leaving small puddles that danced rainbows across their mottled brown spots. The airholes opened and closed like the end of an elephant's trunk as it reaches for peanuts. We clearly heard their breaths, loud and very mammal-like.

A fourth whale surfaced. I took a stroke and cranked the rudder hard with my foot. The whale slipped under the water, then surfaced so close we almost collided. Suddenly, narwhals surrounded us, frolicking in groups of three to eight. We lay our paddles across our spray skirts. The ocean was calm except for a rhythmic low-frequency swell that slurped at the undersides of the nearby icebergs. Occasionally a berg cracked, fractured, and tossed chunks of ice into the sea.

The narwhals visited us for half an hour before they sounded and disappeared. We paddled to shore and sat against sun-warmed rocks.

In the olden days, when the world was new, the first people talked with the animals and danced with the walrus on the bottom of the sea. The walrus liked the people and always offered them food. No one ever went hungry. Those times are past, but even today the bond between animals and people persists. A hunter is too ignorant, inept, and slow to kill an animal. Occasionally, animals pity their poor, frail, human cousins and willfully sacrifice themselves.

That day the narwhals had chosen not to be killed. Instead they brought us the magic that we had traveled so far to find.

24

We arrived in Thule three days later. A guard lounged at the end of a pier and we paddled toward him, across the open bay. It was incredible that he didn't see us.

I called up, "Howdy."

No response.

"Hello up there! It's Jon Turk and Chris Seashore, triumphant Arctic explorers returning from a successful expedition."

No response. He still hadn't seen us or heard me call.

Chris suggested we paddle toward a gray warship, moored to the pier. Surely the stern lookout would see us. We paddled into the hull's shadow, took a photo, and then I called up, "Hey, Dude, anybody alive up there?"

No response, so we continued toward the beach.

Finally, the bow lookout spotted us. "Hey, *you, you*. Who are you? What are you doing?"

Chris whispered, "Don't be a wise guy."

I introduced myself and Chris, and the lookout told us to paddle to shore.

"Are your papers in order? Do you have permission from the U.S. Air Force to enter the base? Did you have permission from the Danish government to enter Greenland via Canada? Did someone stamp your passport at your port of entry?"

"Well, yes and no. Yes, we have permission from the USAF. No, no one stamped our passport at the port of entry."

"Pull your boats up and get out; I'll call the commanding officer."

We did as instructed, and the lookout summoned two more guards to watch us. Geometric rows of buildings extended inland, and military vehicles raced back and forth on the gravel roads. A soda vending machine stood out incongruously on the pier, next to a fire-fighting station. No one asked us about our journey, the land, its animals, or the ice. But one young soldier, not much older than my children, offered me a can of Coke.

I popped the pop-top and handed it to Chris.

"Where'd you get the Coke?" I asked.

"Oh, from the machine over there."

I nodded. "I understand, but how did the Coke get into the machine—to Greenland, I mean."

"Oh, they bring them in by ship, but we ran out so they flew a planeload in on a C–140 transport. You can fly a lot of pop in one of those C–140s."

We were sitting next to 7 million cubic miles of sparkling ice; abundant rivers flowed to the sea; and the Air Force was flying water in from New Jersey. Chris handed me the can, and I took a swig. It was sweet and bubbly.

The commanding officer radioed that he would arrive in about fifteen minutes. The guards lost interest in us, retreated a few steps, and talked among themselves.

Chris spoke softly, "What do you think, Jon?"

"Oh . . . they'll hassle us and then send us to the States on one of the cargo planes that came in on a soda pop run. Maybe they'll fly us to Copenhagen. New Jersey, Copenhagen—it doesn't matter. The expedition ended when the lookout asked us for our papers rather than for information about the land."

Chris leaned against me, and I welcomed the familiar contact. I drifted back to the narwhals in Inglefield Fiord and tried to imagine their deep dive into a world dominated by intense pressure. I peered into the darkness looking for cod but saw instead a family of walrus. Mama was playing the fiddle, Papa was beating a tambourine, and all the little ones were cavorting on their hind feet, waving their tusks, and dancing on the bottom of the sea.

EPILOGUE

Praise be God our Lord, and his blessed Mother St. Mary
who guided and directed and suffered us to go forward without
delivering our souls to the wiles of the Devil who sought our
destruction.

Pedro Sarmiento, in *The Blind Horn's Hate*, Richard Hough

1

Twenty years had passed since I staggered home from the 1890s
bar and decided to sail around Cape Horn. Chris was kneading
biscotti dough; I was listening to music and looking out the window
of our home in the Montana forest. Outside, a doe and its yearling
nibbled brush in the newly fallen November snow.

The phone rang. It was Eric Rice from The North Face. He asked
me if I would test some gear in a cold, wet environment. I said I'd
think of an expedition, hung up the phone, put a stick of wood on
the fire, and turned to face Chris.

"I think I'm going to try the Horn one more time."

She looked up from her flour and egg yolks. "Oh, really?"

2

On December 14, 1996, Mike Latendresse and I paddled to
shore at the southernmost bay of Isla Herschal and walked
through the rain to the abandoned wood-frame Chilean military post.
The windows were blown out and the door had been ripped off its
hinges, but the roof, walls, and floor were sound. A rusted fifty-gallon
steel drum lay on its side in the back room, and Mike rolled it into
the old kitchen.

We fashioned the drum into a crude wood-burning stove and rigged a makeshift flue pipe. I walked outside and gathered damp tinder from the underside of a bush. Mike poured a little of our precious diesel fuel over the sticks and lit a match. Some of the smoke found our flue, but most of it oozed from cracks and rust holes, enveloping the room. The smoke lingered, wandered into dark corners, and then slowly rose out the open windows. A gust of wind herded half the smoke back inside. I added more wet wood, which burned reluctantly.

Mike took off his storm parka, wrung excess water from his wet undergarments, and huddled close to the stove. I did the same, and we stood side by side, breathing the bad air and not saying much.

When our clothes dried and we stopped shivering I suggested, "Let's get dressed, climb up the hill, and have a look."

The ground was boggy and difficult to walk over, and the wind drove steady rain into our faces. Abandoned bunkers and foxholes dotted the hillside. Chile and Argentina had disputed these islands, and the bunkers were built when war seemed probable. We hiked to the ridge and then followed high ground to the summit. The wind pushed against me so strongly that I almost fell backward, but I leaned into the storm and reached equilibrium. Below us, the straits were a chaotic mixture of wind and wave. Beyond the straits, the tundra of Isla Hornos rose toward a high bluff: Cabos de Hornos, Cape Horn, the southernmost extremity of the Western Hemisphere.

Mike and I had been in our kayaks for over a month, following approximately the same route I had paddled alone seventeen years previously. Many aspects of the journey were similar: The fiords and straits hadn't changed; we were cold, wet, and hungry much of the time. But on this expedition we were together, we were skilled, and we paddled responsive boats. We played in the big waves and sailed for sport when reason and prudence told us not to. Hardships were balanced by fun, and I filled my journals with descriptions of the beauty around me rather than with tales of loneliness and suffering. We didn't shipwreck in the surf at Punta Guanaco. Instead, we camped near the site of my previous disaster, made the dangerous crossing during a predawn calm, and continued south along the Cape Horn Archipelago. Now the Horn was in sight.

We were close, but only close. Out of sight, the legendary waves of the Drake Passage crashed against the shore. It would be suicide to paddle today. We'd have to wait.

On the morning of December 16, Mike greeted me with a cheery "Happy birthday, Mr. Fifty-One-Year-Old," and held out a precious candy bar that he had surreptitiously saved from his previous day's rations.

I thanked him and shared it with him. "Nothing like a chocolate hit before the sun is over the yardarm."

I had hoped to round the Horn on my birthday, but the wind raged. I hated the smoky fire and resolved not to add any more wood. If Mike wanted the meager warmth, he could hassle with it. He silently reached the same conclusion, so the fire died. When the smoke cleared sufficiently that my eyes stopped watering, I crawled into my sleeping bag and read one of our three books for the second time.

That afternoon, the barometer began to steady and the wind slackened. About 1:00 A.M. the following morning I was awakened by a strange sound. I sat up in my bag. No, it wasn't a sound; it was the absence of sound! I closed my eyes, tossed in bed, but couldn't sleep. We were ten miles north of Cape Horn and the air was dead calm. I woke Mike.

"It's time to do it."

We packed in the predawn grayness and launched by 3:30 A.M. We paddled south across the straits, then followed the north shore of Isla Hornos west into a gentle swell and headwind. After about five miles we rounded the corner and swung south.

South of Cape Horn, ocean girdles the globe. Pushed by a nearly constant west wind, waves have no beginning or end, just an endless path that started in geologic deep time—after the continents drifted apart to form the Antarctic Ocean. Today, the ancient giants weren't ferocious like young waves born in the turmoil of an Arctic gale. But they had maturity and power.

A kayak, or even a giant supertanker, is like a judo master who rolls with the motion of the opponent but lets most of the energy flow past. An island is different. The shallow shore cuts the bottoms of the waves until the tops rear, growl, bare white fangs, and crash, flinging spume into the air. On the western edge of Cape Horn Island, rock pinnacles stood defiantly to mark the place where a cliff had been, before it had been ground into sand under the continuous assault. The breaking waves reflected back into deep water, producing a cross-swell that lifted the kayak erratically, pushed it sideways, shook the stern, and jiggled the bow.

In the seventeen years since my first Cape Horn expedition, I had paddled a few thousand miles in the Arctic and in uncounted turbulent rivers. My body had learned to control a kayak as it had learned to ski, feeling the motion and responding directly, without intervening verbalization. So my hips rocked with swells and cross-swells as my shoulders paddled southward, toward that last point of land jutting into the sea.

The sky was gradually becoming lighter with the oncoming dawn. My body worked automatically, leaving a space that my mind could drift into. After Greenland, I had succeeded on six consecutive expeditions: two rock climbs on Baffin Island, the ascent of a previously unclimbed peak on the Tibet-China border, kayak traverses in Siberia and the South Pacific, and a mountain bike traverse of Mongolia. Chris participated on all but the Baffin climbs.

The children had grown. Nathan and his wife had a one-year-old, my first grandchild, and Nathan was designing Internet web pages. Reeva was also married and was attending veterinary school at Cornell; she was the mother of my second grandchild. Noey, the youngest, was studying physics in Santa Barbara.

My earlier failures on Cape Horn, The Northwest Passage, and Baffin had receded into ancient history, although they were not forgotten. The failures had been my forty years in the desert to shed the old skin and grow a new one.

We reached the southwest point and turned east. Cape Horn swung into view. About 300 million years ago, 70 million years before the appearance of the dinosaurs, all the earth's land mass was welded together into one giant supercontinent. South America, Africa, and Antarctica were all nestled together. Then subterranean forces tore the supercontinent apart, ripping South America away from Antarctica. The moving tectonic plates ground into one another, shearing rock and creating earthquakes and volcanic eruptions. Cape Horn was formed by separation and repeated collisions and now stands as a thirteen-hundred-foot bluff, the last rock outcrop before land surrenders to the Antarctic Ocean.

The waves pushed from behind now, hurrying us along, inviting us to join them in a race around the world. When I accelerated down the face of a wave, I felt a wind in my face, not an east wind but the wind created by my own speed, surfing the giant comber. We continued eastward until I imagined that we were one paddle stroke short of lying due south of Cape Horn. I stopped. In my fantasy, I saw Drake in a puffy satin shirt and pantaloons, lying on the mountaintop, ankles anchored by a trusted sailor, reaching over the cliff like a bowsprit on a ship. Then I paddled one ceremonial stroke. I had rounded the Horn, completing a journey I had begun a third of a lifetime ago.

Raindrops formed tiny circular wavelets that rode on the giant swells and then dissipated. Rainbows darkened and faded behind Mike's head. The early-morning sun peeked between streaks of gray cloud, played hide-and-seek behind the waves, and then rose high enough to bathe Cape Horn in an orange glow. Mike looked inconsequential in his familiar red boat, red suit, and blue hat—appearing, disappearing, bobbing against the double rainbow in the background.

Rising on a high swell, I noticed waves breaking against an underwater shoal.

Mike asked, "Should we cut between the break and the shore? We've got a quarter of a mile gap to paddle through."

I thought of all the river kayaking I'd done where I had paddled turbulent water, inches from jagged rocks. A quarter of a mile is wider than a large river like the Salmon or the Colorado. Surely we could paddle a kayak through an opening as wide as an entire river. But the tide was dropping. In my imagination, I saw an invisible shoal holding the bottom of a wave long enough to slow it down, while the top raced ahead and crashed into the trough. I felt a kayak, my kayak, *me*, cartwheeling down the face of the breaking wave.

Just when I was about to speak, Mike hollered, "It's too scary. There's not enough control out here."

We paddled outside the break and then turned into a harbor at the east end of the island. My kayak stabilized in the calm water. I was cold and eager to reach shore, but I stopped paddling and looked back over my shoulder. Those giant waves had already slipped from reality into memory.

I imagined a new fold forming in my brain to store the morning's sensations. Ions were racing through neurons connecting that fold to others, so that for the rest of my life, whenever someone mentioned words like *wave*, *kayak*, or *Cape Horn*, I could feel myself surfing down one of the huge waves, hull hissing. Then I could feel the next wave lift me and roll past, unperturbed, on its endless journey around the earth.

I started to paddle the last few hundred yards toward the beach. To experiment with my memory, I quietly spoke the words *grand adventure*. Images of kayaks, rowboats, dogsleds, bivouac ledges, waves, and storms poured out of their folds and crowded together in a mad race to be remembered first. Some of the images were terrifying, others were sodden with fatigue, while many were bathed in bright sunshine and ebullience. They were all mine. I wouldn't discard a single one.

Mike reached shore first, jumped out of his boat, and ran into the water to grab my bow and drag my kayak to shore. I stood awkwardly, took a step, and slipped on the kelp. Mike reached out to steady me.